College Student Development

College Student Development

Leighton C. Whitaker, PhD
Richard E. Slimak, PhD
Editors

The Haworth Press, Inc.
New York • London • Norwood (Australia)

College Student Development has also been published as *Journal of College Student Psychotherapy*, Volume 6, Numbers 3/4 1992.

The Haworth Press, Inc., 10 Alice Street, Binghamton, NY 13904-1580 USA

Library of Congress Cataloging-in-Publication Data

College student development / Leighton C. Whitaker, Richard E. Slimak, editors.
    p. cm.
    "Also published as Journal of college student psychotherapy, volume 6, numbers 3/4 1992"-T.p. verso.
    ISBN 1-56024-313-9 (alk paper).–ISBN 1-56024-314-7 (pbk. alk. paper)
    1. College students–Mental health. 2. College students–Psychology. 3. College students–Mental health services. 4. Psychotherapy. I. Whitaker, Leighton C. II. Slimak Richard E. III. Journal of college student psychotherapy; v. 6, nos. 3/4.
RC451.4.S7C67 1992
378.1'9713–dc20
                                    92-42183
                                        CIP

ABOUT THE EDITORS

Leighton C. Whitaker, PhD, is Director of Psychological Services for Swarthmore College in Pennsylvania, Adjunct Clinical Professor for the Institute of Graduate Studies in Clinical Psychology at Widener University in Chester, Pennsylvania, Editor of *Journal of College Student Psychotherapy,* and a consulting editor for the *Journal of American College Health.* He has authored about 60 publications, including *Schizophrenic Disorders: Sense and Nonsense in Conceptualization, Assessment, and Treatment* (Plenum Press, 1992). Dr. Whitaker has led workshops on college student suicide for national and regional organizations. He served as President of American College Health Association's Mental Health Section in 1990-1991. Dr. Whitaker also maintains a private practice.

Richard E. Slimak, PhD, is Director of Counseling and Associate Professor at the United States Coast Guard Academy. During his twenty years at the Academy Dr. Slimak has taught human behavior, counseling and evaluation, and designed an award-winning peer-based suicide prevention program. The author of numerous articles on college students, Dr. Slimak has presented papers for the Association of University and College Counseling Center Directors, American Association for Counseling and Development, American College Personnel Association, American Association of Suicidology, and the Northeast Counseling Center Directors. Co-Editor with Dr. Whitaker of *College Student Suicide* (The Haworth Press, Inc., 1990), Dr. Slimak also serves as a member of the editorial board for the *Journal of College Student Psychotherapy.* He has led continuing education workshops for the American Psychological Association and served as a visiting professor, lecturer or consultant at Yale University, the University of Connecticut, the University of Massachusetts Medical School, and the United States Merchant Marine, Military, and Air Force Academies. Dr. Slimak resides on a Christmas Tree Farm in North Stonington, Connecticut.

College Student Development

CONTENTS

ALL HAWORTH BOOKS & JOURNALS
ARE PRINTED ON CERTIFIED
ACID-FREE PAPER

College Student Development

Foreword

I am pleased to have the opportunity to write the foreword to this special volume. It allows me to become immersed in a topic near and dear to my heart: providing developmental assistance to students during the college years.

Virtually every college student needs some form of developmental aid at some point in his/her college career. Some lack information critical to understanding or resolving a key developmental task. Others have all the necessary facts but are unable to develop a strategy for resolving a developmental issue. Still others have information and a strategy but cannot assess their situation accurately or gain clear feedback about the validity of key developmental directions. At some time over the course of a college career, one of these deficits may intrude upon a student's developmental progress. The intrusion may occur abruptly, precipitating a crisis, or it may ebb and flow, requiring numerous course-correcting therapeutic episodes (Widseth & Webb, chapter 4). Whatever its specific manifestation, lack of information, strategy, or assessment skill when these become pivotal may well derail optimal development.

Colleges exist to stimulate the development of students. Of the 168 hours available in each week, approximately 16 are used in the classroom and structured to support intellectual development. The remaining 152 hours each week, less purposefully structured, provide a rich environment for the advancement of personal development. The articles that follow probe key research findings, major theories, and important intervention strategies that influence degrees and types of gains that may be made in personal development during collegiate years.

For students, college life provides opportunity and crisis, accomplishment and failure, excitement and despair, energy and exhaustion. The college years clearly tax the adequacy of every student's previous developmental accomplishments. These years bring either rapid developmental advancement or developmental regression. Opportunities arise that will enable students to shed dysfunctional attitudes, values, and interpersonal styles, or allow deeper entrenchment of avoidant or dysfunctional compensatory behavior. Personal dissatisfaction and misery throughout the life-span often can be traced to failed or incomplete resolution of critical developmental challenges of the college years.

Developmental challenges usually encountered during the college years fall into three categories. The need for students to keep up with the pace of development expected of their age cohort characterizes one category of challenge. Clearly each period in the life-span spectrum features tasks that must be accomplished in order to stay on track with one's peers and society's expectations. Developmental tasks that mark the college years involve the ability to express one's self appropriately (communicate, assert); to manage feelings and impulses (anger, hurt, infatuation, jealousy); to establish a firmer identity (sexuality, intimacy, individuation); and to develop a sense of attachment and belonging (family and cultural roots, intellectual and career pursuits).

A second category of developmental challenge associated with the college years involves the relatively predictable crises in which students sometimes find themselves enmeshed. By definition, crisis occurs when a person's normal coping skills are overwhelmed by events and no longer dependably provide stabilization or recovery. Crisis states ensue for a notable percentage of college students when they encounter rejection in romantic relationships, the divorce or death of parents, an eating disorder, failure at critical academic tasks, or substance abuse. Each of these circumstances can cause deep wounds, confusion or alarm, and put the student into a state of crisis. If not adequately resolved, these crises can destroy previous developmental accomplishments leading to developmental regression. In the absence of direct assistance in identifying and resolving problems that fuel such crises, students are at risk for developing dysfunctional compensatory behaviors or seriously compromising their sense of self.

The third category of challenge for college students can be

traced to students' discoveries that disruptive family of origin problems, unresolvable traumatic events in their histories, or chronic abuse during their childhood have precluded development of a solid foundation for establishing a stabilizing self concept. Their emergent personality structure may be characterized by anxiety, constricted emotional expression and relational deficits, and a coping system built upon denial, avoidance, and escape. In the college world, which is usually a more demanding environment than most students have encountered previously, developmental deficits along with their residual unresolved pain, often distress, haunt, and frustrate students' pursuit of academic goals and personal fulfillment.

Focused exclusively on development, this volume contains valuable resources for understanding both the magnitude of the challenges and the diverse influences that the college experience exerts on development. It highlights key problems encountered by students grappling with catching up to or keeping pace with their peers as they move toward individuation and adulthood. It points out the difficulties and sensitivities required of therapists who strive to support and nudge people to more functional and adaptive ways of being (Whitaker, chapter 1). Slimak (chapter 2) weaves developmental theory with contextual complexity into a meta-modular conceptualization which is both usefully solid and realistically fluid. Developmental needs and challenges must be understood contextually. Societal shifts in attitudes and values (Bishop, chapter 3), ethnic background and identification (Cheatham and Berg-Cross, chapter 9), family issues and dynamics (Alishio, chapter 6), and gender issues (Hoffmann, chapter 10; Mann, chapter 11) all of which affect the context within which developmental tasks must be understood, resolved, and the form that resolution takes. In reviewing the turbulence and richness of late adolescence, Rivinus (chapter 8) discusses the deleterious interplay between substance use or abuse and the avoidance of developmental challenges, underscoring the vulnerability of the college student and the value of judicious, educated intervention.

A debt of gratitude is due the authors represented in the following pages. Collectively they have raised our consciousness and broadened understanding of developmental issues. Through their efforts we can see more clearly both the pitfalls and paths to constructive methods for stimulating and supporting students in their developmental journey to adulthood.

David J. Drum, PhD, ABPP
Professor of Counseling Psychology
Associate Vice-President for Student Affairs
Director of Counseling, Learning & Career Service
University of Texas at Austin

Preface

Knowledge of personal development is an essential ingredient in all varieties of effective psychotherapy. This edition provides college counselors and therapists with some of the most important developmental perspectives needed in today's work with students. We have tried to address both the general and the particular, the constant and the current considerations in college student development.

Chapter 1, "Psychotherapy as a Developmental Process," by Leighton Whitaker, Swarthmore College, Pennsylvania, illustrates the importance of developmental knowledge in terms of how students' personal histories including the cultural influences in their lives interact to determine the dilemmas and challenges facing them and all who work on campuses today. Richard Slimak of the U.S. Coast Guard Academy in Connecticut then delineates in Chapter 2, "A Student Development Metamodel for University and College Counseling Center Professionals," theoretical context for succeeding chapters. Dean John Bishop, University of Delaware, depicts in Chapter 3, "The Changing Student Culture: Implications for Counselors and Administrators," the particular changes which present new challenges for the 1990s.

Our next four chapters offer more specific frameworks for understanding our work in developmental terms. In Chapter 4, "'Toddler' to the Inner World: The College Student in Psychotherapy," Jane Widseth and Richard Webb of Haverford College, Pennsylvania, build on their previous articles in the *Journal of College Student Psychotherapy* by elucidating students' needs to alternate inner and outer explorations, just as the young child must have a secure home base to make possible their venturing out into the world. In Chapter 5, "Developing *Typically* in the College Years," O.W. Lacy, Emeritus, Franklin and Marshall College, Pennsylvania, outlines enduring Jungian personality types and their importance for understanding the interaction of the constitutionally given and the acquired. In Chapter 6, "Applying Trans-Generational Family

Theory and Therapy to College Student Psychotherapy," Kip Alishio, Miami University, Ohio alerts us to the considerable relevance of knowledge of family systems in our work though we do tend not to do family therapy per se. Chapter 7, "Findings of the Survey of Undergraduate Concerns: Anxieties, Academics, and Ambitions," by Sarah Klagsbrun describes and discusses her work when she herself was an undergraduate at Princeton University, New Jersey. It is the most recent of several student contributions to the *Journal of College Student Psychotherapy.*

Our final four chapters address some especially important specific developmental concerns. In Chapter 8, "College Age Substance Abuse as a Developmental Arrest," Timothy Rivinus of Brown University, Rhode Island, shows how alcohol and other drugs tend to block personality growth and, as college counselors and therapists may add from their own observations, how continuing substance misuse short-circuits our work with students. Chapter 9, "College Student Development: African Americans Reconsidered," by Harold Cheatham of Penn State University and Linda Berg-Cross of Howard University, Washington, D.C. shows how knowledge of Africentricity can be used creatively in an intervention model to promote African American college student development. Chapter 10, "Gender Paradoxes in College Student Development," by sociologist Frances Hoffmann, of the University of Missouri, depicts what is now known about the growing convergence between men's and women's development in contrast to their persistent gender differentiation. Thomas Mann of Pennsylvania's Devereaux Foundation, in Chapter 11 discusses "The Influence of Gender Identity on Separation Related Depressive Phenomena in College Men and Women," showing that, analogous to Frances Hoffmann's views, men and women are both more similar and different than appears on the surface.

Inevitably, we have not covered all of the important topics in college student development but we hope that the reader will find in this volume much that will be helpful in counseling, psychotherapy and in work with students generally.

Leighton C. Whitaker, PhD
Richard E. Slimak, PhD

Chapter 1

Psychotherapy
as a Developmental Process

Leighton C. Whitaker

SUMMARY. Psychotherapy as an effective developmental process requires both knowledge of personality development in general and knowledge of the person's particular developmental influences, including cultural. Among the latter, commercial culture and peer culture, as well as family influences, are especially powerful forces that college psychotherapists need to understand in depth. Several case examples are used to illustrate the influence of social conformity pressures and how the psychotherapist can further perspective and understanding. Alcohol and other drugs, violence perpetration, machismo training and the excesses of the beauty industry are discussed in the context of developmental psychotherapy.

This chapter explicates the importance and usefulness of a developmental framework for psychotherapy with special attention to the needs of college students.

Psychotherapy is potentially most effective when done within a knowledgeable developmental model, regardless of whatever other orientation a therapist may have. The process of psychotherapy, is itself developmental and should be attuned to helping meet a client's developmental needs. As Basch (1988) says,

Psychotherapy, as I see it, is applied developmental psychology. The therapist uses his or her knowledge of normal devel-

---

Leighton Whitaker, PhD, is Director of Psychological Services for Swarthmore College, Swarthmore, PA 19081.

1

opment to reach some conclusions about the reasons for a patient's malfunctioning and how one may enter the developmental spiral either to foster or to reinstate a more productive, or at least less destructive, developmental process. (Basch, 1988, p. 29)

Ideally, the therapist is guided both by the developmental model and the individual client's uniqueness, so that as the particular psychotherapy process is being informed by the model, the model is informed by the psychotherapy process. Therapists thus have a method of learning simultaneously about the individual client, the psychotherapy process, and the model.

USING A DEVELOPMENTAL MODEL

College psychotherapists who are attuned to students' special developmental needs, as well as suitably trained and experienced as therapists, will be able to recognize and utilize the many advantages of a developmental model. Effective utilization requires: ascertaining a given student's developmental stage(s); being able to relate a student's difficulty in the present stage of life to earlier difficulties; realizing how development is being helped or hindered by current interpersonal and environmental influences; gearing therapy to help the student advance to a further stage of growth and/or helping to consolidate a certain stage.

Without a knowledgeable developmental model, treatment tends to be static and out of tune with the person's inevitable developmental needs. The results may appear innocuous but often harm will have been done. For example, the current fashion of simply "targeting symptoms" may effectively stultify growth by obscuring underlying developmental dilemmas and giving everyone involved, including the student, the message that developmental needs are unimportant or even non-existent. Since symptoms themselves are typically signs of underlying dilemmas, symptom targeting by itself tends to reduce developmental opportunities by masking them and may even assure blocking of development.

Mary was a college senior whose presenting symptom was panic attacks. She had avoided seeing a therapist until her attacks became overwhelming and threatened to stop her college career as they became increasingly unaffordable in the face of greater academic and personal challenges. She wondered if the therapist would give her something to eradicate her symptom.

The therapist inquired into her developmental history and learned that the attacks began at age four. Her alcoholic grandfather had decided one day to park his car by the roadside and to deliberately drink himself to death. Mary's father, after discovering his own father's dead body, came home and told his family, whereupon Mary began to cry. Father responded to her crying by telling her over and over again not to cry. Father did not let himself cry either. Mary learned her lesson well and carefully, albeit at the cost of panic attacks, never cried again.

If the therapist had simply responded to Mary's request for drug treatment to target her symptom, her developmental blockage would have been reinforced. Instead, as Mary could then readily see from her own account, she could elect to address her symptom as an invaluable developmental opportunity. In the process of learning not to stifle her feelings, including her long overdue grief reaction, she could not only lessen her panic attacks as they would lose their motivating power but she would be able to stop and correct a basically morbid family-originated process that had damaged her father and then herself. On the other hand, she could choose a treatment that would simply target her symptom. In either case, she would have a meaningful choice made possible by understanding the derivation and probable cause of her symptom. Whereas she had no choice at age four, or even throughout childhood, she did now.

When students are enabled to see and to take seriously their own developmental needs, they become empowered by beginning to understand themselves, find a better sense of direction, and actively collaborate in their own therapy. Then, instead of being the passive recipient of some treatment which is chosen for them and done to them, they can fully participate in and "own" the therapy process and the results.

The developmental approach to assessment and psychotherapy is inherently intriguing, like a mystery story, as therapist and student work together to gather clues and to reach important realizations. Thus the learning aspect of the developmental psychotherapy process begins to engender motivation and important realizations in itself. It results in the student's learning to learn, especially to develop the ability to learn about oneself, an ability that tends to increase and carry beyond the actual period of psychotherapy. Developmentally-oriented psychotherapy thereby serves a preventive function since the student has learned and keeps learning how to avoid being blocked from self-understanding.

As implied by Mary's wondering if the therapist would just give her something to make her symptom go away, there is always at least some resistance to the learning process. Resistance can take many forms. Among students, intellectualization and rationalization are common. "Is there any hard evidence that my panic attacks are psychologically determined?" "My grandmother had panic attacks, so they must be inherited!" "Maybe I have a chemical imbalance and that's causing my problem"; "That historical stuff I told you about was a long time ago, and besides I haven't thought about it."

As therapists learn, if they have succumbed to the lure of responding with intellectual arguments, debate may merely stiffen resistances. Though such intellectual defenses invite collusion in the form of intellectual debate, they tend to be highly speculative and proliferative, especially since the motivation behind them is to avoid getting at the truth. The therapist has to deal with the fear motivation which would avoid realization. As a young man said eloquently about his own resistances, "The unfolding of the truth is the inevitable scare."

The resistances are there for protection which, at least historically in the person's life, was needed to ensure survival, and therefore to make at least some development possible. So what is needed is cultivation of a further developmental perspective. In Mary's case, the therapist noted that when she was age four, and indeed during her entire life at home, it was important, indeed probably essential, for her not to cry. Crying would have meant threatening her father intolerably, making him extremely angry, and suffering even more severe admonitions not to cry, so she would have had to stifle further her normal need to grieve and to grasp emotionally what had happened.

The therapist then sets up a vivid contrast effect in order to make a crucial distinction. "When you were living at home and growing up, you certainly could not have afforded to cry or grieve. You needed to protect yourself in order to survive and you learned well how to survive." The therapist might then pause and say "I wonder if that's true now though, right here. Is it still so dangerous to cry? I wonder if your solution back then is actually the problem now?" Thus the therapist conveys an understanding to Mary of her dilemma and, further, shows a possible way out.

This therapeutic approach teaches a method of understanding which helps the student to master various kinds of dilemmas, whether we call them stalemates, double binds, or "catch 22s," in other words those many situations in which one may feel "stuck." Often such dilemmas can be resolved by understanding matters within a developmental framework which contrasts then and now.

Generally, the therapist can begin by asking how matters got to the present impasse. The student may have brought forward, quite intact, some assumption which made perfect sense back when but which has little or no validity now. The answer to this dilemma is not to deny the validity of the student's survival strategy when it was formed, or even as it was carried forward in time, but rather to acknowledge its validity when it was formed and then to question its validity for the present and the future.

Even after the student has realized the contrast, at least by grasping it intellectually, the therapist may see resistance to giving up the old defense, a defense that is now admittedly the problem. The therapist then needs to cultivate a still further developmental process. Often the student needs to realize and begin to grieve three kinds of losses that will be experienced in giving up the old pattern of defense.

The first loss relates to realizing what "useless" time, effort and misery have been spent in the service of the system of defensive conformity to the old situation. As a student remarked, "I wish I hadn't spent all those years like that!" Since the realization of loss is inherently sad, the student needs to be or become *able* to be sad, contrary to the mistaken popular notion that people shouldn't be sad–they should just be "happy"–and that to be sad is to be depressed (Whitaker, 1990).

The second loss relates to leaving the psychological field in which one was close to the people adjusted to in terms of conformity of outlook. When Mary began to let herself cry, she became out of harmony with the ethos of her father who did not let himself cry and forbade her to cry. By changing her old ways, she felt estranged from that system of being that had helped her to survive. Realizing that one is truly losing the old connectedness is also, normally, a sad experience.

The third kind of loss is closely connected to the second. When one leaves a psychological field, one usually leaves behind those in the field, at least if those others will not change.

> A student who had flunked out of college, like his sister, then made remarkable progress in psychotherapy, reentered college and was about to graduate. He reported a dream in which he had nearly reached the top of a hill but refused to walk any further unless his sister, who continued in real life to be dysfunctional, could be brought along with him. All three kinds of his "losses occasioned by improvement" needed to be explicitly recognized and grieved before he could proceed further.

THE CONCEPT OF "NORMAL" DEVELOPMENT

Implicit in any developmental model of personality is the assumption that some forms of development are more desirable than others, at least within given contexts. When the interpersonal and cultural contexts themselves are considered normal, they may be considered rightfully dominant in importance. For example, to say that an individual is "maladjusted" or a "misfit" is to say he or she has failed to develop in harmony within a presumably normal cultural context.

On the other hand, when individuals are seen as more important than the cultural context–even a presumably normal context–we think more often of accommodating them, even if they are quite idiosyncratic, especially if they are persons who can make an outstanding contribution to society. For example, Isaac Newton, a genius who revolutionized the scientific view of the world, was strikingly eccentric and so out of harmony with others as to be considered mad by his contemporaries (Storr, 1990). However, Newton was also regarded as one of the greatest scientists of all time and was honored for his contributions. Similarly, the poet Emily Dickinson was an extreme recluse who was hardly in touch with other people except in a one way manner through her writing. Yet society has recognized the great value of her quite "deviant" and idiosyncratic contributions to the world's literature.

Simply equating a typical pattern of development in a particular culture with normal development rests on the incorrect assumption that the culture itself is wholly normal. The psychotherapist should refrain, therefore, from merely practicing some psychology of adjustment, not only out of respect for the individual and because the individual may contribute to society, but because every society itself has morbidity promoting features. As psychiatrist Arthur Deikman documents in his book, *"The Wrong Way Home: Uncovering the Patterns of Cult Behavior in American Society,"* at least the tendency to cult forms of behavior, with its inherent bigotry, is omnipresent in society. The conforming person who uncritically and essentially unthinkingly simply adjusts to a pressure group becomes likely to take out his or her own resentment on persons outside the group who are not in conformity. "The more authoritarian the human social system, the more likely a separatist world view will arise because any anger or resentment stimulated in the follower by his or her submission to the leader requires displacement onto other persons–the outsider, the infidel, the non-believer" (Deikman, 1990, p. 104). Insidiously, the cult tendency inevitably destroys the integrity and well-being of the insiders also.

Colleges and universities, like other social institutions, are subject to the morbidity enhancing features of society in general as well as their own morbid tendencies. One has only to think of the common general societal promotion of heavy alcohol use and its particularly emphatic, though often denied, promotion in colleges. First year students, whether or not accustomed to drinking, are initiated on many campuses by drinking rituals which in many cases, directly and indirectly, promote disability and even death. Though use of alcohol and other drugs is probably less for youth bound for college than for the general population of youth:

> There's a higher incidence of alcohol use on college and university campuses than in the U.S. population at large. Eighty five percent of college students drink beverage alcohol compared with 70% of the general population. . . . However, it still is overlooked that the highest source of mortality in the late adolescent and young adult population is alcohol and drug related motor vehicle fatalities. (Rivinus, 1988, p. 4)

Students who fail, as it were, to "fit in" with alcoholic culture may be snubbed socially and be considered maladjusted.

> John was a college junior who had fit into his campus culture group quite well. But he decided to see a therapist after being upset by experiencing in himself and among friends some extreme instances of destructive behavior while under the influence of alcohol and marijuana. He realized in his sober moments that his "getting wasted" was at odds with his own upbringing and ideals. But the desire to fit in with his peers and the attractions of a macho style of behavior made passively "going with the group" all but irresistible despite parental disfavor, academic mediocrity, deteriorating health, and a sense of self-betrayal. Thus John was "stuck."
>
> The therapist emphasized looking at John's life developmentally. John recalled at length his early life, his parents' ideals, and his own adolescent rebellion. He saw that he had really stopped determining his own development, had disowned his past and was trying to fit in with his present sub-culture as if that was a desirable adjustment. His major in college, which he had chosen for merely "practical reasons," held no fascination for him. He saw his future as fatefully limited to a humdrum job, onerous obligations, and lacking any joy or

creativity. He could not conceive of how his relatively happy childhood and the values he had developed early in his life could ever be expressed. He seemed to be acting out a basically depressive lifestyle with the implicit assumption that his positive early life experiences were or should be dead and useless. "Getting wasted" appeared to mean destroying his early identity.

As John saw his life in developmental perspective, he began to actively determine his own future, a future that he would form and "own." He sifted through what he wanted from his past and what he wished to change in accord with his ideals. The late adolescent and early adulthood developmental need to do this sifting relative to one's upbringing was being met. He changed his college major to one that excited his interest and imagination, formed some new friendships, and maintained some old friendships but on his own terms. His old friends who were immersed in the drug culture, macho behavior and cynicism, had to relate to him quite differently. At first they contested and belittled his efforts to change but he began to be respected for his efforts and the friends were provoked to look more carefully at their own lives with the sobering realization, as it were, that they could also change. Thus John became successfully maladjusted and provocative relative to the prevailing morbidity of his peer group.

College psychotherapists especially should apprise themselves of the recent and current negative cultural developmental influences that impact so greatly on students' lives. It is not enough to look only at students' relationships and experiences with parents, although they are crucial determiners of personality development. Peer relationships together with mass communication and commercial culture play increasingly important roles beginning in early childhood, especially since our institutions have done little to counter these influences until very recently. Peer relationships and pressures probably outweigh whatever colleges do to influence students through either the academic or student affairs curricula as sociologist Frances Hoffmann (1992) has noted in her contribution to this volume. Psychiatrist and pediatrician Timothy Rivinus

(1988) illustrates, in his reflections on his own rather typical kind of experience, the powerful interactive influence of authorities modeling drug use and denying its inherently damaging effects, including the consequent peer pressure to use drugs:

> My parents, forbearers, teachers and mentors taught me nothing of the dangers of substance use. Substance use was "a given" in the family and culture in which I grew up. It was also a given in college and medical school, a social and accepted form of pleasure. No strings attached. In college I learned that drinking was "a thing to do." In medical school I learned from my peers that drugs could produce ecstasy and nothing else. (Rivinus, 1988, p. 3)

The present generation of college students has been raised largely by television which, on the whole, massively promotes morbid behavior by means of both its mode and its content. The mode, which is that of induced passivity and vivid visual and auditory sensation, promotes unthinking, uncritical acceptance of the content. By contrast, the printed word has to be read, a more active process inviting real thinking which is active and more likely to be critical. The content of both the big and small screens models and highlights destructive behavior on the whole.

The vast majority of TV programs have been most influential abusive and exploitative babysitters. For example, according to the National Council on Alcoholism, "A child will see alcohol consumed an average of 75,000 times on TV before he or she is of legal drinking age" in addition to 100,000 television ads for beer that the average child sees during the same formative years (Johnson, 1988, p. 78). Similarly, the average entering college student has passively witnessed an ever increasing number of murders on both the small and big screens, and invitations to imbibe caffeinated beverages, to eat principally unhealthy foods, to diet in various faddish ways, and to react to disagreement violently. Video culture, perhaps most extremely in the form of video tapes, promotes morbidity massively. Witnessing all of this violence tends to program people for both internally and externally directed violence.

Since students have been reared increasingly by TV since 1950 and TV, as well as movies, has become increasingly violent, it should not be surprising that both youth murders and suicide have risen rapidly also. Colleges and universities can expect more campus violence including both internally and externally directed forms. For example, according to the Centers for Disease Control (1991a), suicide rates for youth 15-19 years old have quadrupled from 1950 to 1988 (2.7 per 100,000 in 1950 to 11.3 in 1988). In a survey of the United States and its territories, 27% of grade 9-12 students reported serious thought about committing suicide.

Similarly, the survey showed that "approximately one of every five high school students carried a firearm, knife, or club at least one time during the 30 days preceding the survey" (Centers for Disease Control, 1991b, p. 683). Males carried weapons approximately four times as much as females. The extent of the violence problem now reaching colleges and worsening as a future dilemma is also implied in the Federal Bureau of Investigation data showing that in the decade of the 1980s more than 11,000 people in the U.S. were murdered by high school youth using firearms, knives, or blunt objects.

Popular magazines induce conformity to ideals that are merely commercially motivated and thereby strive to get young people to eschew their natural attributes in favor of expensive artificial habits and images. The current epidemic of eating disorders clearly owes much of its motivation to these pervasive social influences (Gordon, 1989, 1990).

College campus efforts to counter commercially motivated morbidity are still miniscule and mild compared to the massive influence of commercial culture, whether the comparison is in terms of money invested, pervasiveness of presentations, or persuasive force. For example, even in magazines which one might think would be devoted to psychological and physical well-being, such as *Psychology Today* or *Sports Illustrated,* any of the rare inducements to stop smoking cigarettes or drinking alcohol are overwhelmed by sensational pictorial ads promoting smoking and drinking, the two overall most destructive drug uses. The "Marlboro man" still epitomizes "real manhood," which is achieved ostensibly through using the drug which, by itself, accounts for half of all untimely deaths in the United States. Like popular magazines, television overwhelmingly pairs alcohol and sometimes even cigarettes with sports accomplishments and images of ideal athletes. Though, or more likely because, alcohol decreases muscle strength and coordination in both the short and long runs, beer and baseball are paired during commercial breaks between innings to suggest the opposite. Illustrating how aggressive and manipulative of the law advertisers can be, Virginia Slims cigarettes are paired with womens' tennis even on television where the cigarette trade name is emblazoned on a huge backdrop, thus getting around the injunction against direct cigarette ads on TV.

But college psychotherapists can contest and help change otherwise compelling destructive life patterns promoted by commercial culture, through psychotherapy and through influencing campus community norms. Students who seek counseling or psychotherapy tend to question the status quo since, often, the status quo has not been working satisfactorily for them. Furthermore, the mode of developmentally oriented psychotherapy suits students' generally undernutured need to learn to think actively, critically and with a view to their long-term well-being.

To help students in any thorough way, therapists must continually educate themselves about the morbidity induced by popular culture, a culture which represents itself mythically as normal. Therapists have to see through the myths themselves if they are to help their student clients develop the insight to reject such myths in favor of their own well-being. College psychotherapists can then also be better consultants to campus organizations interested in promoting healthy lifestyles.

Typically, pop culture, with its often exclusively commercial motivation, comprises campaigns to induce conformity to a supposed group norm which is advanced by public relations and advertising efforts. The commercial marketeers attempt to influence a mass market number of people. For example, beauty advertisers target virtually all females but especially adolescent girls and young women who are anxious to fit in with what becomes peer culture. The trick is to convince as many females as possible that they are naturally and inherently deficient and therefore need the product to be acceptable as persons and as sexual objects. To do so, the marketeers promote unnatural images which are impossible to attain without the product. Naomi Wolf (1991), in her book *The Beauty Myth: How Images of Beauty Are Used Against Women,* masterfully, relentlessly, and devastatingly exposes the psychology and methodology of the many ploys used by the beauty industry. For example, among the excesses of the many injurious beauty industries,

> The trend toward breast surgery is created by a culture that blocks out all breasts that are not the Official Breast, calls imagery left over from this editing "sex," keeps women ignorant of their own and other women's bodies, and provides a little monitored service . . . (Wolf, 1991, p. 247)

She ascribes the burgeoning cosmetic surgery business to the profit motive which turns out to be quite antithetical to confident sensuality. "The surgeon's market is imaginary, since there is nothing wrong with womens' faces or bodies that social change won't cure; so the surgeons depend for their income on warping female self-perception and multiplying female self-hatred" (Wolf, 1991). Her book makes clear that both women and men are losers in this kind of commercial onslaught that distances the sexes by idealizing artificiality. Her quarrel is not against sexuality, which she wishes to nurture, but against its spoilers. Therefore she argues against the beauty industry which ostensibly promotes sexual attractiveness but functions quite effectively to suppress female sexuality and, in turn, to de-eroticize male-female relationships.

Increasingly, advertisers are pairing sex and alcohol. Colt 45 malt liquor is supposed to enable successful seduction every time. As noted in Newsweek, citing ads by Miller Genuine Draft, Coors Light, Keystone, and Old Milwaukee, "Bikinis and beer have long been a popular marketing mix. But after a recent period of relative enlightenment, brewers have sunk to new lows . . ." (Newsweek, June 24, 1991, p. 6). In the light, or should we say darkness, of commercial culture, it is not surprising that so many youth have deep, inextricable imagos combining alcohol and other drugs, deprecatory sex, and food fetishes.

> Joyce began to see a college psychotherapist because she had an eating disorder and was depressed. In relating her developmental history, she noted that she had dreaded her physical growth beginning at puberty. She planned to try to maintain a boy-like appearance, to be like the models she saw in magazines who seemed more similar to pre-adolescent boys than grown women. So her ideal was to stop developing. But she began to develop into a full figured woman. By the time she reached college she was a "failure," someone who hated herself for not achieving her ideal. She envied women with "stick figures" who looked like the models she continued to view obsessively in magazines. Accordingly, she did a great deal to hurt herself and her body, by binging and purging, drinking heavily, smoking marijuana, and pursuing males who were deprecating of her. Meanwhile, she deprecated males who were both interested in and respectful of her.

Her psychotherapy focused on constructing and understanding the history of the influences which had led to her "adjustment." Family use of food in substitution for other gratifications formed part of the basis of her self-destructiveness, which combined with the massive influence of the beauty industry, caused her to deprecate herself in myriad ways. She began to "see through" these influences and to become assertive in nurturing her considerable intellectual, social and physical assets. On the way, she completely overcame her eating disorder and drug dependency as the motivation for them evaporated. She was also less depressively inclined and able to choose a career.

Myriam Miedzian (1991), in her book *Boys Will Be Boys: Breaking the Link Between Masculinity and Violence,* exposes the complementary male mythology, that to be a "normal" and acceptable male, one must learn to be violent and keep proving that one has been thus become a man. She clearly documents the power and pervasiveness of this influence from the cradle to the grave and at all levels of society. In her chapter on "Real Men, 'Wimps,' and our National Security" (p. 18), she documents how the machismo ethos has done much to serve patriotism, "manhood," and war while destroying empathy for the victims of war and blocking the development of negotiating skills and the efforts of those men and women who would find alternatives to destructiveness. She links the glory of war with the cultivation of bigotry.

Discussing how sports are taught, Miedzian emphasizes the connection between winning at any cost and the inevitable generalization of this philosophy to one's whole life and the consequent ease with which one practices both physical and psychological violence. Thus the "normal" rearing of males has quite abnormal, morbid effects. Machismo culture induces men to engage far more than women in murder, suicide, and other forms of violence, including war (Whitaker, 1987).

But women too are being brought more and more into the violence culture as reflected in their committing more violent crimes themselves as well as being victimized by others and themselves. Increases in female cigarette smoking, eating disorders, and recourse to damaging forms of "cosmetic" surgery in the past decade are examples of greater externally induced but now internally mediated self-destructiveness.

Though commercial culture often induces distinctive forms of morbidity according to gender, it ensures, as it were, that both sexes will begin to be heavily influenced as soon as they can see and hear. The media increase the numbers and destructiveness, year by year, of the violent acts targeted at all children beginning in the earliest childhood years. While no country comes close to the United States in terms of overall TV violence, we are especially adept at making sure, with the most advanced modern technology, that children are more thoroughly programmed for violence. "On American TV, childrens' weekend daytime programs averaged 15.5 violent acts per hour in 1988. Evening time programs averaged 6.2. On all three networks childrens' weekend programs have long been and continue to be three to six times more violent than evening prime-time programs" (Miedzian, 1991, p. 209). "American children watch TV an average of twenty-four hours a week. This is more time than they spend in school. By the time they are eighteen years old our children have viewed approximately twenty-six thousand murders on the screen" (Miedzian, 1991, p. 211). Parents have only to allow their children to be absorbed in popular television to ensure that they will have a dedicated and expertly abusive babysitter.

ISSUES OF AUTONOMY VS. DEPENDENCY

Adolescence may be largely an invention of modern Western society at least in the economic and, inevitably therefore, emotional senses. Our society on the whole presses for more and more education which delays economic and emotional autonomy. Arguably, more education usually eventuates in greater autonomy in the long run, but it also creates more dependency in the not so short run, and the dependency conditions often delay the development of some forms of responsibility. Economic dependency often exacts a high price emotionally, analogous to the long term consequences of borrowing money at a high rate of interest.

Some parents might say that, if "youth is wasted on the young" as George Bernard Shaw claimed, it is because youth are not paying for it. At least that is the view some parents may begin to have as they themselves pay ever escalating college costs. As the parents of a recent college grad noted, it was as if they had paid out of their net earnings each year the entire cost of a new Cadillac car without receiving any of the cars. Since college costs have outpaced inflation for the past ten years, both parents and college students are often hard-pressed to earn the continually greater amounts of money required. Most often, even when college students contribute substantially, it is not nearly enough to work their way through college.

The college years are more or less representative in our culture of a transitional period that may mark the end of adolescence and the development of ability to lead one's own life. In recent years, however, the college years are less representative of nearness to full autonomy. Students are more likely to return home after college and/or go on to graduate school. In either case they are not fully in "the real world" of relatively autonomous functioning. Thus certain forms of dependency–whether on parents or school or, often, both–tend to continue unabated. Such prolonged dependency is rife with opportunities for conflict.

The child/adult wants freedom of a kind and may well resent the still controlling ways of parents or school. Parents feel, naturally enough they suppose, that they want some say as to how their money is spent. And schools tend still to be at least somewhat in loco parentis, if only to protect themselves; though they have eased off in recent decades, many colleges are rethinking the matter now and tending to exert more control.

As in many tense situations, humor may serve both to illustrate and defuse the tension between parents and children. Columnist Art Buchwald (1990) satirized the college student's stay at home in his column "Parent-child bout when college is out." He observes that "Most experts give the honeymoon three weeks from the moment the student was picked up at the airport to the hour the father yells at his child, 'When are you going to get a job?'" (Buchwald, 1990, p. 2-D). And of course many students have heard and can effectively satirize the tales told by parents of their own wonderfully noble early life struggles. For example, there is the proverbial story of the parent as a young child walking 10 miles through snow and bitter cold just to get to school. Such a story may be devilishly effective if told to current college students who have grown up without much opportunity to experience physical hardship or the memory lapses that facilitate exaggeration.

The so-called "boomerang generation," comprising college grads who return to the nest and thereby strain their parents' patience and purses, may be attributable chiefly to financial pressures.

> Most starting salaries haven't risen to meet the level of escalating housing costs. And rare is the college grad who spent his or her academic career building up a bank account instead of joining classmates on Spring Break excursions. So what you have is a generation of young professionals who want to move away but who plainly cannot afford to. (Diamond, 1990, p. 49)

As a result of our basic, and continually rising, commitment to higher education together with rapidly escalating education and housing costs, the dependency vs. autonomy conflict may be higher than ever before. It is a conflict tailor-made to cause great distress to both parents and students unless it is explicitly addressed and at least partially resolved. How can college psychotherapists address this developmental dilemma wherein education, which is designed to increase autonomy in the long run, mitigates against the development of autonomy for many more years than the natural biological timetable?

Perhaps the answer resides in clearly recognizing that there is no perfect answer, that there will always be major stress, and that each party must learn about the other party's problems and viewpoints. Of course, the conflict itself takes myriad forms, and college therapists usually hear just the student's viewpoint. Therefore, therapists may have to ask certain questions which enable a better reading of the parental position by considering the parents' own developmental histories.

> Student: I got into this big argument with my parents about next summer. They want me to take some dumb job slinging hamburgers. That won't help me learn anything. Besides, my parents make a lot more money per hour than I can make. And, anyway, what I'd like to do is just take it easy for a couple of months, maybe go to Europe like some of my friends.
>
> Therapist: Where are your parents coming from? Did they go to college? What was it like for them?
>
> Student: Well, yeah, they went to college but they make a big deal of how they did it. Mom used to sling hash at some place and Dad was a laborer or something in the summers. But you can't work your way through college now, like they say they did. They're just being unfair.
>
> Therapist: So they have some strong feelings about what they did and they would like you to do something like they did?
>
> Student: Yeah, I guess so, but that doesn't seem fair because things have changed.

Therapist: You're right that things have changed. But both you and your parents have very strong feelings about all this. You and they are coming from very different places. You feel justified and they feel justified. I guess we can see why. Do you think that they want you to make a financial contribution for the spirit of it as well as the money? Would it make them feel appreciated?

Obviously, just a brief interchange like this is quite unlikely to produce a complete resolution, but it may get the dilemma unstuck and more productively oriented.

Therapists also hear students' accounts of parental practices which seem to use money to inhibit their child/adult's development.

Gary was an extremely hard-working and accomplished student who tended to be popular but who never had money for social activities. His girlfriend found various ways to pay for the modestly priced events that they did attend, albeit seldom without anguish on his part. Gary's parents took the position that he should work all summer to earn money for college and, during the academic year, should both get excellent grades and work part-time to pay his academic expenses. They seemed expert at making sure he would have no economic latitude though they themselves were well off financially. Nothing Gary could say was effective in changing their minds. At the heart of the matter was a covert determination to control their son in puppet-like fashion. To complete the dependency trap, they showed strong disapproval when he considered seeing a college psychotherapist who "would just stir things up."

Hopefully, parents and their college students share a common goal: promoting the students' personal growth and autonomy. But given the impositions, of prolonged adolescence and expensive preparations for "real life in the adult world," it may be difficult for them to keep focused on this common goal. Therapists can help by carefully distinguishing between strengthening versus morbid forms of dependency and thereby avoiding enabling support for morbid dependencies and cultivating interest in strengthening forms. Education is a clear example of a generally strengthening form of dependency. By becoming educated, people become more able to care for themselves and others. And the process of education instructs people in constructive forms of interdependency.

Psychotherapy should also be a strengthening form of dependency both in terms of the goal and the process. As in education, the process can teach constructive interdependency as therapist and student work together to develop the helping relationship and further the common goal of strengthening the student.

The stigmatizing of psychotherapy is often premised on confusing weakening with strengthening forms of dependency. Every therapist has heard the complaint that someone might become dependent on psychotherapy, as if psychotherapy is inherently a weakening form of dependency. Yet the same complainer may have no notion that the psychotherapy, if carried out well, is replacing really weakening forms of dependency such as food or drug dependency. Usually such a complainer is denying the very existence and significance of the morbid dependencies.

This denial-motivated confusion is superbly illustrated by popular media presentations. During professional sports events shown on television, one hears messages to youth to "stay off drugs" paired with advertisements to drink beer on every possible occasion. The message becomes beer equals baseball and beer contains no drug. Thus denial and hypocrisy are taught relentlessly using the most advanced technical means.

> A Clint Eastwood movie shows the hero, who is trying to inveigle himself into acceptance by a macho cult, sitting at a bar where he proves to the other men in the bar how tough he is by demanding and drinking literally every concoction that the bartender can offer. He then gets up on his feet so that everyone is quite impressed. Then another man offers the hero a "drug" (marijuana perhaps) whereupon the hero declares "No, I'm too high on life."

Since such messages are directed much more to males than females, it is not surprising that males shun psychotherapy much more than females on the average, as well as commit many more suicides, murders, and other violent crimes.

TREATING THE STUDENT WELL

As discussed previously, a developmental model for psychotherapy means discovering how a student's problems have evolved as adjustments to developmental dilemmas, and providing perspectives on how the student can now afford, as it were, to be different. The treatment process itself must embody both this growing knowledge and a therapeutic attitude that is in accord with what the student can now afford to be. In essence, psychotherapy as an effective developmental process requires the therapist to empathize with the old adjustment strategies, and to help with the inevitable vicissitudes of giving them up.

Treatment as a therapeutic concept needs to be linked closely to how we can treat people well in the general sense. Too often, treatment professionals fall into a narrow definition of treatment that disregards the person's basic developmental needs while providing a technical form of treatment. Since how one is treated as a human being in the overall sense tends to be internalized, the manner in which the therapist treats the student–whether poorly or well–has critical developmental significance. Treating the student well means that the therapist is caring and respectful, and not just competent in terms of technical expertise. Implicitly, therapy goals include helping to build these caring and respectful qualities within the student.

Since change means giving up old adjustments which have been vitally needed, resistances to change often have a phobic quality. It is as if the student says, even after some insight is gained, "I can't change; I feel stuck," implying that something dreadful will happen if she or he does change.

A first year college student approached her first class with dread though, or more likely because, she was highly motivated to succeed. Throughout her high school years she had been taunted and often treated sadistically by her female peers as someone who threatened them because she was "too smart and too pretty." She adjusted to this treatment by what she called "fitting in" which meant getting heavily involved in the peer drug culture, missing classes and developing an eating disorder that served to make her "dumb," sick and less attractive.

On the morning of her first college class, she managed, as it were, to have an argument with her boyfriend and to have a "panic attack" which prevented her from attending class. In her therapy session later that day she recalled thinking that her boyfriend, who was not going on to college, might "feel bad" if she succeeded. In other sessions, she was able to recall specific instances of being punished by girlfriends for being smart and pretty.

Now possessed of some insight, she further resisted success by claiming, rather triumphantly it seemed, that she had already doomed herself because she had missed the vital first class. In addition to noting her triumphant manner and her defensive use of this further convenient handicap, the therapist pointed out that the girls who had tortured her were no longer in a position to do so and that humoring her boyfriend would not be good for either of them. Furthermore, it was vital for her to see that the therapist cared about and respected her in the sense of treating her as a worthwhile human being entitled to a life in accord with her interests and desire to develop her potential. In this process, it was the student's "dumb and ugly" defensive self-image pitted against the therapist's steadfast insistence that she was smart and attractive but afraid of attack. She then went on to do quite well in college as she "saw through" her developmental history.

In conclusion, the developmentally oriented psychotherapist has to see through developmental dilemmas in their family, peer culture and commercial culture forms in order to help students realize their own potential. Targeting symptoms is expedient; developing one's potential to understand and guide one's life is wise.

REFERENCES

Basch, M.F. (1988). *Understanding psychotherapy: The science behind the art.* New York: Basic Books Inc.

Buchwald, A. (1990). Parent-child bout when college is out. *The Philadelphia Inquirer,* June 12, 2-D.

Centers for Disease Control (1991a). Attempted suicide among high school students–United States, 1990. *Morbidity and Mortality Weekly Report, 40*(37), 633-635.

Centers for Disease Control (1991b). Weapon-carrying among high school students–United States, 1990. *Morbidity and Mortality Weekly Report, 40*(40), 681-684.

Diamond, D. (1990). The boomerang generation. *Applause,* July, pp. 49, 50.

Deikman, A.J. (1990). *The wrong way home: Uncovering the patterns of cult behavior in American society.* Boston: Beacon Press.

Gordon, R.A. (1989). Bulimia: A sociocultural orientation. Chapter 4, pp. 41-55, in L.C. Whitaker & W.N. Davis (Eds.) *The bulimic college student: Evaluation, treatment and prevention.* New York: The Haworth Press, Inc.

Gordon, R.A. (1990). *Anorexia and bulimia: Anatomy of a social epidemic.* Cambridge, Mass.: Basil Blackwell, Inc.

Johnson, W.O. (1988). Sports and suds. *Sports Illustrated,* 8/8/1988, p. 78-79.

Miedzian, M. (1991). *Boys will be boys: Breaking the link between masculinity and violence.* New York; Doubleday & Co., Inc.

Newsweek (1991). Peripicks: Great moments in advertising. June 24, p. 6.

Rivinus, T. M. (1988). Introduction in T. M. Rivinus (Guest Editor) *Journal of College Student Psychotherapy,* vol. 2 (3/4), and in T. M. Rivinus (1988, Editor) *Alcoholism/ Chemical Dependency and the College Student.* New York: The Haworth Press, Inc.

Storr, A. (1990). *Churchill's black dog, Kafka's mice and other phenomena of the human mind.* New York: Ballantine Books.

Whitaker, L. C. (1987). Macho and morbidity: The emotional need vs. fear dilemma in men. *Journal of College Student Psychotherapy,* vol. 1 (4), 33-47.

Whitaker, L.C. (1989). Myths and heroes: Visions of the future. *Journal of College Student Psychotherapy,* vol. 4(2), 13-33.

Whitaker, L.C. (1990). Countering cultural myths to help prevent college student suicide. *Journal of College Student Psychotherapy,* vol. 5(3/4), and Chapter 4, pp. 79-97, in L. Whitaker & R. Slimak (Eds.) (1990). *College student suicide.* New York: The Haworth Press, Inc.

Wolf, N. (1991). *The beauty myth: How images of beauty are used against women.* New York: William Morrow and Co.

Chapter 2

A Student Development Metamodel for University and College Counseling Center Professionals

Richard E. Slimak

SUMMARY. This chapter attempts to build a bridge between student development theory and the university and college counseling center. The bridge relies on the developmental work of William G. Perry, Arthur W. Chickering, and David Drum, and the philosophical work of Huston Cummings Smith. The bridge takes the form of a three-dimensional metamodel which is not dependent on time or the generation presently attending American colleges and universities. A case study is presented to assist in the explication of the metamodel.

Much has been written about student development within the past two decades. Beginning with the transitions from student personnel, through student affairs, to student development theories and their applications, the literature has focused almost exclusively on the various "offices of student life" at American institutions of higher education. This focus has almost been to the exclusion of the university or college counseling center. Too often counseling centers are seen by others, as well as themselves, as emotional remediators rather than developers.

Richard E. Slimak, PhD, is Director of Counseling and Associate Professor at the United States Coast Guard Academy. Address requests for reprints to Richard E. Slimak, PhD, Cadet Counseling (ssl), United States Coast Guard Academy, 15 Mohegan Avenue, New London, CT 06320.

Theorists abound in student development. Many, like Maslow (1962), Kohlberg (1984), and Erikson (1968), have their under pinnings centered in a more general human development arena. Others, like Chickering (1969), Drum (1980), Perry (1990), and Morrill, Oetting and Hurst (1974) are focused exclusively in American higher education. Yet, there appears to be, only a narrow and unsteady bridge to the world of the university and college counseling center.

This metamodel is intended to provide a construct for counseling center professionals in their developmental work with students. In addition, this construct should ensure that developmental issues are not lost when the immediate therapeutic agendas are central in the counseling process.

THE METAMODEL'S BACKGROUND

This model is intended to serve as an everyday construct for the therapist in terms of their work with students in American higher education settings. It should have utility for both remediation and development since it is an "active" model that intends to chart a course during the years of college in terms of seven "dimensions" that Arthur W. Chickering set forth in *Education and Identity* (1969). These dimensions are housed within three "domains" of the person that Huston Cummings Smith postulated (1971). The activity or movement within the model transits the time line of the undergraduate years through incorporating the three "modes" of William G. Perry's *Forms of Intellectual and Ethical Development in the College Years: A Scheme* (1970) and, to a degree, Mary Field Belenky et al.'s *Women's Ways of Knowing* (1986).

Dimensions

Arthur W. Chickering (1969) reviewed the literature on adolescent and young adult development in the late 1960s and formulated seven major "vectors" of student development for both men and women in undergraduate higher education.

Chickering's first vector is *achieving competence*: developing competency in the intellectual, physical, and manual skill areas as well as interpersonal and social interactions. The second vector deals with two primary young adult emotions, aggression and sex, and is termed *managing emotions*. The third vector is *becoming autonomous*: the understanding of the interdependence of emotional, financial, and physical independence. The fourth vector, *establishing identity*, is ". . . an inner consistency of values, emotions, beliefs, and determinants of behavior" (Hurst, 1978, p. 116). *Freeing interpersonal relationships*, the fifth vector, is a function of the other four vectors, and as ". . . White (1958) observes, relationships become less anxious, less defensive, 'less burdened by inappropriate past reactions, more friendly, more spontaneous, more warm, and more respectful (p. 343)'" (cited in Chickering, 1969, p. 15). The sixth vector, *clarifying purposes*, includes ". . . occupational, marital, socioeconomic, avocational, and general life style goals. It implies intentionality of direction in life" (Hurst, 1978, p. 116). The final vector, *developing integrity*, involves belief systems which guide behavior. This vector is threefold: including humanizing values, personalizing values, and developing congruence.

Domains

Previous models of college student development have been, primarily, functions of psychologist's research. The "domains" of this model are housed in the work of a philosopher. Huston Cummings Smith (1971), professor of philosophy at the Massachusetts Institute of Technology and, later, Syracuse University, while delivering a Phi Beta Kappa commencement address, reflected on a sabbatical year in Tibet and said:

> For at its best education is not mere *in*formation; it is *trans*formation. As *e-ducare,* the drawing forth of that which is potentially best in man, it seeks transformation of the human spirit into a life of quickened perception, heightened interest, nobler aspiration, and deepened community. (p. 2)

It was during the year in Tibet that Smith, as serendipity would have it, happened on one of two monasteries that trained their lamas (monks) to ". . . chant in an extraordinary way, a way which enabled individual lamas to sing multiple tones simultaneously" (op.cit., p. 3). In a sense, the lamas were trained to sing solo cords: ". . . 'solo' in the sense that one voice does the singing, 'chords' in the sense that the voice is sounding multiple (3) tones simultaneously" (op.cit., p. 3). After playing a recording of this "haunting, holy sound" (op.cit., p. 3) Smith turned to the commencement audience and said:

> Just as the lama was sounding three tones simultaneously–a first, a third, and a faintly audible fifth–I hope that your lives, too, will sound three notes in concert. (op.cit., p. 3)

The first tone is a metaphor for the student's *public life*: the community, nation and world overlapping in their lives in terms of "job" or "occupation" pursued to earn a living and the volunteer work assumed.

In harmonized accompaniment with the public life is a second tone, the *personal life*–or inter-personal life. No less important than the public life, this "domain" is ". . . families, friends, neighbors, and the love and mutuality that give rise to these" (op.cit., p. 6) as well as the concomitant tensions and conflict generated by these interactions.

While the first and second tones (public and personal lives) are clearly discernable, there is a third tone in the background, barely audible, which represents *our private or inner life*. This life, no less important than the other two, is our intra-personal life, hidden, perhaps unconscious, which lends a gyroscope to our being. Smith (1971) sees in this life a ". . . final, private recess . . . (in which) . . . we assume our stance toward the world, feeling at home in it or alienated from it" (p. 7). This life is not appropriate to be revealed since we cannot reveal it–not with any degree of clarity (Smith, personal communication, October, 1981) without the assistance of a skilled therapist. Certainly, this domain is the traditional turf of the university and college counseling center.

Modes

Temporal movement in this meta-model occurs with the model's modes. The modes owe their origins to the work of William G. Perry (1970), David Drum (1980), and Mary F. Belenky, Blythe M. Clinchy, Nancy R. Goldberger and Jill M. Tarule (1986) which cover three decades of research.

Perry (1970) developed a nine position model that could be described in four stages: simple dualism, complex dualism, relativism, and commitment in relativism. Criticism has been levied against the model because it focuses on a restricted population (Harvard and Radcliffe students) with both the sample and the interviewers or raters being primarily male. Nevertheless, Perry's work is a significant contribution and its influence is seen in the later works of Drum (1980) and Belenky et al. (1986).

Drum's (1980) model is Chickering (1969)–like in its seven dimensions and Perry (1970)–like in its three modes: basic, expansive, and refined. In a sense, the modes reflect Perry's dualism, relativism, and commitment in relativism.

Belenky et al. (1986) focused solely on women and included not only current students, but alumnae and women in the ". . . 'invisible colleges'-human service agencies supporting women in the workplace were not part of the study's focus which is almost exclusively families and schools (op.cit.). While crediting Perry for a foundation, Belenky et al. (1986) emerged from their qualitative research with a five major category model:

> *Silence*, a position in which women experience themselves as mindless and voiceless and subject to the whims of external authority; *received knowledge*, a perspective from which women conceive of themselves as capable of receiving, even reproducing, knowledge from the all-knowing external authorities but not capable of creating knowledge on their own; *subjective knowledge*, a perspective from which truth and knowledge are conceived of as personal, private, and subjectively known or intuited; *procedural knowledge*, a position in which women are invested in learning and applying objective procedures for obtaining and communicating knowledge; and

constructed knowledge, a position in which women view all knowledge as contextual, experience themselves as creators of knowledge, and value both subjective and objective strategies for knowing. (p. 15)

For the purposes of this metamodel elements of all three theorists are incorporated in three "modes" that are intended to reflect potential temporal growth during the traditional four undergraduate years at an American college or university.

The first mode, evident during the freshmen year, is termed *dualism*. This mode, which inevitably is brought to college with all the other appurtenances of home and high school, is the absolutistic right wrong, good bad, black white position of all or nothing. Perry's (1970) simple and complex dualism, Drum's (1980) basic mode, and Belenky et al.'s (1986) silence and received knowledge, all have elements in this first mode.

The second mode, sometimes evident at the inception of the freshmen year, but usually appearing more during the sophomore year is termed *relativism*. It is characterized by the diminishing of dualism's absolutes and the taking on of new possibilities for behavior. Perhaps the best term to describe this stage is experimentation. Perry's (1970) conceptions of temporizing (a prolonged pause) or escape (immersion in this stage of "anything goes" without acknowledgment that it is a stage leading to further growth) are potential obstructive behaviors for some students that are worthy of therapy. The term "sophomore slump" may be used by the layman to describe temporizing or escape. Perry's (1970) relativism, Drum's (1980) expansive mode, and Belenky et al.'s (1986) subjective and procedural knowledge all contribute to this second mode.

The third mode is, hopefully, evident in the later part of the junior year and during the senior year. Sadly, American higher education accelerates the second mode, relativism, but, historically, has done little to facilitate the integration which characterizes the third mode called *commitment in relativism*. A function of the seemingly polar experiences of dualism and relativism, commitment in relativism (also termed "enlightened dualism" by Perry) is characterized by the re-introduction of an internal gyroscope in the student's life. The "gyroscope" has rights and wrongs that are unique to the student without the need to proselytize or demand that others live by them. Perry (1970) is the source for the term "commitment in relativism" with Drum's (1980) refined mode and Belenky et al.'s (1986) constructed knowledge contributing to the development of the metamodel's third mode.

The dimensions and domains of the metamodel exist in and of themselves independent of time. It is the modes which are temporally dependent which make the metamodel dynamic during the undergraduate years (see Table 1). In the third mode there is, implicitly, an understanding and celebration of the dignity of others in a way that, as Jean Baker Miller would have it, this interdependence actually fosters independence (cited in Hoffman, 1989, p. 10).

THE METAMODEL

It is important to understand that the modes (dualism, relativism, and commitment in relativism) and the domains (public, personal, and inner) are considered to be independent of the times and generations. However, the dimensions may well be a function of the "moment." Chickering's seven developmental vectors serve as the dimensions for this metamodel and one, in particular, may immediately be seen as dated. With ". . . 60% of men graduating from college in recent years return(ing) home and stay(ing) there at least a year" (Hoffmann, 1989, p. 6), "becoming autonomous" may well not fit the economic realities of the times. In fact, Drum's (1980) "physical self" dimension may be much more appropriate for the 1990s. Just as universities and colleges are subject to re-evaluations to maintain accreditation, so too must these dimensions be re-validated if they are to be workable for the counseling center professional.

CASE STUDY

Jim, a senior, came self-referred to the counseling center with presenting issues of positive self-concept and concomitant questions regarding the career direction he had chosen and been preparing himself for the last 3 years. With parents divorcing during his early teens, Jim abandoned his parents early for emotional support and, ostensibly, relied heavily on his peers for emotional sustenance. The reality was, however, that be never fully engaged his peers in reciprocal support. He "gave" but never "risked" asking for anything in return. An excellent hiker and camper, avid gourmet cook, masseur, accomplished sailor and rower, Jim nevertheless felt "empty" in his undergraduate environment. This "emptiness" was fueled by peer rejection in terms of his chosen career. Interestingly, adults already successful in the career found Tom accomplished and someone with whom they wished to work. However, Jim was noted for not completing requisite labor-intensive, low-reward tasks for adults in his chosen career.

In terms of the metamodel for student development, Jim appeared relativistic in terms of most of the dimensions and somewhat caught or temporizing in this mode. With his public and personal domains intertwined and an inner domain yet to be heard, therapeutic efforts focused on separating the public and personal domains into two distinct notes and facilitating the development of the inner mode. By encouraging the development of an independent, fuller personal mode with "commitment in relativism" considerations, a perspective was gained on the negative public intrusion into the personal mode that seemingly resulted in the "self-concept" difficulties. Additionally, psychometrics confirmed the career direction and by gaining developmentally in his personal mode, Jim was able to feel more confident about the proper position his public mode must assume. In addition, other dimensions of development (in terms of the metamodel) began to show signs of positive movement.

CONCLUSION

This student development metamodel for use by university and college counseling center professionals is intended to be incomplete. It may even appear "fuzzy" to some. In a sense, its incom-

Table 1

The Metamodel

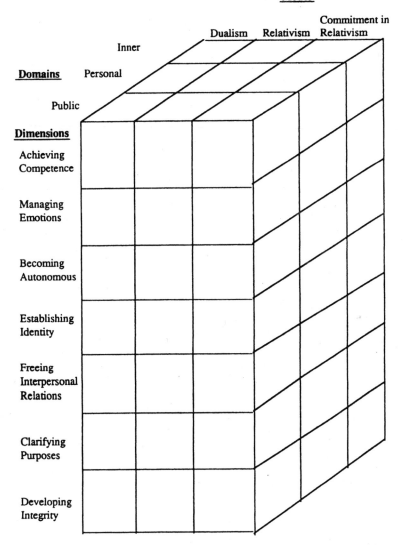

pleteness and fuzziness are endemic. The "cube" which provides a home for the model is not intended to be absolute. Rather, it is a reflection of graphics and a humble attempt to simplistically display human complexities. Even spirals or inter-connected three-dimensional paraboloids, children of the computer world of graphics that they are, cannot in our wildest dreams account for all of the richness and textures in the threads of the tapestries that partly comprise the humanness of our clients.

To fully plumb this metamodel one needs a working understanding of the efforts of William G. Perry, Huston Cummings Smith, Arthur W. Chickering, David Drum, and Mary F. Belenky et al. With this understanding should come the realization that this metamodel cannot fully encompass all of their contributions.

Emotional remediation has been the perceived task of the university and college counseling center. Inevitably this involves the inescapable pain and sadness of life. This model attempts to introduce a richer, fuller fabric of development to a counseling process increasingly seen as "too few fingers for too many holes in the dike." Huston Cummings Smith (1970) said:

> This is what life is like:
> beauty mingled with sadness.
> Its sadness you cannot escape.
> Try not to miss its beauty either . . . (p. 1)

REFERENCES

Belenky, M. F., Clinchy, B. M., Goldberger, N. R., and Tarule, J. M. (1986). *Women's Ways of Knowing: The Development of Self, Voice, and Mind.* New York: Basic Books Inc.

Chickering, A. W. (1969). *Education and Identity.* San Francisco: Jossey-Bass Inc., Publishers.

Drum, D. (1980). Understanding student development. In W. H. Morrill, J. C. Hurst, and E. R. Oetting (Eds.), *Dimensions of Interventions for Student Development.* New York: John Wiley & Sons.

Erickson, E. H. (1968). *Identity: Youth and Crisis.* New York: Norton.

Hoffmann, F. L. (1989) Developmental issues, college students, and the 1990's. *Journal of College Student Psychotherapy,* 4, 3-12.

Hurst, J. C. (1978). Chickering's victors of development and student affairs programming. In C. A. Parker (Ed.), *Encouraging Development in College Students*. Minneapolis: University of Minnesota Press.

Kohlberg, L. (1984). *The Psychology of Moral Development*. New York: Harper & Row, Pub., Inc.

Maslow, A. J. (1962). *Toward A Psychology Of Being*. Princeton: Van Nostrand Reinhold Co., Inc.

Morrill, W. H., Oetting, E. R. and Hurst, J. C. (Eds.) (1974). *Nine Outreach Programs*. Fort Collins: Colorado State University Press.

Perry, W. G. (1970). *Forms of Intellectual And Ethical Development In The College Years*. New York: Holt, Rinehart and Winston.

Smith, H. C. (1955). *The Purposes of Higher Education*. New York: Harper & Row, Pub., Inc.

Smith, H. C. (1958). *The Religions of Man*. New York: Harper & Row, Pub., Inc.

Smith, H. C. (1965). *Condemned To Meaning*. New York: Harper & Row, Pub., Inc.

Smith, H. C. (1971, June). *The Vital Cord*. Commencement address presented at Hobart and William Smith Colleges, Geneva, New York.

White, R. W. (1958). *Lives in Progress*. New York: Dryden Press.

Chapter 3

The Changing Student Culture: Implications for Counselors and Administrators

John B. Bishop

SUMMARY. A review of the literature on the values, behaviors, and attitudes which college students bring to institutions of higher education, focusing particularly on how these have changed across generations of students. Changes in career, social and political values are discussed, as well as the personal behaviors which have been investigated in studies of academic honesty, alcohol and other drug use, suicide, and eating disorders. Attitudes and behaviors about sexuality, interpersonal violence and multicultural differences are also reviewed. Some implications which the current student culture creates for counselors and student personnel administrators are identified and discussed.

One of the recurring challenges for college and university personnel is to develop and maintain an understanding of the college student population. Changes in that population may require adjustments on the part of the institution, ranging from those that directly relate to the activities which occur in the classroom to those which involve other areas of campus life. In this sense, an institution of higher education is similar to many other social institutions that

John B. Bishop, PhD, is Dean of Counseling and Student Development at the University of Delaware. Address correspondence to: Center for Counseling and Student Development, University of Delaware, Newark, DE 19716.

strive to meet the needs of a changing constituency, but the population which our colleges and universities serve is more transient and changeable than most.

Changes in the student culture have a great impact on campus life in general and for the work of student personnel professionals in particular. The type of communication which student personnel professionals purport to foster between themselves and students is very dependent on a thorough understanding of the student culture. In fact, the effectiveness of such personnel may be, in large part, related to their understanding of students.

The purpose of this chapter is to review some of the most recent research on college students and the culture which they bring to college and university campuses and to identify some implications of these findings that counselors and administrators need to consider.

VALUES

The role of values in understanding human behavior is well established. Individuals use their values as standards of evaluation in determining what is good or bad, true or false, right or wrong, desirable or undesirable, important or unimportant. Young (1961) pointed out that what a person *values* is not necessarily what a person *wants*. That is, people sometimes act differently than they believe they should act. For example, most individuals might agree that it is important to carefully explore the political platforms of all candidates before voting, but the populace does not follow such a practice in actuality. Thus, individuals do not always behave in ways that are consistent with their stated beliefs and values. Nonetheless, philosophers, psychologists, and other behavioral scientists have written volumes about the concept of value and the power it exerts on human behavior (Young, 1961).

The values of college students are influenced by family, friends, religion, personal experiences, and societal factors. Their perceptions, motives, goals, interests, and decision-making processes are closely related to the systems of values they hold. A good place to start understanding college student behavior, or to compare one generation of college students to another, is to consider some of the research about the career, social, and political values of this population.

Career Values

In a 1990 survey of college freshmen, Astin (1991) indicated that the most frequently noted reason students reported using in deciding to go to college was "to get a better job (78%)." The second most popular reason was "to be able to make more money (73%)." When asked what kinds of objectives are essential or very important, the most frequent response of college freshmen was "being very well-off financially (74%)." Conger (1988) notes that this concern with material values is much higher among today's high school and college students than it was 20 or even 10 years ago.

In the early 1980s, Levine (1983) observed that college students were becoming more competitive and professionally ambitious. One possible interpretation of this change is that the importance which college students are placing on material values is stimulating such competitiveness. It is difficult to determine if this change in materialistic values is due to a form of greed intentionally created by our society (e.g., pursuit of the "good life") or a response to a lack of confidence in the economic future of our society, or both. The economic realities which current students face are different than those typically confronted by earlier generations. For example, the rising cost of higher education itself results in many students having to find part-time employment to help pay college expenses and, at the same time, finding themselves with substantial financial debts upon graduation. It has become more likely that college students will not be able to achieve the same standard of living as their parents enjoy.

Research on the changing female sex role supports the contention that the career values of college students have been changing. Fiorentine (1988) reviewed the results of the American Council on Education annual survey of freshmen students from 1969 to 1984 and found a dramatic increase in the value which women students are placing on status and attainment goals, such as being rewarded well financially and being recognized as an authority in their field.

One result of this change is that male and female students are more similar in their value constellations than has been the case in the past, although the data does not indicate that women have relinquished their more traditional interest in domestic or nurturant goals. Fiorentine (1988) concludes that an "amalgamation" of the female sex role is occurring, suggesting that females are acquiring some male-like goals while retaining some that are traditionally female. Some of the traditional gender differences in the values and career aspirations of college students are decreasing and existing theories of sex-differentiated career aspirations may be limited by the norms on which they are based.

As noted elsewhere (Bishop, 1990), today's students are increasingly concerned about getting good grades in order to be more competitive for available jobs or admission to graduate or professional schools. They also appear more likely to select an academic major that offers the best prospect for employment rather than for other types of satisfaction. In short, the career values of today's students appear to be increasingly shaped by financial considerations.

Social and Political Values

Consonant with college students appearing increasingly concerned with material success, surveys of student attitudes and characteristics indicate a marked decline in interest in social and/or political issues. Astin's most recent survey of college freshmen showed that only 21% are interested in influencing the political structure, 26% would participate in a community action program, 34% would get involved in programs to clean up the environment, and 43% see it as important to influence social values (Astin, 1991). In a recent review of literature on adolescent values, Conger (1988) concluded that the vast majority of today's students have no interest in becoming involved in protests, contributing to the larger society, or working to correct social and economic inequities. Furthermore, long term trends indicate significantly less interest in political activities and "helping others in difficulty." Levine (1980) reminds us that some student characteristics have remained stable over many generations, while others have oscillated or changed from time to time. The present generation, however, is larger, more diverse, and less influenced by the family and the schools than any of its predecessors.

The social and political values which have become more important to adolescents recently may be those which emphasize the possibilities of "self-realization" (Conger, 1988). Support for issues of equality, self-determination, and freedom for women has increased since the 1960s. Opportunity for self-expression and self-improvement has become increasingly important. The heightened interest young people have demonstrated in their own physical health and well-being is one positive example of such a value. Other manifestations of this interest in self-improvement are seen in more material ways, including the financial concerns referred to earlier.

Lavin and Prull (1989) note that social scientists have frequently attempted to capture the essential characteristics of recent generations of college students. The students of the 1950s were characterized as traditional and conforming, those of the late 1960s and early 1970s as alienated from society, those in the late 1970s and early 1980s as the "me generation," and the current generation of students is seen as more politically conservative, egocentric, and less committed to social and/or political change. Furthermore, Lavin and Prull's (1989) analysis of four samples of college freshmen at intervals spanning 1969 through 1987 showed that college students have become increasingly impulsive, indicating less regard for the consequences of their actions. This attitude may be more noticeable in personal and interpersonal behavior than in social and political arenas and is often viewed as having negative consequences.

Another indicator of the social and/or political values of a group may be the extent to which it is knowledgeable about current events. Lucas and Schmitz (1987) surveyed 863 college students and found that, while 80% thought it was important to be informed about current events, only 12% claimed to be well-informed. Most of the respondents, therefore, acknowledged that their actions did not necessarily follow their stated beliefs in regard to the attention they gave to events occurring beyond their own day to day activities. This finding also suggests that today's college students are not greatly interested in social and/or political issues.

PERSONAL BEHAVIORS

The personal behaviors of college students have always been of concern to the counselors and administrators who have responsibilities for their general welfare. Boyer (1987) notes the current ambivalence or uncertainty about the responsibilities of colleges and universities for student behavior. Judicial systems and residence life operations struggle to define standards that can be expected or required, even when legal regulations are quite clear. Likewise, counseling and health service personnel often discuss how much they ought to intrude into the personal lives of students when health-related issues are brought to light. Where the responsibility of the institution begins and where it ends are difficult questions in terms of striking a balance between the rights of students and institutional concerns. Counselors and administrators have had to be increasingly attentive to issues of academic honesty, alcohol and other drug misuse, suicide, and eating disorders.

Academic Honesty

In a review of studies focusing on academic honesty, Jendrek (1989) reported results indicating that between 40% and 90% of students admit cheating. Examples include a survey of business students in which 49% reported cheating (Tom and Borin, 1988); another in which 56% of students enrolled in agriculture, technology, and engineering reported that they have cheated (Singhal, 1982); and a study that found 88% of premedical students and 58% of medical students sampled reported cheating (Sierles, Hendrickx, & Circle, 1980). Ludeman (1988) surveyed 208 United States colleges and universities and found that 29% of the responding institutions reported that academic dishonesty was on the increase, while only 8% indicated a decline in such activity.

Some researchers are skeptical about the magnitude of the cheating which has been reported. Karlens, Michaels, and Podlogar (1988) argue that what students *say* about their behavior and what they actually *do* may differ. There is some evidence that different research designs, such as those employed by Nelson and Schaeffer (1986), produce markedly different results from those obtained in studies based solely on questionnaire data. Karlens, Michaels and Podlogar (1988) call for more empirical investigations to explore the types of actual cheating and the circumstances in which students are more likely to cheat.

Institutions of higher education are concerned about actual cheating and the reasons for it. Singhal (1982) reported a study in which 68% of students believed that competition for grades is the major reason for cheating. In comparing students who cheat and those who do not, Haines, Diekhoff, LaBeff, and Clark (1986) found the former to be less mature and morally developed, less likely to be paying for their own education, and more likely to attribute their behavior to external circumstances, even though they acknowledge that cheating is wrong.

Alcohol and Other Drug Misuse

Drinking alcohol has been a popular pattern of student behavior for many years. Rivinus (1988) noted a higher incidence of alcohol use on college and university campuses than in the United States population at large. Increased attention has recently been given to the drinking behaviors of college students because of the effect it has on a wide variety of other behaviors (Saltz & Elandt, 1986) and, in particular, its perceived connection to antisocial activities (Hirschorn, 1987). Saltz and Elandt (1986) found in their literature review that approximately 90% of college students have consumed alcohol and that the heaviest drinkers tend to live off-campus or in fraternity/sorority houses, have lower grade point averages, and experience more negative consequences related to drinking. The authors recognized the difficulty in distinguishing between causation and mere correlation in many of the studies. Additionally, it should be noted that some attempts to conduct longitudinal studies of drinking patterns have been complicated by changes in the legal drinking age.

Continuing concern about the use and abuse of alcohol by college students is demonstrated in numerous ways. Dannells (1991) noted a great increase in campus judicial cases related to alcohol, while Maney (1990) reports that much attention has been devoted to heavy drinking because of its relationship to other areas of concern, such as mental health problems, depression, interpersonal conflicts, and suicide tendencies. The realization that adult children of alcoholic families are at higher risk for developing alcohol-related problems than those who come from nonalcoholic families has led to special outreach efforts at some institutions. Rivinus (1988) points out that the motivation for colleges and universities to increase programming regarding alcohol is not just to protect students, but also to avoid the liabilities that may be associated with the role of alcohol in accidental deaths, suicides, rapes, and other violent acts. Perhaps the good news is that some studies have shown that efforts to educate students about alcohol are effective and can have a positive impact (Gonzalez, 1986).

Other drug use patterns of behavior have also been studied. Carter and Sedlacek (1983) compared samples of freshmen students from 1973 and 1983 and found a decline in the use of barbiturates, marijuana, and hashish, but an increase in the use of amphetamines and cocaine. The use of beer, wine, hard liquor, and cigarettes appeared to change little over time. The 1983 class of freshmen was more likely to oppose the legalization of marijuana, think that drug dealers should be turned in to the authorities, and less likely to feel sorry for people on drugs. A similar study compared the attitudes of freshmen in 1978 and 1988 (Kohatsu & Sedlacek, 1989). The 1988 freshmen were found to be generally more conservative about drug use and more concerned about the addictive properties of drugs and their physically deleterious effects, whereas the 1978 sample was more worried about the illegality and psychological effects of drugs. The 1988 freshmen were also less likely to favor the legalization of marijuana and were more concerned about driving a car while drunk.

Anabolic androgenic steroid use is of increasing concern to college and university officials. Lopez (1990) reported that some athletes use steroids in an effort to derive the maximum benefits from physical training, but that others are using such substances simply to "look good." The personal side effects of using steroids range from those that are embarrassing and annoying to those that have the potential to be deadly. Additionally, the aggressiveness which may result from steroid use often impacts others. Haupt and

Rovere (1984) have expressed great concern about the information and credibility gap which exists between the users of steroids and the medical/scientific community.

Suicide

In a review of the literature about suicide among American college students, Slimak (1990) noted the interest researchers have taken in studying the incidence of suicide ideation, attempts, and actual deaths in the student population. While many of the reported studies have been completed in specific institutions and must be generalized with some caution, the findings are, nonetheless, generally troubling. For example, Westefeld and Furr (1987) found that 81% of a sample of 962 students reported being depressed, 32% had suicidal ideations, and 4% had histories of actual suicide attempts. Carson and Johnson (1985) surveyed a population of 218 students and indicated that 20% had seriously considered committing suicide. This same group reported more symptoms of stress than the students who had not considered suicide as an option. In addition, Sherer (1985) reported that 42% of a sample of 149 college students said they had either suicidal ideations or had contemplated a method for killing themselves.

This particular student behavior deserves special attention because, as Bernard and Bernard (1982) have suggested, the college environment itself may serve to amplify certain problems and actually contribute to the increase noted in self-destructive and suicidal behaviors. In fact, Westefeld and Pattillo (1987) have pointed out that the suicide rate is estimated by some to be approximately 50% higher for college students than it is for a comparable population that does not enroll in higher education. Schwartz's (1990) analysis of both governmental and health service records found the opposite to be true: the incidence of student suicide is lower than that of their age and sex matched peers. Even in light of these conflicting contentions, there can be no debate over the fact that the suicide rate for the 15-24 age group is rising, while the rate for the remainder of the population in the United States is relatively stable (Slimak, 1990).

Eating Disorders

The incidence of eating disorders among high school and college-age women became a topic of much concern during the decade of the 1980s. Mintz and Betz (1988) noted that there has been some difficulty in the attempts which had been made to determine the actual frequency of eating disorders because of the wide array of operationalized criteria used to define the problem. To address this issue, a study was conducted by Mintz & Betz using an eating-disorder continuum to classify behaviors. Of the 643 women subjects, 3% were classified as bulimic, 61% were found to engage in chronic dieting, binging or purging alone, or subthreshold bulimia, and only 33% reported what could be considered normal eating habits. Furthermore, the degree of disturbed eating was strongly correlated with lower self-esteem, more negative body image, a greater tendency to endorse sociocultural beliefs about the desirability of female thinness, obsessive thoughts about weight and appearance, and the interference of weight and appearance concerns with other aspects of life. One implication of this study is that the "normal" eating behaviors of college women varies from that which would be considered as healthy eating behavior.

Dickstein (1989) concluded that the current college environment may, in vulnerable female students, facilitate and foster the occurrence of bulimia. Cesari (1986) expressed concern about the degree to which bulimia has become a "fad" behavior among college women. That is, many students engage in behaviors that do not satisfy the diagnostic criteria for clinical bulimia, but that does not imply that there is no need for serious concern. Eating disordered behavior is clearly related to both physical and psychological health issues. The recognition of the problem and the factors in the college environment that contribute to it have led to the development of some significant approaches to treatment and prevention (Whitaker & Davis, 1989).

INTERPERSONAL BEHAVIORS AND ATTITUDES

The relationships which students have with their peers, parents, and others may be the cause and/or the result of the way they perceive themselves and the social order. College students live in a society in which interpersonal behaviors are often a focus of attention, with their varying perceptions, wants, and goals leading to individualized patterns of behaviors. Some of these interpersonal behaviors and attitudes are particularly powerful and evident in the student culture.

Sexuality

Abler and Sedlacek (1989) studied the sexual attitudes and behaviors of college freshmen from 1972 to 1987. Their findings suggest that students are becoming more liberal in their behavior as well as in some of their attitudes, as indicated by the reported incidence of sexual intercourse and increasingly liberal personal sexual codes. However, students apparently are taking the AIDS risk into consideration in modifying their sexual behaviors. Most sexually active students reported that they either were in a monogamous relationship with a partner whose sexual history was known or used condoms for sex with multiple partners.

In a review of the literature about the sexual attitudes and behaviors of college students, Spees (1987) concluded that from 1974 to 1985 there was an increase in overall sexual activity, an emerging openness to discussing sexual issues with peers and trusted adults, a growing concern about rape, and greater awareness by male students of their responsibility for contraceptive behaviors. In a similar vein, Conger (1988) reported that, from 1970 to 1985, adolescents increased their incidence of premarital intercourse and were much more likely to live together as unmarried couples. Additionally, the percentage of adolescents who oppose legalized abortion or who view having children outside of marriage as morally wrong appears to be decreasing.

Violence

Interpersonal violence on college campuses is often under-reported and sometimes denied. Roark (1987) indicates that some of the most common forms of violence experienced by college students include rape, assault, harassment and hazing, in spite of our institutional commitments to enlightenment, education, student development, and personal safety. Factors which appear to underlie the various forms of campus violence include: a population that is developmentally vulnerable to peer pressure, feelings of invincibility, and new freedoms; a societal legitimization of pro-violent values; changes in the sex role socialization process; prejudice and discriminatory stereotypes; and the use of alcohol and/or other substances which increase the likelihood that individuals will engage in what would otherwise be prohibited behaviors.

Roark (1987) notes that courtship violence, referring to aggressive acts in dating relationships, has been the subject of much recent research. For example, Bogal-Allbritten and Allbritten (1985) surveyed college students' experience with different kinds of interpersonal violence (e.g., verbal threats, pushing or shoving, slapping, punching, choking, or assault with an object or weapon) and found that 61% had personal knowledge of another student who was involved in an incident of courtship violence and 19% reported at least one personal experience. Worth, Matthews, and Coleman (1990) reviewed other studies which reported that from 21% to 53% of college students have been victims of courtship violence. Such figures are disturbing, particularly in view of Makepeace's (1981) contention that many victims of such violence would not choose to report it. Furthermore, Lo and Sporakowski (1989) found that courtship violence is mostly reciprocal in nature, with many women being as likely as men to use violence as a means of conflict resolution, and most college students willfully choose to remain in dating relationships despite the presence of violence.

Acquaintance rape, or a sexual assault that is committed by someone who is known by the victim, appears to be increasing on college campuses. Koss, Gidyez, and Wisniewski (1987) surveyed over 7,000 students and found that 84% of the reported rapes were perpetrated by acquaintances. A similar finding was reported by Aizenman and Kelley (1988) in a study in which 22% of the college female subjects had been involved in acquaintance rape, while another 51% indicated that they had successfully avoided such attempts. They noted that college women are vulnerable targets, particular in view of the obvious physical differences in size between the sexes, and the sex role stereotypes which portray males as aggressive and females as passive. Educators are, in response to this problem, attempting to develop and support acquaintance rape prevention programs (Neff, 1988; Pace & Zaugra, 1988).

Dealing with Differences

There has been a great deal of attention focused on the ways in which this generation of college students reacts to those who are different from themselves. Discriminatory behaviors towards those of different races, genders, or ability are of particular concern. Only 21% of the freshman class of 1990 indicated that racial discrimination is no longer a major problem in America (Astin, 1991).

DeCoster and Mable (1981) indicated that students claim to appreciate the educational advantages of living in a pluralistic campus environment, yet minority populations are more tolerated than embraced, more feared than understood. Research continues to lend support to that contention. To illustrate, Sedlacek (1987) reviewed studies which focused on the experiences which African-American students have in traditional institutions of higher education and found that such students, when compared to Caucasian students, perceived greater levels of hostility and racism and often feel isolated and lonely. Studies continue to show that the attitudes of Caucasian students toward African-American students have remained rather consistently negative across a wide variety of situations. In addition, there are recent reports of more overtly racial incidents on many campuses (Farrell, 1988; Hayes, 1988).

Because many colleges and universities are making efforts to create more multicultural and diverse student bodies, researchers have also examined the attitudes of college students towards many different kinds of special populations, such as those with physical disabilities (McQuilkin, Freitag, & Harris, 1990), older people (Schwalb & Sedlacek, 1990), women (Etaugh & Spiller, 1989) and lesbians and gay men (D'Augelli, 1989; D'Augelli & Rose, 1990). In general, such studies suggest that most minority populations on college campuses continue to be regarded with indifference, prejudice, and/or fear by those in the traditional majority population.

IMPLICATIONS FOR COUNSELORS
AND ADMINISTRATORS

The types of changes in the student culture which have been reviewed above have implications for counselors and administrators in institutions of higher education. The involvement of such personnel in professional development programs, efforts to communicate what is known about students to others, considerations of the impact of societal changes on higher education, and the development of educational programming are all related to the current state of the student culture.

Professional Development. One of the most obvious features of the student culture is that it does, indeed, change. Such change has a direct relationship to the professional development obligations of those who work in colleges and universities. It is the responsibility of all professionals in counseling and higher education administration to engage in the continuing development of their professional skill and understanding to ensure that they are able to function effectively and provide competent services to their various clientele.

Professionals must increase their competencies as practitioners in order to meet accepted standards of practice and the changing needs of students. For example, eating disorders in the college population are much more evident than in preceding generations. It is also true that many college counselors had little or no training to enable them to understand the issues which surround eating disordered behavior. In order to be able to provide services to students who have new or emerging types of problems, continuing professional development efforts must be made. Otherwise, professionals will function in an increasingly smaller sphere or risk engaging in what might well be considered unethical practice. Today's effective practitioners, almost by definition, are those counselors and administrators who rigorously pursue professional development programs that will keep them abreast of the needs of their clientele and competent to serve them well.

Interpreting the Student Culture. It is reasonable to assume that counselors and other student personnel professionals are knowledgeable about various aspects of the college student culture. Their day-to-day contact with students is likely to be both extensive and intensive, resulting in a considerable array of demographic and developmental data. Such information is of obvious value in understanding the student culture and interpreting it to others, but its usefulness is often limited because it is not organized in a meaningful way and/or communicated to others in a systematic fashion. The absence of an objective data base has often diminished the value of what counselors and administrators may know about students. Anecdotal accounts of experiences with students may be of some interest, but generally do not seem to influence the institutional decision-makers who preside over the lives of students.

Bishop and Trembley (1987) have argued that there is a role for student personnel practitioners in contributing to the base of data about students, but such personnel often neglect to report their observations in ways that facilitate wider understandings. For instance, the career concerns of students, reports of behavioral problems, data about physical health issues, and accounts of interpersonal violence are all examples of information which might be held by counselors and student personnel administrators. Again, however, these potential interpreters of the student culture have been limited by not organizing and systematizing their data.

Developing a data base need not require a large investment of time or sophistication in research design and statistical analysis (Bishop & Trembley, 1987). Organizing information in an understandable form may be the most important feature in explaining what is known about the student culture and is certainly the first step in communicating it to others. Furthermore, the ability of counselors and student personnel administrators to maintain their own professional competencies is related to how well they understand their changing clientele. Having meaningful data certainly enhances the probability that such understanding can be established and continued.

Societal Influences. Today's college students have grown up in a world that is rapidly changing. The population is increasingly multicultural in nature, the economy is influenced by international factors, and the society is intensely competitive. Some of the problems which are confronting college students now are substantially different than those experienced by previous generations.

It has become more common for college freshmen to arrive on campus with significant histories with drugs, alcohol, sex, eating disorders, and other behaviors that did not emerge in previous generations until later in adult life. Increasingly, they come from single-parent homes and have fewer sources of personal support available to them. Additionally, while experience may be viewed as a "teacher" of sorts, not all exposures to adversity will result in improved ability to handle adversity. Just because college students have more adult-like experiences in their lives, it is not logical to conclude that they are more mature or able to handle those experiences well.

Roscoe (1987) cautions those who might recall their own college experiences as similar to those of today's students. Such caution is important for counselors and administrators in higher education, but also relevant for faculty members who often find it difficult to understand the need for various types of student services that have been developed recently. Research evidence (e.g., Koplik and DeVito, 1987) shows that today's students are more troubled and concerned about the future, and report higher distress in all aspects of their lives than was true even 10 years ago. It is logical to assume that the rapid changes which are occurring in our society will continue to have a direct influence on the lives of college students and the higher education environment.

Theory and Educational Programming. Student development theorists appear to have been on target often with their conceptualizations of issues college students must confront. For example, Chickering (1969) discussed the importance of learning to manage two major impulses: aggression and sex. Much research on the behaviors and attitudes of college students has been done in regard to these impulses, adding to both our practical knowledge and theory development. It is necessary, however, to recognize both the advantages and the limitations of attempting to develop a model of college student development. Perhaps the advice of Knefelkamp, Widick, and Parker (1978) needs to be remembered: the search for a comprehensive model of student development will likely be ill-fated, although the temptation to force various models together might be strong. Various theories make contributions through their descriptions of the process of developmental change which students go through in the context of higher education, but the true test of any theory or model may be in the determination of whether or not it is helpful in guiding practice. Theory is valuable as a source of awareness, as a way of organizing our thinking about students, and as a key to developing insight about possible courses of action (Knefelkamp, Widick & Parker, 1978). It should also be the stimulus for conducting research which, in turn, will contribute to the theory building process. Student personnel practitioners need to continue to develop and test the theories upon which their work is based if the profession as to progress further.

It is also encouraging to recognize that intentional efforts to influence the behaviors and attitudes of college students can be effective and that it is possible to do successful educational programming outside of the classroom. Successful interventions on campuses have been reported that address issues such as date rape (Pace & Zaugra, 1986), alcohol education (Burrell, 1990; Gadaleto & Anderson, 1986), dealing with AIDS (Burke, 1989; Cramer & Baron, 1990), eating disorder behavior (Hotelling, 1989; Sesan, 1989), racism (Henley & Arnold, 1990), and others. The leadership role of counselors and student personnel administrators in developing and delivering such educational programs is an important one. As noted elsewhere (Bishop, 1990), the consultation roles of such personnel may need to be expanded to maximize the development of educational programs to the magnitude needed to address emerging areas of concern in the student culture.

CONCLUSION

There is ample research evidence available to demonstrate that the student culture in our institutions of higher education is rapidly changing. Professionals who deal with college students have a special obligation to be cognizant of these changes and to help others understand them. Because of our rapidly changing society, the student culture may be altered more frequently and dramatically in the future than it has been in the past.

REFERENCES

Abler, R.M. & Sedlacek, W.E. (1989). Freshman sexual attitudes and behaviors over a 15-year period. *Journal of College Student Development, 30,* 201-209.

Aizenman, M. & Kelley, G. (1988). The incidence of violence and acquaintance rape in dating relationships among college men and women. *Journal of College Student Development, 29,* 305-311.

Astin, A.W. (1991). *The American freshman: National norms for fall 1990.* Los Angeles: American Council on Education and University of California at Los Angeles.

Bernard, J.L. & Bernard, M.L. (1982). Factors related to suicidal behavior among college students. *Journal of College Student Personnel, 23,* 409-413.

Bishop, J.B. (1990). The university counseling center: An agenda for the 1990's. *Journal of Counseling Development, 68,* 408-413.

Bishop, J.B. & Trembley, E.L. (1987). Counseling centers and accountability: Immovable objects, irresistible forces. *Journal of Counseling and Development, 65,* 491-494.

Bogal-Allbritten, R.B. & Allbritten, W.L. (1985). The hidden victims: Courtship violence among college students. *Journal of College Student Personnel, 26* 201-204.

Boyer, E.L. (1987). *College: The undergraduate experience in America.* New York: Harper & Row, Pub., Inc.

Burke, C. (1989). Developing a program for student peer AIDS educators. *Journal of College Student Development, 30,* 368-369.

Burrell, L.F. (1990). College students' recommendations to combat abusive drinking habits. *Journal of College Student Development, 31,* 562-563.

Carter, R.T. & Sedlacek, W.E. (1983). *Sex differences in student attitudes and behavior toward drugs over a decade* (Research Report No. 8-83). College Park: University of Maryland, Counseling Center.

Cesari, J.P. (1986). Fad bulimia: A serious and separate counseling issue. *Journal of College Student Personnel, 27,* 255-259.

Chickering, A.W. (1969). *Education and identity.* San Francisco: Jossey-Bass Inc., Publishers.

Conger, J.J. (1988). Hostages to fortune: Youth, values, and the public interest. *American Psychologist, 43,* 291-300.

Cramer, D.W. & Baron, A. (1990). AIDS in the workplace: A workshop for university personnel. *Journal of College Student Development, 31,* 80-81.

D'Augelli, A.R. (1989). Homophobia in a university community: Views of prospective resident assistants. *Journal of College Student Development, 30,* 546-552.

D'Augelli, A.R. & Rose, M.L. (1990). Homophobia in a university community: Attitudes and experiences of heterosexual freshmen. *Journal of College Student Development, 31,* 484-491.

Dannells, M. (1991). Changes in student misconduct and institutional response over 10 years. *Journal of College Student Development, 32,* 166-170.

DeCoster, D.A. & Mable, P. (1981). *Understanding today's students.* New Directions for Student Services, No. 16. San Francisco: Jossey-Bass Inc., Publishers.

Dickstein, L.J. (1989). Current college environments: Do these communities facilitate and foster bulimia in vulnerable students? In L.C. Whitaker & W. N. Davis (Eds.), *The bulimic college student: Evaluation. treatment and prevention.* New York: The Haworth Press, Inc. Also published as *Journal of College Student Psychotherapy, 3,* 2/3/4.

Etaugh, C. & Spiller, B. (1989). Attitudes toward women: Comparison of traditional-aged and older college students. *Journal of College Student Development, 30,* 41-46.

Farrell, C. (1988, January 27). Black students seen facing "new racism" on many campuses. *Chronicle of Higher Education,* pp. Al, A36-38.

Fiorentine, R. (1988). Increasing similarity in the values and life plans of male and female college students? Evidence and implications. *Sex Roles, 18,* 143-148.

Gadaleto, A.F. & Anderson, D.S. (1986). Continued progress: The 1979, 1982, and 1985 college alcohol surveys. *Journal of College Student Personnel, 27,* 499-509.

Gonzalez, G.M. (1986). Trends in alcohol knowledge and drinking patterns among students: 1981-85. *Journal of College Student Personnel, 27,* 496-499.

Haines, V.J., Diekhoff, G.M., LaBeff, E.E., & Clark, R.E. (1986). College cheating: Immaturity, lack of commitment, and the neutralizing attitude. *Research in Higher Education, 25,* 342-354.

Haupt. H.A. & Rovere, G.D. (1984). Anabolic steroids: A review of the literature. *The American Journal of Sports Medicine, 12,* 469-484.

Hayes, L. (1988, June 16). Resurgence of racism seen on campuses. *Guidepost,* pp. 1,4.

Henley, B. & Arnold, M.S. (1990). Unlearning racism: A student affairs agenda for professional development. *Journal of College Student Development, 31,* 176-177.

Hirschorn, M.W. (1987, March 25). Alcohol seen number 1 campus abuse problem despite concerns about student's drug use. *Chronicle of Higher Education,* p. 1.

Hotelling, K. (1989). A model for addressing the problem of bulimia on college campuses. In L.C. Whitaker & U.N. Davis (Eds.), *The bulimic college student: Evaluation, treatment and prevention.* New York: The Haworth Press, Inc. Also published as *Journal of College Student Psychotherapy, 3,* 2/3/4.

Jendrek, M.P. (1989). Faculty reactions to academic dishonesty. *Journal of College Student Development 30,* 401-406.

Karlens, M., Michaels, C., & Podlogar, S. (1988). An empirical investigation of actual cheating in a large sample of undergraduates. *Research in Higher Education, 29,* 359-364.

Knefelkamp, L., Widick, C., & Parker, C.A. (Eds.). (1978). *Applying new developmental findings.* New Directions for Student Services, No. 4. San Francisco: Jossey-Bass Inc., Publishers.

Kohatsu, E. L. & Sedlacek, W.E. (1989). *Freshmen attitudes and behavior toward drugs: A comparison by year and gender* (Research Report No. 8-89). College Park: University of Maryland, Counseling Center.

Koplik, E.K. & DeVito, A.J. (1986). Problems of freshmen: Comparison of classes of 1976 and 1986. *Journal of College Student Personnel, 27,* 124-131.

Koss, M.P., Gidyez, C.A., & Wisniewski, N. (1987). The scope of rape: Incidence and prevalence of sexual aggression and victimization in a national sample of higher education students. *Journal of Consulting and Clinical Psychology, 55,* 162-170.

Lavin, T.J. & Prull, R.W. (1989). Student personality traits and values across generations. *Journal of College Student Development, 30,* 407-412.

Levine, A. (1983). Riding first class on the Titanic: A portrait of today's college student. *NASPA Journal, 20,* 3-9.

Levine, A. (1983). *When dreams and heroes died.* San Francisco: Jossey-Bass Inc, Publishers.

Lo, A.W. & Sporakowski, M.J. (1989). The continuation of violent dating relationships among college students. *Journal of College Student Development, 30,* 432-439.

Lopez, M. (1990). Steroids in athletics: One university's experience. *Journal of College Student Development, 31,* 523-530.

Lucas, C.J. & Schmitz, C.D. (1987). Social awareness and knowledge of current events among college students. *College Student Journal, 21,* 162-167.

Ludeman, R. (1988). A survey of academic integrity practices in U.S. higher education. *Journal of College Student Development, 29,* 172-173.

Makepeace, J.M. (1981). Courtship violence among college students. *Family Relations, 30,* 97-102.

Maney, D.W. (1990). Predicting university students' use of alcoholic beverages. *Journal of College Student Development, 31,* 23-32.

McQuilkin, J.I., Freitag, C.B., & Harris, J.L. (1990). Attitudes of college students toward handicapped persons. *Journal of College Student Development, 31,* 17-22.

Mintz, L.B. & Bets, N.E. (1988). Prevalence and correlates of eating disordered behaviors among undergraduate women. *Journal of Counseling Psychology, 35,* 463-471.

Neff, L. (1988). Acquaintance rape on campus: The problem, the victims, and prevention. *NASPA Journal, 25,* 146-152.

Nelson, T. & Schaeffer, N. (1986). Cheating among college students estimated with the randomized-response technique. *College Student Journal, 20,* 31-325.

Pace, D. & Zaugra, J. (1988). Model of a date rape workshop for college campuses. *Journal of College Student Development, 29,* 71-372.

Rivinus, T.M. (Ed.). (1988). *Alcoholism/chemical dependency and the college student.* New York: The Haworth Press, Inc. Also published as *Journal of College Student Psychotherapy, 2,* 3/4.

Roark, M.L. (1987). Preventing violence on college campuses. *Journal of Counseling Development, 65,* 365-371.

Roscoe, B. (1987). Concerns of college students: A report of self-disclosures. *College Student Journal, 21,* 158-161.

Saltz, R. & Elandt, D. (1986). College student drinking studies 1976-1985. *Contemporary Drug Problems, 13,* 117-159.

Schwalb, S.J. & Sedlacek, W.E. (1990). Have college students' attitudes toward older people changed? *Journal of College Student Development, 31,* 127-132.

Schwartz, A.J. (1990). The epidemiology of suicide among students at colleges and universities in the United States. In L.C. Whitaker & R.E. Slimak (Eds.), *College student suicide.* New York: The Haworth Press, Inc. Also published as *Journal of College Student Psychotherapy, 4,* 3/4.

Sedlacek, W.E. (1987). Black students on white campuses: 20 years of research. *Journal of College Student Personnel, 28,* 484-495.

Sesan, R. (1989). Peer educators: A creative resource for the eating disordered college student. In L.C. Whitaker & W. N. Davis (Eds.). *The bulimic college student: Education. treatment and prevention.* New York: The Haworth Press, Inc. Also published as *Journal of College Student Psychotherapy, 3,* 2/3/4.

Sierles, F., Hendrickx, I., & Circle, S. (1980). Cheating in medical school. *Journal of Medical Education, 55,* 124-125.

Singhal, A.C. (1982). Factors in student dishonesty. *Psychological Reports, 51,* 775-780.

Sherer, M. (1985). Depression and suicidal ideation in college students. *Psychological Reports, 57,* 1061-1062.

Slimak, R.E. (1990). Suicide and the American college and university. A review of the literature. In L.C. Whitaker & R.E. Slimak (Eds.), *College student suicide.* New York: The Haworth Press, Inc. Also published as *Journal of College Student Psychotherapy, 4,* 3/4.

Spees, E.R. (1987). College students' sexual attitudes and behaviors, 1974-1985: A review of the literature. *Journal of College Student Personnel, 28,* 135-140.

Tom, G. & Borin, N. (1988). Cheating in academe. *Journal of Education for Business, 1,* 153-157.

Westefeld, J.S. & Pattillo, C.M. (1987). College and university student suicide record-keeping procedures: The case for a national clearinghouse. *Journal of College Student Personnel, 28,* 34-38.

Westefeld, J.S. & Furr, S.R. (1987). Suicide and depression among college students. *Professional Psychology: Research and Practice, 18,* 119-123.

Whitaker, L.C. & Davis, W.N. (Eds.). (1989). *The bulimic college student: Education, treatment and prevention.* New York: The Haworth Press, Inc. Also published as *Journal of College Student Psychotherapy, 3,* 2/3/4.

Worth, D.M., Matthews, P.A., & Coleman, W.R. (1990). Sex role, group affiliation, family background, and courtship violence in college students. *Journal of College Student Development, 31,* 250-254.

Young, P.T. (1961). *Motivation and emotion.* New York: John Wiley & Sons.

Chapter 4

"Toddler" to the Inner World: The College Student in Psychotherapy

Jane C. Widseth
Richard E. Webb

SUMMARY. The way students use psychotherapy in their undergraduate years is reminiscent of the image of the "refueling toddler." Developmental factors lead students in late adolescence to seek exploratory therapy and then to step away from the therapy. Three clinical examples help to illuminate this observation. The authors use this developmental observation to argue against policies for time-limited psychotherapy in college years.

The college student's experience is replete with the task of negotiating separations and losses and with the simultaneous or overlapping challenge of individuating a coherent and stable sense of "self." We, the authors, are but two of the many who have written in some fashion about this complicated developmental weave or "sonata" (see Webb and Widseth, 1988, 1991a, and 1991b, and Webb, Widseth, and Bushnell, 1991).

In looking to these separation-individuation issues, we, as authors and college psychotherapists, have drawn particular inspiration from the seminal works of Peter Blos (1979), Christopher Bollas (1987), and Margaret Mahler (1975, 1979) and her col-

Jane C. Widseth, PhD, is Psychological Counselor, Haverford College, Haverford, PA 19041. Richard E. Webb, PhD, is Director of Psychological Services, Haverford College, Haverford College, Haverford, PA 19041.

leagues. Blos writes of the "recrudescence" of early separation issues in the life of the adolescent, a notion developed from a different perspective by Bollas. Mahler's work seems especially relevant because of her down-to-earth and yet very rich and poignant descriptions of the child's evolving sense of separateness from the "mother."

In our work, we have found it useful to rely upon Blos' and Bollas' notion that early developmental concerns re-emerge in both a familiar and a new way at later stages, including those faced by college students. We have found the language of Mahler especially useful for applying this notion to students. We find it helpful in describing how college students, 17-22 years of age, approach the exploration of their "inner" worlds, and we see the understanding that emerges from this description as relevant for appreciating how students approach the psychotherapy they seek out at psychological services or counseling centers.

In this article we discuss briefly some of the separation-individuation concerns pertaining to the late adolescent college student. We then note the relevance of such understanding for appreciating the pattern, which many students demonstrate (Webb et al., 1988, 1991), of entering and leaving their psychotherapeutic work. Although all people are "babes in the woods" when it comes to exploring their unconscious lives, we think there is some advantage in and basis for thinking particularly, in developmentally normative terms, of late adolescent college students as being "toddlers" to the inner world.

DEVELOPMENTAL CONSIDERATIONS

From the perspective of Mahler, the toddler is the very embodiment of the word "curious" as she or he first begins to break out of the symbiotic relationship to the "mother." If let out of the parent's arms, the toddler will explore the environment fully and freely, oblivious to dangers. At a later age or developmental phase, that same toddler will look very different. Now, perhaps with the experience of some hurtful falls and bumps, the toddler seems to need the parent's presence, at least in terms of being within eyesight or earshot, to explore the environment. At this stage, the toddler seems to need to "refuel" in order to sustain his or her curiosity and does so by periodically returning to the parent for brief holding or touching. Later in time, with even greater experience of the world now to draw upon, the toddler seeks a "rapprochement" with the parent, and curiosity seems to be paired with the wish for the active participation of the parent. In an ideal sense, the child later moves on to sustaining curiosity when independent of the parent.

The image of the toddler pertinent to college students in the transition from childhood to adulthood is characterized by a much more complicated curiosity and exploration. It is no longer a focus so easily characterized as the world around and external to the "toddler." While it is true that much in the new college environment may be categorized as "outside" or external to the student, a critical difference between the toddler of the early years and the "new" toddler of adolescence is the addition of self-consciousness and reflective thinking. And the addition of this capability makes all new exploration an exploration which can shift fluidly in its relevance as to whether it is most saliently an exploration of the "external" world or of the new toddler's "internal" world. Blos writes of the adolescent's challenge of reworking internalized objects. This process begins, usually, in the physical presence of the home and family. Later, this exploration occurs at college, in other words, in the context, in most cases, of a very real and physical separation from parents and familiar relationships.

This process, which is so important to understand, can be obscured by all the new tasks at hand for the new college student who must "out there" make new acquaintances, negotiate social customs, and face important academic responsibilities. The late night hours are often spent talking about political issues, musical interests, past sexual histories, values, and otherwise "frolicking about." Such contacts are important for generating so much of the excitement that radiates from students and for sustaining their curiosity to seek more of such exchanges. But it is important to remember that the "fresh start" that is so often spoken of by students, as what they look for in their coming to college, seems clearly to reflect the students' intentions to rework their sense of who they are. Jonathan Slavin (1987) notes that, "Once out of the family arena the adolescent becomes quickly engaged in a highly charged and very compelling relationship to a new setting–a setting characterized not only by very real differences with the family environment, but infused as well with fantasies of anticipated temptations, gratifications and possibilities for revision of oneself and one's relationships that have been revitalized by the upheavals of puberty" (Slavin, 1987, p. 7).

Bollas' (1987) notion of the "transformational object" also reminds us of the complicated underlying unconscious "workings" that are so much a part of this activity and which help define what may be sought from the college environment. He writes of the search for re-experiencing the early connection with the mother. This early connection is a process wherein:

> . . . before the mother is personalized for the infant as a whole object, she has functioned as a region or source of transformation . . . with the infant's growth and increasing self-reliance, the relation to the mother as the other who alters the self changes to a person who has her own life and her own needs . . . The ego experience of being transformed by the other remains as a memory that may be reenacted in aesthetic experiences, in a wide range of culturally-dreamed-of transformational objects (such as new cars, homes, jobs and vacations) that promise total change of internal and external environment, or in the varied psychopathological manifestations of this memory. (Bollas, 1987, p. 28)

ENTERING AND LEAVING PSYCHOTHERAPY

When students come to us at our college for a psychotherapeutic consultation, we try to impart to them in one fashion or another that we can offer them an opportunity to explore their concerns and to "brainstorm" together about "what's going on." We try to remember, more or less privately and despite diverting pressures that come from the student, as well as colleagues from other departments within the college and our own narcissism, that we are not the holders of special wisdom about how to live life nor the holders of special powers to take away anyone's anxiety or pain or joy or whatever. We operate essentially on an assumption that the more "data" a person has, the better chance the data-gatherer can make a "good" decision. And what "expertise" we might claim is that we are sometimes "pretty good" at hearing "between the lines" and "under" what people tell us.

We start, then, from a position that seeks not to define the scope of the work for the student who seeks our consultation. We try to position ourselves neither as the "mother" who offers "refueling" (e.g., solace) nor as the "mother" who defines for the "toddler" what areas are safe to explore and what ones not. We, in essence, try to allow ourselves to become open to the inner world that the student is bringing to us rather than a moderator or definer of it.

As a consequence of this posture, which we describe above, we have had opportunity to observe how students naturally approach psychotherapy through their years at our college. And in this sense the image of the refueling toddler (Mahler et al., 1975), seems pertinent to us for understanding how college students use us for psychotherapy. Just as the toddler finds explorations of the *external* world exciting for a time and then needs a respite, so do we find the new toddler, the undergraduate student, often fascinated with explorations of his or her *internal* world. But also like the toddler of the early years, we find the toddler of the college years to have fluctuating capability to stay with the exploration. Although this capability is always different for each individual, depending upon the status of the undergraduate's negotiation of his or her separation-individuation from parental figures (Webb and Widseth, 1991a), we find, generally speaking, that undergraduate students seem typically to need a rest, to "refuel" from the exploration. At this point, we are of the impression that this is particularly true of first year and sophomore students. They seem to come for a time for exploration of their inner worlds and then to back away and seek a rest from this work. They, more than the older undergraduate students, juniors and seniors, seem hopeful that as they leave their family and old friends that "new solutions" and "answers" to their lives will be found "out there," somewhere external to themselves, somewhere in their new setting of college. Consequently, they seem to "tire" or to have less patience for "looking inside" for answers than their older peers. As Slavin (1987) aptly says, "All adolescents, including those with incipient and more crystallized forms of pathology, approach the transition from the family setting with a similar set of beliefs and convictions: that 'out there' in a new setting and in a new relationship, solutions are possible that were not available previously" (Slavin, 1987, pp. 7-8).

Quite often, these students, who tire and pull back from their inner explorations return to us to continue their work later in their tenure at the college. At times they take yet another respite in the work before returning to it a third time. While we think our students, particularly, are inclined to be psychologically-minded, we do not think that this characteristic can fully explain our findings.

Here, more specifically, is what we have found. In each recent graduating class, 36% or more met with a counselor or therapist in our service at least once for help with personal concerns during their college career. Of the 369 student-clients in four years of records, 37% had 1-3 sessions in our service over their *entire* college careers, 28% had 4-10 sessions, 19% had 11-20 sessions, and only 15% had more than 20 sessions. In this same group, over four years, roughly one out of three students came in for two or three *series* of appointments.

We consider that: (1) The findings serve to open to more critical thinking any explanation that a student's leaving his or her therapy work may be categorized, conventionally, as "resistance"; it is resistance, but there is a developmental factor which needs consideration. (2) Since undergraduate students, when freely allowed to utilize the psychotherapy consultation service, do not flood into long term psychotherapy, why do so many services feel the need to be the refueling parents who set limits on the exploration? Our findings, in the context of an appreciation of the complicated structure of the individuation process, address the choice of time-limited psychotherapy for work with undergraduates. We think that the argument for a time-limited modality as the treatment structure of choice, because the therapist is considering the "dependency" sensitivity of the students, should be considered a substantial oversimplification. Similarly, we think our findings allow counterpoint to those clinicians heavily invested in a more educational approach to counseling, a "focus-limited" approach. The inner world is a critically important focus for the new toddler no matter how ambivalently it is held by him or her. Do we truly provide an informed service to our students by hearing only part of their ambivalence? Are we offering the best education to our students if we consciously set out to ignore what is a critical aspect in the scope of what they seek to discover, whether that be inside or outside of the classroom? Our findings suggest that we can leave the limiting to the student.

CLINICAL EXAMPLES

To give a sense of our work, we offer here three examples, two of students who fit into our "exploration-rest" pattern, students who came in for a series of appointments and then sought a rest from the work and then returned later (Webb, Widseth, & Bushnell, 1991). The first is a student who came for but one series of appointments.

Example I: "Sara" sought therapy in October of her sophomore year and had seven sessions. When she first spoke with the therapist, she said that her boyfriend had urged her to seek help. He thought she was "too dependent," and she acknowledged that she did feel "totally dependent." Sara said that when he talked about breaking up with her, she felt "shattered." In the next few sessions, she went on to describe how she felt worthy and loveable when he was with her and warm to her. If he were away, she felt he must be angry with her; otherwise, he would be with her. She and the therapist talked about how he might have studying or other things to do, and not be angry with her.

In the fifth session, the therapist wrote in her notes that the underlying feelings of the sessions had changed and that she, the therapist, felt more warmth toward Sara. In the sixth session, Sara announced that she was going to discontinue her therapy. She felt that her relationship with her boyfriend was going well, and even more importantly, she felt good away from him during the recent Thanksgiving break, and that, while she had missed him, she had nevertheless had a wonderful holiday at home. She noted also that she had learned in her sessions that not everything that went wrong in their relationship was her fault. She now recognized that he had problems, too. By the end of that session, she decided to continue her therapy.

In the seventh session, Sara talked about her boyfriend breaking up with her. She was angry with the way he mocked her in front of their friends. She then opened up about her family of origin, said that she felt like her father just before her parents got a divorce, and that she hated herself for feeling this way. Just after this seventh session, Sara called to cancel her next. She told the receptionist that she had "too many things to do right now," and that she would call next semester if she "needed to." She never called back.

This student, Sara, can be seen as having deep-seated problems with self-esteem, but unable to sustain a continued exploration. It is noteworthy that in her last session, during the last week of classes, she opened up about her experience of her father in the parents' divorce. One glimpse of that distress seemed to lead her to discontinue further meetings. She reminds us of the baby who walks a bit on her own and then sits down, and refuses to walk for several more months. One can only imagine that the new territory was too scary.

Example II: We described our work with "Lisa" in an earlier paper (Webb, Widseth, & Bushnell, 1991). To summarize, Lisa came to our service for three series of sessions during her college career, four her sophomore year, ten as a junior, and 18 as a senior; all with the same therapist.

Lisa, a college sophomore, came in after a day in which she collapsed "out of control." The triggering incident was the insensitivity of a guest professor who smoked a cigarette in class. When Lisa confronted him after class about college policies restricting smoking in classrooms, the professor was not sympathetic. He felt that he needed to smoke during class. She burst into tears and sobbed for the remainder of the day with her boyfriend. Lisa thought back to earlier times when she wanted an empty room with sound proofing so that she could make as much noise as she wanted. The therapist wondered why she needed to be alone. Was it to be alone, or was it to protect others from her rage? Lisa told the therapist that her mother forced her to see a counselor in high school, but that she, Lisa, had refused to talk. The therapist wondered if she felt her mother did not want to hear what she would say. Lisa said her mother had trouble mothering because of her own experiences of being physically abused as a child.

After two or three sessions, Lisa felt more in control and less like revealing the "messy" thoughts and feelings inside. She was afraid to assert her needs for fear of losing friendships. By the fourth session, she was focused on her studies, the work needed to complete the semester.

In the second series, beginning right away first semester of her junior year, she revealed a history of trauma. Lisa was four years old when she and her mother were in a car accident. Their car burst into flames and Lisa was trapped initially, got third degree burns from her shoulder to her ankles, spent three weeks in the hospital, and eventually had seven surgeries. When the therapist winced over the pain and anguish of such an experience, Lisa stated unequivocally, "If I touch that hurt, I will vaporize."

Lisa spent several sessions talking about her relationship with her boyfriend. She couldn't decide whether to stay in the relationship or not. Over the fall vacation, she went home to visit her family. When she returned to college, she was happy about her visit home. She had a good time with her parents, and she felt relieved when her parents didn't hang on to her when she needed to leave. She worried that her parents would be "upset" because she wanted to be a "guest" in their home. The therapist and Lisa then went back to an earlier theme: Lisa's feeling destructive of her mother and the mother's emotional and physical abuse of her. When the therapist said "You're feeling uneasy about being hurtful like your mother," Lisa responded in such a way that the therapist felt her (the therapist's) comment was abusive. Lisa said she wanted to feel stable and in control. She and the therapist understood in that context that Lisa didn't want her equilibrium upset by exploring these "lurking, nagging issues." Over the next few sessions, Lisa acknowledged a sense of "rot and corruption" inside her but that she was afraid of exploring these feelings for fear of losing control. In the tenth session, she said, "This is my last counseling appointment for a while; I need a break." She felt more settled and less like she had to come for sessions. She had once again found her studies pressing. Also, she and the therapist understood that she had to go on "auto pilot" in preparation for some stressful upcoming events, including further diagnostic surgery and a four week winter break at home. She put it this way: "The only way I can deal with all of this is to say with a smile: 'I've gotten through worse, so I can get through this period. Just don't think about it!'"

The 18 sessions in the final series spanned the period from mid September to early March of her senior year. In this third series, the first meeting followed her having broken up with her boyfriend. She was surprised that they had broken up, but was relieved, since she felt a need to have time for other friendships and relationships. Clearly, the approach of graduation was on her mind. She appreciated the sense of freedom and independence gained after the step away from the boyfriend.

The theme of blowing up at others reemerged. It came out first in her talking about the boyfriend whose "blowing up" used to terrify her, just as when her mother used to blow up at her. Lisa remembered how at home she used to be very, very careful; for eight years, she and mother were unable to speak without fighting. Lisa then talked about crying all the time. She had to be on guard to check her mother's mood. The therapist commented on how hard, as a child, she had to work, and the therapist also pointed out how Lisa noticed that the therapist had a cold. Lisa added that not only was she being careful about the therapist's mood, but also knew she gained friends by being attentive to others. Lisa went on to talk about needing to blow up at her family but being afraid to, because she still needed them. She hoped that in the future she might be able to blow up at the therapist. The therapist reminded her of her feeling unsettled by the pace the therapist had set in past sessions. Lisa said, "I came here hurting but wanting bandaids. Now I'm not hurting so much, and I know how to bandaid myself." Lisa had, in an earlier session, revealed that the "digging in the past" had undercut her foundation. She said that she needed to stay more in the present.

The theme of controlling the pace continued as she explored her own fear of getting too loose. She worried a lot about her violent fantasies, for example her thoughts of buying glassware and hurling it at a wall. The next several weeks she was "storming mad" at the college, her boss, her roommates, and finally the old boyfriend. It turned out that in the middle of their relationship, the boyfriend had had an affair. He was so upset and felt so guilty that he became furious with himself. At that time, she took care of him instead of telling him how she felt. But now, two years later, she confronted him. The outcome of their confrontation was that he decided to move off campus and to break up with her. In this tumultuous period, she had bad dreams, talked about difficult menstruation, described the trauma of the car crash, and told her major professor that she was not applying to graduate school. She cancelled additional appointments in order to finish her exams and paper before Christmas.

After a six week hiatus, she talked about a wonderful Christmas visit with her family and talks with alums who affirmed her reservations about the college and who then proceeded to write letters in support of her concerns. Beginning her job search, she realized how tired she was of taking care of others. She felt exhausted. When two firms offered her interviews for attractive jobs, she spoke of receiving wide-spread affirmation from friends and of the possibilities of developing new relationships. In that context, she turned to the issue of her anxiety over sexuality. She revealed that when she felt sexually stirred, she felt deep threat.

In the penultimate session, she talked about her happy spirits and good weeks, and her fear that if she were to address the issue of sexuality, she would collapse. She revealed that she had visited the old boyfriend. That day they had felt comfortable sexually together and had gone to a movie. Afterwards they had returned to his apartment where he had cooked a meal. She ate part of the dinner and then left. She felt overwhelmed with sadness. Rather than stay with him, she decided to go home so that she could get up early to prepare for the next day. The therapist commented that Lisa had found the work sustaining but needed to leave to get herself ready for what is next in her life. Lisa agreed, saying that she wanted to go home and read a book. In the last session, two months before graduation, she returned to her sadness at leaving the boyfriends' apartment and turned to her sadness at leaving the therapist. She was, nevertheless, enjoying new books and new friends; she felt ready to move on.

In essence, Lisa established the work still to be done and her decision to step away from the work. The acknowledgement by the therapist of her need to set the pace was important to her, because she felt the respect for her needs and decisions.

Example III: Our third example is work with "Al," who sought therapy for three series spanning over five years.

Al saw a therapist eight times spring semester of his first year, because he was "depressed" about his relationship with his girlfriend who allowed fondling but no sexual intercourse. The therapist wondered at the time about some underlying competitive issues with an older brother and about Al's residual feelings about his parents' divorce. The therapist wrote in his concluding note that each session opened with Al worrying about not having sex, but that each session evolved toward a discussion of how closeness and intimacy were the "real" issues. Al ended his sessions before the end of the semester saying that, although he was not having sex, he was enjoying some new friendships and generally feeling "better." The therapist wondered to himself whether Al was beginning to struggle with feeling dependent upon him.

Al returned for therapy about one year later, the spring of his sophomore year, and, at his request, met with a different therapist. He could offer no clear explanation as to why he did not choose to return to the first therapist. He met with the new therapist for nineteen sessions, discontinued during the summer, but returned at the start of the fall semester and continued until the midpoint of his junior spring semester.

During this period Al again was preoccupied with sexuality. He was still a virgin, he announced, but his focus seemed to deepen. He seemed much less pressured to focus on "when" he would have sex and was much more open to sharing his concerns about what having sex meant to him. In fact, he told the therapist at the end of the fall semester that he had suspended even "looking" at women while he looked within himself during this time in therapy.

During this fall period Al spoke of how "wary" he was of his sexual fantasies. He was frightened that his fantasies and desires might be viewed as "exploitive, silly, and wrong." He coped by "misting over" his feelings and expressing them through participating in a heavy metal rock group, which he experienced as highly erotic. He was angry that he felt he had to inhibit his feelings, and yet he did not want to be criticized for them. He was confused about what women felt and thought about sex. He spoke about a symposium he attended and his preoccupation with a woman talking about how she liked to belch and fart and to say, "cunt" and "fuck," in contrast with a current girlfriend of his who announced that she didn't really want a sexual relationship.

Al's talk about sex during this series soon led him to sharing much about his childhood history. His father and mother divorced when he was a grade-schooler. The marriage turned towards divorce soon after the father suggested that the mother, a victim of childhood sexual abuse, improve her sexual responsiveness by having an affair. Mother took father up on this suggestion and felt more gratified by the extra-marital relationship. Al spoke of his father's absence after the divorce and feeling abandoned. As a single parent, Al's mother proceeded to have a number of sexual partners, with whom the love making was sometimes audible to Al. Her bedroom was "off limits" to him and his brother, but she did not cover her body from their view around the house. Al remembered masturbating excitedly, albeit with intense guilt, while looking at a book about sexual techniques that he found in his mother's room.

With such history now considered in the therapy work, Al noted feeling comfortable with women as Platonic loves or as objects of sexual pleasure; he understood that he was uncomfortable fitting together these two forms of connectedness with the same partner. He came to understand that to be clumsy and virginal was to feel childlike and incestuous. He revealed his private feeling and thoughts increasingly. He told the therapist with embarrassment that when he imagined his mother having sex with men he imagined her holding on to the man and at the same time crying tears of hurt and pain. He then said he had trouble thinking of his penis as something soothing and pleasure-giving instead of hurtful and burning. He told of his first experience touching a woman's vagina and his preoccupation the next day with continually washing his hand to rid it of the "smell."

Al returned to his therapy work after the recess between semesters and introduced his feeling separate and far away from his parents and his brother. His brother had recently announced that he would be taking a job in Australia. Al was soon in a "tizzy" . . . falling in love; in two weeks he was sleeping regularly with his girlfriend, and they were having intercourse. After missing an appointment, Al came in to say that he wanted to discontinue his work, that he wasn't sure he had anything more to say even though he also felt frightened that, if he wasn't seeing the therapist, something "awful" would happen.

Three and a half months later Al saw the therapist for one appointment during the summer recess. He shared that his girlfriend had broken up with him.

Al did not return to his therapy work during the fall semester of his senior year, and he took a leave of absence from the college the next two semesters after that to attend a special school pertaining to his academic major. A month into his last semester of his senior year he returned for ten therapy sessions.

During this last series, Al seemed to pick up where he had left off two years ago. He began by telling of being lonely and how he felt he was "beating around the bush." He quickly was able to hear his alluding to sexual concerns, and he began speaking more freely about his fear-tinged fascination with women. He spoke of the play *MacBeth* and of the witches "flashing and thrusting the nothing, the vagina, between their legs at MacBeth." As the witches had the power over MacBeth so, he felt, did women over him. He spoke of how when he masturbated and "let loose," he then had nothing left but the ejaculate and "Who would want that?" The work continued in this vein with considerable weaving back and forth between his sexual concerns and his concerns of finishing his senior thesis and graduating. His exploration of "who" the therapist was to Al became important also. He spoke of the therapist as the missing man, the "father," with whom he could talk about his penis and about being a man. He spoke about feeling himself to be his father's child and yet feeling that in his relationship with his father he would "cast the net and yet come up empty." In the final session Al parted, expressing his gratitude by asking the therapist whether he could put a plug in for our Psychological Services in his senior year exit interview.

CONCLUSION

The sketches of interviews with "Sara," "Lisa," and "Al" exemplify the exploration/rest dynamic that we have described.

Lisa articulates her need for vacations from the work as due to (1) pressing events, like diagnostic surgery and graduation, which call for her full attention and (2) exploratory therapy undercutting "my foundation." She needs her resources to attend to events pressing upon her, and feels the therapy is too unsettling.

It is revealing to compare the material revealed in a first set of interviews (Sara) to material from three sets of sessions (Lisa, Al). One gets the sense of Sara's difficulties working through separation-individuation and only a glimpse of the history of her problems. In contrast, Lisa's and Al's basic problems get elaborated more fully. Lisa's difficulty with her destructive feelings and Al's anxiety over sexuality gain more and more depth of expression. One sees how the therapeutic triangle, the three foci comprising current life situation, history, and transference (Malan, 1979) gets filled in with details.

All of us as young therapists, especially when fresh from internships in psychiatric settings where assessment and diagnosis are central activities, hear with alarm certain revelations from students. We may hear about a schizophrenic sibling, divorce of parents, or the trauma of a traffic accident as causes of deep-seated problems for which psychotherapy is needed. We may then shift into a mode of diagnostic interviewing familiar to us and then into the stance of recommending a referral for long-term, intensive psychotherapy. With experience, however, we begin to learn that students often feel either misunderstood by the diagnostic efforts or not ready to follow through on the referrals. And gradually more and more we see the wisdom in an early supervisor's advice: "Stay *with* the client, whatever he or she is talking about." Students have taught us that while they know the parents' divorce or car accident was traumatic, they want to talk about what is happening to them *now*. They are quite often not ready to open up the hurt too widely; as Lisa said, "If I touch that pain, I will vaporize." The college psychotherapist needs to be available for exploration of what they want to talk about and neither hold on too tightly, insisting that the exploration continue and focus on what the therapist thinks is important, nor push away, insisting that the student not get "too dependent" or in "too deep."

Explicit time limits are unnecessary, because most students won't sustain the exploratory psychotherapy and because there are limits already set by the college calendar. Furthermore, where a college or university has a policy of time-limited psychotherapy for students, such a policy influences the way the student and therapist work together. As Robert May (1988) notes, the student may arrive already ready to fight and/or the student and therapist may split off the anger at "the administration" for imposing the end of sessions. May also comments on the difference between active and passive endings. He differentiates ". . . between a good-bye you choose and one that is forced upon you. The latter tends to evoke the trauma of helpless losses: the child whose parent dies, the jilted lover, the knowledge of the inevitability of illness and death" (May, 1988, p. 65). May goes on to ask, "But what of the sadness of choosing to leave? What of the difficult recognition that one's own development requires a turning away from people you cherish?" (p. 65). We would add: What of the recognition that development requires a struggle with what to explore, how far to go with that exploration, and when to do it?

REFERENCES

Blos, P. (1979). *The adolescent passage.* New York: International Universities Press.

Bollas, C. (1987). *The shadow of the object: Psychoanalysis of the unthought known.* London: Free Association Books.

Mahler, M.S. (1979). *The selected papers of Margaret S. Mahler. Vols. 1 and 2.* New York: Jason Aronson.

Mahler, M.S., Pine, F., and Bergman, A. (1975). *The psychological birth of the human infant.* New York: Basic Books, Inc.

Malan, D.H. (1979). *Individual psychotherapy and the science of psychodynamics.* London: Butterworths.

May, R. (1988). The scope of psychotherapy. Chapter 4, pp. 57-100, in *Psychoanalytic psychotherapy in a college context,* edited by R. May. New York: Praeger.

Slavin, J.S. (1987). Readiness for psychotherapy in late adolescence: Considerations for the provision of clinical services on a college campus. Paper presented at the Fall Conference of the Philadelphia Society for Psychoanalytic Psychology, Philadelphia, Pennsylvania, September 19.

Webb, R.E. and Widseth, J.C. (1988). Facilitating students' going into and stepping back from their inner worlds: Psychotherapy and the college student. *Journal of College Student Psychotherapy, Vol. 3(1),* 5-15.

Webb, R.E. and Widseth, J.C. (1991a). Students we don't refer: "Holding" the unheld. *Journal of College Student Psychotherapy, Vol. 5(2)*, 19-42.

Webb, R.E. and Widseth, J.C. (1991b). With memory but no desire: Thinking of Bion in doing college psychotherapy. *Journal of College Student Psychotherapy, Vol. 5(3)*, 29-50.

Webb, R.E., Widseth, J.C., and Bushnell, D. (1991). Further comments: Facilitating students' going into and stepping back from their inner worlds. *Journal of College Student Psychotherapy, Vol. 5(3)*, 67-80.

Chapter 5

Developing *Typically* in the College Years

O.W. Lacy

SUMMARY. A development progression is outlined which dove-
tails with and expands the life-span theory of Erik H. Erikson and
the type conceptions of W. Harold Grant into six stages, the span
in years of each of which is roughly divisible by seven: *Early
Childhood* (Birth to Seven), which includes Erikson's Trust v.
Mistrust, Autonomy v. Shame/Doubt, and Initiative v. Guilt, and
in which the child establishes Extraversion or Introversion; *Late
Childhood* (Seven to Fourteen), Erikson's Industry v. Inferiority
and the establishment of the Dominant function; *Adolescence* (Fourteen to Twenty-One), including Erikson's Identity v. Role Confusion and the raising into consciousness of the Auxiliary function;
Young Adulthood (Twenty-one to Thirty-Five), Intimacy v. Isolation, and the practice of the Tertiary; *Mid-Life* (Thirty-Five to
Forty-Nine) Generativity v. Stagnation, and the bringing under
some control of the usually unconscious Inferior; and finally, *Mature Adulthood* (Forty-Nine to Seventy) Erikson's Integrity v. Despair in which the conscious and differential use of all functions
allows approaching the ideal of individuation.

In our efforts to predict, (to anticipate, to appreciate, to control,
to influence, to understand, to modify and/or to explain, etc.) the

A graduate of Hampden-Sydney College, Dr. O.W. Lacy received his doctorate in clinical psychology from the University of Pennsylvania; since 1953 he has
filled a variety of teaching, counseling, and deaning positions at Hampden-Sydney, Trinity (CT), and Franklin and Marshall colleges, whose continuing support
of his research and writing is gratefully acknowledged. He is Director, *Emeritus*,
Counseling and Career Services, Franklin and Marshall College, Box 3003,
Lancaster, PA 17604-3003.

behavior of others, we utilize a variety of schemes based on diverse categories Among the shibboleths more often employed in this categorizing process are, for example, our notions about age, sex, race, religion, and/or educational attainment, some of which, some of the time, in combination or individually, increase the likelihood of more accurate predictions. In the last decade or so Carl Jung's theory of psychological type (Jung, 1971), as extended and operationally articulated by Myers (1980), has provided an increasing number of college counselors and therapists with another useful means of understanding others–and ourselves. Less well known, even to those interested in type, are the seminal concepts of W. H. Grant about the sequence each type follows as it unfolds throughout life. This chapter proposes to apply the theory and techniques of type to personality development, especially in the college years.

TYPE THEORY IS A PSYCHOLOGY OF CONSCIOUSNESS

It cannot, at the outset, be emphasized too strongly that the theory of type is a theory of consciousness. Late in his long life Jung said of his book, "*Psychological Types* . . . was an effort to deal with the relationship of the individual to the world, to people and things. It discussed the various attitudes the conscious mind might take toward the world, and thus constitutes a psychology of consciousness . . . [It] yielded the insight that every judgment made by an individual is conditioned by his personality type and that every point of view is necessarily relative" (Jaffé, 1963, p. 207). As we shall see, this consciousness has to do with people becoming aware of their psychological preferences which unfold throughout life from conception to death. It is clear that Jung conceived the preferences to have their origin in the individual's biological heritage: "As a general psychological phenomenon, . . . the type antithesis must have some kind of biological foundation" (Jung, 1971, p. 331). While he did not have the benefit of knowledge of the last three decades' spectacular advances in molecular biology, our current scientific knowledge would appear to lend credence to his belief.

THE ATTITUDES OF CONSCIOUSNESS

Current type theory asserts two basic polar *attitudinal* preferences: First, how we prefer to invest our energies, interests, and attention: either in the outer, objective world of people, things, and actions (Extraversion) or in the inner, subjective world of thoughts, feelings, memories,and images (Introversion) In the extraverted attitude the psychic energy flows to the outer object; in the introverted attitude, the psychic energy flows from the object to the subject. And, second, how we prefer to live our 'extraverted lives: whether in the Judging mode, planning, deciding, ordering, and regulating or in the Perceptive mode, seeking experience, flexibility, spontaneity, understanding, and adaptation.

THE FUNCTIONS OF CONSCIOUSNESS

The theory, further, relates these attitudes to two fundamental mental *functions*, each of which can be experienced in two opposing ways: *Perception* in terms either of facts as revealed by the Senses or of the iNtuitively experienced trends, possibilities, patterns, inherent in those facts, and *Judgment* (the process of decision making), either by Thinking, a process which is analytical, linear, logical, objective, and quantitative, or by Feeling, a global, evaluative, subjective, qualitative process.

THE HIERARCHIC NATURE OF THE FUNCTIONS

Jung proposed, further, that one of the four mental functions came to be used with more differentiated consciousness, grace, skill, enjoyment, and competence than the others and thus became dominant. Since this dominant function could be focused either extravertedly on the outer world or introvertedly on the inner, Jung's scheme yielded eight types. In the culminating Chapter X of *Psychological Types*, each of Jung's eight was elucidated, as Myers (1980, p. 17) observes, "in sharpest focus and with maximum

contrast between its extraverted and introverted forms; consequently, he describes the rare, theoretically 'pure' types, who have little
or no development of the auxiliary." Indeed, in a tome of 987
paragraphs, Jung devotes only a few to the nature of the auxiliary;
yet these establish the relationship of the auxiliary to the dominant
and to the attitudes:

> . . . I have no desire to give my readers the impression that
> these types occur at all frequently in such pure form in actual
> life . . . Closer investigation shows with great regularity that,
> besides the most differentiated function, another, less differen-
> tiated function of secondary importance is invariably present
> in consciousness and exerts a co-determining influence . . . Its
> secondary importance is due to the fact that it is not, like the
> primary function, valid in its own right as an absolutely reli-
> able and decisive factor, but comes into play more as an
> auxiliary or complementary function (1971, p. 405).
>
> Hence the auxiliary function is possible and useful only in
> so far as it *serves* the dominant function, without making any
> claim to the autonomy of its own principle. For all the types
> met with in practice, the rule holds good that besides the
> conscious, primary function there is a relatively unconscious,
> auxiliary function which is in every respect different from the
> nature of the primary function. (1971, p. 406)

It was the genius of Katherine Briggs and Isabel Myers to realize
the vital importance of the balancing auxiliary to the well developed personality. It provides for the Extravert access to the inner
life, for the Introvert entry into the outer, for the dominant Judger,
support from the perceptual mode, and for the dominant Perceiver,
a sustaining judgment. Applying Jung's criteria that the auxiliary
function must be different in every respect from the primary and
"useful only in so far as it serves the dominant," in *Introduction
to Type* and later in Chapter 9 of *Gifts Differing*, Myers rewrote
Jung's descriptions of the so-called "pure" types mediated by the
auxiliary's ameliorating effects.

To illustrate his point that "the unconscious functions likewise
group themselves in patterns correlated with the conscious ones,"

(1971, p. 407), Jung used dominant thinking with sensing auxiliary: "thus, the correlative of conscious, practical thinking may be an unconscious, intuitive-feeling attitude, with feeling under a stronger inhibition than intuition." Unfortunately, he turned away from this opportunity to proceed to a full scale developmental psychology of type, dismissing "these peculiarities . . . [as] of interest only for one who is concerned with the practical treatment of such cases."

THE INTERWEAVING OF FUNCTIONS AND ATTITUDES

Jung postulated that if the dominant were extraverted then the other three, less differentiated functions would be introverted (and, of course, if the dominant were introverted, the other three would be extraverted) asserting, for example, that for the extravert:

> the most differentiated function is always employed in an extraverted way, whereas the inferior functions are introverted; in other words, the superior function is the most conscious one and completely under conscious control, whereas the less differentiated functions are in part unconscious and far less under the control of consciousness. (1971, p. 340)

Again, discussing the Introverted Thinker (his own type, INTP):

> The counterbalancing functions of feeling, intuition, and sensation are comparatively unconscious and inferior, and therefore have a primitive extraverted character that accounts for all the troublesome influences from outside to which the introverted thinker is prone. (1971, p. 387)

Following the Jungian "received wisdom," Myers (1987, p. 9) also proposes that the three lesser functions are all typically expressed in the attitude opposite to that of the dominant.

Believing that Jung erred in this particular, I concur with other students of typology (Brownsword, 1987, Grant, Thompson, and Clarke, 1983, Kroeger and Thuesen, 1988, and Jefferies, 1991) that the balance is not one against three, but rather that two functions are preferably extraverted, and two introverted. My experience teaches me that if the dominant be extraverted, so too its tertiary; and if the dominant be introverted, so also its tertiary. Let me here digress briefly to cite two case histories to illustrate my conviction that in this matter the facts do not support the received wisdom.

TWO CASE HISTORIES

Case 1: Sylvester (Extroverted Feeling with Intuition, ENFJ). This Ph.D. in Higher Education and university administrator is an especially close friend of two psychologists, both of whom, with the assurance both of training and extensive practice, claim a considerable degree of expertise with the concepts of type and its prediction. Since early on the shared relationship of these three has involved frequent visits among the three to each others' places of employment and homes. Sylvester, as we shall call him to assure anonymity, in the early years of the friendship, perhaps annoyed by the psychologists' "typetalk," scoffed at the notion of type, calling it "mumbo-jumbo" and the MBTI, a pencil and paper Ouija Board.

It was no trouble at all for the psychologists, both INFPs, to deduce from Sy's incessant flow of conversation, the preponderance of which had to do with his concerns, plans, schedules, and activities for the welfare of the threesome, that he was surely E-FJ. Both "experts," moreover, observed in his home study and university office a multiplicity of gadgetry, in his workshop and garage an incredible array of tools and equipment each with a special function (not just an all purpose hammer, but a large sledge, a small sledge, three sizes of claws, two different ballpeens, a magnetized tack hammer, large and small wooden mallets, large and small rubber mallets, *ad infinitum*–I resist the temptation to catalog the similar arrays of shovels, rakes, saws, screwdrivers, pliers, wrenches, boots, hats, raingear, backpacks, canoes! Under this onslaught of the practical, factual, material, the two psychologists concluded that Sy's auxiliary was Sensing. and the tertiary, the invisible iNtuition.

Subsequently, Sy subjected himself to the MBTI, and on several repetitions has always come out ENFJ; he himself "owns" to that type, and reports that his dominant feeling is best supported by his inner inspirations about the possibilities he sees in most situations–and the psychologists ate their crow cold and raw! Even Sy admits that his extraverted sensing is at best childlike, only apparently practical in the larger scheme of things, and at worst, childish.

Case 2, Ricardo (Extraverted iNtuition with Thinking, ENTP). At thirty five, an economist with solid Ivy League masters and doctorate and valuable experience in quality liberal colleges, this academic dean and vice president is already marked as an administrator with much further to go in the Academy. Noted as an "idea" man, the fecundity of his imagination has always illuminated his teaching and research, and has made him inspiring not only to his students but now also to his administrative colleagues and subordinates, and perhaps more importantly to trustees and alumni. Hearty, affable, and jovial, it is easy to mistake him for an ENFP, but many a student or colleague has come away from a conference, on grades or budget, dismayed by an apparently inexorable coldness in decision when the matter came down to the final push against shove: in those moments Rick epitomizes that "central core of chill," which, in Lord Snow's *The Corridors of Power*, Hector Rose, that quintessential civil servant, had identified as the one indispensable ingredient of character for the consistent winner in power contests.

Both cases illustrate that the behavior the observer sees is neither pure dominant nor, as I conceive it, pure tertiary, neither pure perception, nor pure judgment, just as the drop of water on my window is neither observedly two parts oxygen and one part hydrogen. The point has often been made in the type literature that the extravert shows her/his best to the world (the dominant), and the introvert, his/her second best (the auxiliary). The broader point made in both of these cases is that what is generally seen by the outside observer in the case of extraverts is behavior indicative of both the dominant and tertiary functions, and in the case of the introvert, indications of the auxiliary and inferior. What we see, in other words, in the introvert's behavior is her/his second best colored by his/her worst; in the extrovert's, his/her best, colored by her/his next-to-worst! It takes real trust–or great stress–for the introvert to reveal the introverted functions; and in spite of the extraverts' general tendency to share all parts of themselves, their introverted functions may be completely overlooked.

In general, behavior associated with the dominant functions is likely to be described by an assortment of adjectives such as: adult, civilized, enlightened, finely discriminated, graceful, kind, polished, urbane and so on; those associated with the inferior: animalistic, awkward, benighted, cruel, grossly stereotyped, rough, savage, etc. The adult behaving in the grip, so to speak, of the auxiliary will appear to the observer as' being especially adolescent, and in like fashion, the adult being led by an unruly tertiary will appear as most disappointingly childish. While in most situations behavior not moderated by the exercise of the dominant is, at the very least, likely to be deemed inappropriate, in fact each of us throughout life carries within the burdens not only of the adult, but also of youth, child, and animal in varying degrees of conscious differentiation and self recognition.

GRANT'S STAGES OF TYPE DEVELOPMENT

Among type theorists, Grant is, I believe, the first to have proposed an age-based developmental sequence. In the early 1970s, he proposed, in MBTI workshops, a scheme based on six stages, each more or less six years long: early childhood (birth to six), later childhood (six to twelve), adolescence (twelve to twenty), young adulthood (twenty to thirty-five), mid-life (thirty-five to fifty), and the "golden years" (whatever is left).

While in the main Grant's model makes a great deal of sense, I shall, going along through the model's outline, suggest that the span of Grant's time periods be lengthened to multiples of seven since these seem to me more in keeping with our knowledge of development in general, with certain institutionalized "points of passage" in our own and many other cultures and with the lengthening average life expectancy. The number *seven*, moreover, with its rich connotations in the religions, traditions, and mythologies of many cultures, is also more numinous. Considering the proposed time spans, the reader should bear in mind that they are not rigid to the minute, hour, month, or even year, but are approximations or general tendencies, and that as in most things psychological, the notion of variability around a central tendency is to be expected.

While Jung clearly felt that type is genetically based, the influence of the environment in the life-long development of type is critical: whenever the environment forces "such a falsification of type . . . the individual becomes neurotic later, and can be cured only by developing the attitude consonant with his nature" (1971, p. 332). When, for example, my gentle, left-handed mother began as a small girl to write naturally with her preferred hand, an insensitively cruel stepmother would plunge the offending hand into a bucket of scalding-or icy-water. Mother throughout her life wrote a beautiful Spencerian script, with her right hand; and always the gentle INFP, she would only say of her stepmother, "She was determined to do what she thought was right. I never liked her."

Early Childhood (Birth to Seven): [Compare with Erikson's (1950) first three stages, **Trust v. Mistrust, Autonomy v. Shame/Doubt,** *and* **Initiative v. Guilt.** *By seven almost all children are in school, no longer taught, supervised, and cared for solely by parents].* Grant does not include this period in his formal "stages" but note the emphasis Erikson puts on the learnings and growth to be expected in these years.

Jung, in discussing the influence of biological inheritance in determining the preferred manner of investing the libido, noted "the fact that children often exhibit a typical attitude even in their earliest years" (1971, p. 332). My close observation of the manifest behavior of my three daughters *in utero*, observations supported by those of their mother, suggests a positive correlation of intrauterine activity with a later preference for extroverted behavior both in childhood and adulthood. Somewhat to my surprise, furthermore, a former student, then the Chief of Neonatology at a major West Coast medical school, emphatically agreed with my hypothesis that it is often possible to observe prenatally the preference for extraversion or introversion.

As for the other preferences, Grant and his colleagues appear to be accurate in observing, each of us enters upon the human journey with an original endowment, psychic as well as physical, a certain identity which is present even in the womb . . . Prior to the emergence of a distinct ego the infant and the small child is given . . . through the spontaneous movements of the psychic organism a 'get acquainted' period, so to speak . . . Each child is given the opportunity to gain, through undifferentiated experience, a basic familiarity with all four functions. This period is a time for random and tentative dabbling in the expression and development of the four functions" (Grant et al, 1983, p. 20).

Later Childhood (Seven to Fourteen): [Compare Erikson's **Industry v. Inferiority.** *By seven almost all children are in some sort of school situation, usually being taught all subjects by one teacher. By fourteen almost all young people have passed puberty and are in schools being taught by different teachers for different subjects].* After the initial early childhood period of indeterminate sorting out and trying on of the four functions, the model suggests "then, at six, the child's particular personality begins to develop and show itself more clearly. More specifically, there is the *spontaneous emergence* [emphasis supplied] of one of the four functions as the one which throughout life will be dominant in the personality. . . . And this preference, in the first stage of development between six and twelve will be accompanied by a preference of attitude in the exercise of the preferred function" (Grant et al., 1983, p. 20).

The later years of a "normal" childhood should, then, be occupied, in this model, with the perfecting of the dominant. In childhood, for example, Ricardo would have been concentrating on the myriad possibilities, patterns, complexities, and meanings he was finding in the world about him. And Sy would have been found concentrating in that same outer environment on service to others,and harmonious personal relationships, characterized by gentle, tender, compassionately warm expressive behavior.

Adolescence (Fourteen to Twenty-One): [Compare Erikson's **Identity v. Role Confusion.** *In this period more than in any other, the pressures of the peer group are exceptionally strong. Sexuality is a major issue as is independence. In the main, the actual workaday world does not intrude so much on consciousness, but this is the time of important decisions about educational and vocational careers].* At age twelve [say rather, *by* fourteen], Grant proposes (1983, p. 21) that a seeming disengagement from the earlier expression of the dominant occurs *spontaneously* [emphasis again supplied] with a tendency actively to express the second, auxiliary, function; and that the auxiliary's expression will typically be in the attitude opposite to that normally associated with the dominant. Thus in the adolescent years the typically developing young person, while not forsaking nor abandoning the dominant but, indeed, continuing to perfect it, will also be largely occupied with the establishment of a second function, in the conscious modality opposite to that of the dominant, this auxiliary operating as an Aaron, as it were, to the dominant's Moses, to balance, buttress, and buffer.

To illustrate with different types: Nancy, Introverted Feeling with Intuition (INFP), would in adolescence, having in late childhood quietly and unobtrusively developed a caring sensitivity quite similar to the exuberant Sy, but, intensive and limited to a few compared to his expansive concern with many, would have gone public, as it were, with possibilities, patterns, and meanings not unlike Rick's in their broad range and diversity, yet pursued far more intently than would be his style, and withal still colored and governed by her feeling judgment.

John, Introverted Thinker with Sensing (ISTP). Exactly opposite to Sy, he would have been noted in the lower grades as quietly easygoing in most things but surprisingly tough-mindedly logical to the point of defiance–or passive resistance–in matters involving equity issues, good in the analytical and quantitative aspects of his studies, and certainly more concerned with justice than mercy. Now acquiring at every turn a host of factual information, he is now not nearly so solitary, often enjoying the company of others in sports, practical projects like rebuilding an antique car, learning an instrument and playing in a group, or getting involved in practical environmental or other service projects.

Young Adulthood (Twenty-One to Thirty-Five): [*Compare Erikson's* **Intimacy v. Isolation.** *General education ends and we either eagerly go to work or work at specializing in a career, and just as eagerly begin a marriage and family*]. The young person passing into young adulthood, starts the development of the tertiary, in the same conscious modality, but opposite to the auxiliary; and expressed in the attitude associated with the dominant, and therefore opposite to that associated with the auxiliary. Again, neither dominant nor auxiliary is abandoned, but there is manifest emphasis and energy devoted to "experimenting" with the tertiary, to purposive raising one's consciousness of it and its uses, especially in situations not high in risk to the ego.

Eric, Extraverted Sensing with Thinking (ESTP). In the last year or so of college, Eric finds himself, more and more making decisions on the basis of personal values rather than his heretofore tried and true logic. Often he may find himself expressing openly feelings in a rather embarrassing, childish way But he finds his increased sensitivity to the feelings of others an asset in his dealings with others.

Julia, Introverted Sensing with Feeling (ISFJ). Concurrently with the transition from college into the "real" world, Julia has rather surprised herself for no longer arriving at decisions by open, frank discussions about appropriate values with her circle of friends. Instead, often to the dismay of those friends, her conclusions are very private and much more frequently analytical and logical than global and value based. Her friends wonder if she is becoming hard-hearted, more concerned about what are her rights, or her just dues, in contrast to her previous reputation as the Martha of the crowd, always willing to wash up the dishes, set an extra place, go the extra mile, on foot, in the rain, without an umbrella.

Mid-life (Thirty-Five to Forty-Nine): [Compare Erikson's **Generativity v. Stagnation.** *Suddenly "the world is too much with us, late and soon, getting and spending, we lay waste our powers, little we see in nature that is ours." The family, home, and career(s) appear generally to be established and are now being nourished; but reevaluations and reassessments in these fourteen years may, none the less, for some bring crises and conflict].* In this period according to Grant's model, the person is called on to deal consciously with the inferior function. It will be recalled that for Jung three of the functions, under the aegis of the dominant, could be used consciously by the typical adult to deal with the demands of life, but that the fourth or inferior tended to remain undifferentiated from the unconscious; furthermore, usually as a result of excessive stress, when the inferior did break through into control of consciousness, the person's behavior would best be characterized as brutish, savage, cruel, animalistic, and the person would be seen by others as not him- or herself. This conscious engagement with the inferior clearly is best practiced in low risk, low stress, often recreational, situations. And whenever this consciousness raising with respect to the inferior is undertaken, a quantum increase, figuratively speaking, will be necessary in the libidinal investment.

Polly, Extroverted Thinking with Intuition (ENTJ). In the mid-life passage, Polly finds herself impelled, as it were, to get in touch consciously with her feelings so that she can express them in a controlled way, without letting them control her. Often her emotional expressions are, at best harsh, rough, aggressive, and negative, but as the years proceed, she learns to use her highly differentiated powers of analysis to build logical "loops" that insure a reflection of her growing sensitivity to the feelings and concerns of others. And she is also able to express her own feelings and opinions, both positive and negative, in a more differentiated, less all-or-none, explosively overwhelming way.

Ron, Introverted iNtuitive with Feeling (INFJ). Faced now with the challenge to treat consciously his heretofore inferior, extraverted sensing, Ron begins to attend with greater interest the myriad facts and details of his environment. At this point he may begin piano lessons, take up gardening, furniture building and repair, trail construction and maintenance, or other such like practical, hands-on activities. Used to his long recognized and tolerated tendency to ignore the all-important fact in the pursuit of one of his inspirations, his long time friends may have much occasion to marvel at his "compulsive" attention to the most minute detail, the elaboration of his scheme of organization, and his exacting demands for a similar punctiliousness on the part of others with whom he now wishes to share his interests.

Mature Adulthood (Forty-Nine to Seventy and perhaps more) *[Compare Erikson's* **Integrity v. Despair***. The "Golden Years." There are about fourteen years before "normal" retirement; perhaps twenty eight or more years of life expectancy left].* In this stage the type development model presumes that the person has, to a greater or lesser degree, completed the cycle of bringing into consciousness when appropriate all four of the mental functions. Although Sensing, iNtuition, Thinking, and Feeling will typically follow the person's lifelong hierarchic pattern from dominant through auxiliary and tertiary to inferior; none the less, at will, by conscious investment of more libido, by consciously increasing psychic energy, the person can, as it were, employ the needed function extravertedly or introvertedly to respond to the demands of the situation.

The person can now, as never before, be free to exercise all her or his qualities and strengths, can resort to a vast accumulation of years of data, facts, and impressions, can voyage deep into inner or outer space on the richest tapestries of fantastic fancy, can explore the heights and depths of interpersonal relationships, and can participate in the good fight to extend the boundaries of justice, individual freedom, and universal brotherhood. In short this is the time when the crowning, culminating differentiation, individuation, may be fulfilled. This individuation, Jung says, is a process of differentiating the individual from the collective norm, of building up those particularities of the individual which are "already ingrained in the psychic constitution" (1971, pp. 448-449).

Calling individuation a process of coming to wholeness in life's journey, Grant et al., suggest it can be described in six propositions, freely paraphrased below.

We come to wholeness or approach full individuation:

1. when we achieve the power or freedom to utilize each of the four functions;
2. when we utilize all four of the functions in harmony despite the tension inherent in the dynamic interplay of these polarities;
3. through six distinct periods of life in which the individual's preferred ways of focussing energy, perception, and judgment are interwoven in a contrapuntal or helicoidal way;
4. not *sui generis* but in a variety of environments: physical, social, cultural each of which interacts with our preferences in a range of ways from the subtle to the coercive;
5. not inevitably: full, absolute wholeness is more often a goal not fully attained; and finally,
6. when the failures and negatives associated with persons and the influencing surround can provide opportunity and challenge to further growth. (1983, p. 180-185)

This abbreviated account of Grant's developmental conceptions about type's life-long sequencing has allowed none of our illustrative cases to be fully expanded; on the contrary, constrained by limitations of space and time, we have had to content ourselves with presenting only two of the possible sixteen types at each of the four periods of life when the functional focus of consciousness is differentially emphasized. The reader interested in learning how, under this model, all of the sixteen types may be expected to develop typically in each of the life periods is urged to consult Grant, Thompson, and Clark's Appendix B (1983, p. 215-248).

IMPLICATIONS FOR COUNSELORS

In this section I turn to what I hope will be some practical suggestions for therapists and counselors, suggestions based on a point of view indebted not only to concepts of type, but also to Erikson's life stages, for the two seem mutually helpful. It will be recalled that Erikson held that the successful resolution of the conflict characteristic of any particular stage of development is based on the successful integration of those which preceded. Similarly I would suggest that at each stage unless the appropriate consciousness of preference has been attained, subsequent levels will, at best, be flawed, and the person to reach a fuller maturity must mend the flaw.

Consider that the traditional college-aged student, not much under seventeen or over twenty-four is usually seen as late adolescent or early adult. (To be sure, with the increasing presence of the non-traditional student on campus, the counselor may more often be called on to deal with persons presumed to be in the later stages of development.) Thus, "normal" problems, from the point of view of Erikson, most likely will concern the complexities of the *Identity v. Role Diffusion* and/or *Intimacy v. Isolation* dilemmas; and "normal" problems in type development will be the recognition and practice of the auxiliary and, perhaps, the establishment of the tertiary. Less "normal," for Eriksonian development, will be failures to have resolved the earlier questions involving *Trust v. Mistrust*, bodily *Autonomy v. Shame/Doubt*, *Initiative v. Guilt*, and *Industry v. Inferiority*; for type development, less "normal" will be failures in recognition and acceptance of the basic preference for the domain where the libido shall best be invested, **I** or **E**, and of which of the psychic functions, **S, N, T,** or **F,** shall be dominant.

To summarize the task of this critically formative period of struggles to identify the self in terms of career, independence, and capacity for loving adult intimacy, here is Erikson's story of Freud crisply, laconically replying to the question, "What should a normal person be able to do well?" . . ."Leiben und arbeiten!" (1950, p. 129).

One begins, obviously, with the here and now, the problem placed by the student on the counselor's "plate," and the counselor has only about a half dozen or less chances to clean the platter. Though the total number of counseling sessions may in a relatively few cases be quite large, generally the counselor may expect to have somewhere between three and six sessions with a typical undergraduate client; this estimate of the average number of sessions has remained relatively constant over the last two or three decades, without regard to size of institution, theoretical orientation of the counselor, and client-declared reason for making the contact.

Lacy, Frank, and Kirk (1976) found, however, significant differences on indices of personality taken on university entrance between those later seeking counseling to resolve career or educational decisions or choices and those seeking counseling for personal reasons, or giving no reason at all. On the *Omnibus Personality Inventory*, the latter group scored higher on scales measuring estheticism, impulse expression, and psychological complexity; admitting to more attitudes and behaviors that characterize the socially alienated and emotionally disturbed, they appeared more sensitive, and more likely to report feelings of depression and isolation. Such findings suggest that the people in the Choice/Decision/Information group may well be dealing with the more "normal" problems of their age level, while those in the Personal/No Statement group may exhibit more deep-seated problems.

Over nearly four decades as dean and counselor, I have discussed with hundreds, maybe thousands, of young people their concerns about love and/or career; seldom was it possible to make a clear cut separation and deal with the one to the exclusion of the other. Usually early on we would get into their results on the Strong Interest Inventory and the MBTI. As a matter of course, most of them had no difficulty whatsoever knowing what their preferences were, and most of the time the patterns of preference were well differentiated. What the use of both instruments did was to confirm certain positive aspects of their personalities, to say to them, as it were, "It's ok to be you." And, especially with the Strong, and more recently with the MBTI, as more specific type related educational and career data has become available (Myers and McCaulley, 1985, MacDaid, McCaulley, and Kainz, 1986), the students were helped to focus and particularize their continuing explorations about possible educational and vocational paths. Holland's General Occupational Themes as explicated by the Strong, in addition to their utility in pointing up general career possibilities, if framed as *searches* for vigorous involvement with the physical environment (R), for truth (I), for beauty (A), for love, including the Greeks' meanings for *eros*, *philos*, and *agape* (S), for power and clout (E), and for order (C) often were powerfully stimulating in opening the way to clarifying discussions about the values currently and, possibly, permanently important to them.

In a sense one can say these "normal" concerns of the Late Adolescent and Early Adult periods, such as choice of educational programs and career paths, problems of intimacy and of independence, and the like, are the general concerns of all in the institutions we serve; for example, coaches and professors, financial aid officers and treasurers, deans and food service dieticians, medical and development staff, all may lay claim to some part of this action and, doubtless, might find many of the ideas presented here useful. But as psychotherapists and counselors we have, in the sensitive area of psychological dysfunction, special expertise and special responsibilities both to the individual student and to our institutions. It is demonstrably economically cost effective, to say nothing of the far more important savings of human potentialities, to prevent dysfunction if possible rather than to wait to heal it.

In addition to those openly voiced, a multitude of the concrete issues raised by college students are often pervaded with unspoken concerns over sexual expectations and identifications, and these concerns seem especially intense for those whose innate preferred

dominant function is both judgmental and runs counter to the ste-
reotypic expectation for their sex. Of the four polarities which
together determine a person's type, only **TF** consistently shows
differences associated with sex. In often repeated studies of various
samples and populations, with various ages, occupations, and educational levels, males appear to prefer Thinking in the proportion 3:2
and females to prefer **F** in the same proportion, 3:2. Since the dominant in normal development is presumed to be established in the
years of later childhood, the so-called latency period, these facts of
type may not seem to be so remarkable to the middle school young-
ster concerned more with competency in learning, in sports, and the
like, but with the onset of puberty, all the rules seem to change, and
all sorts of new, and, if only because new, anxiety-laden sexual
concerns are obtruded into consciousness or behavior.

If the developmental theory of type outlined here holds, it would
be expected that the introverted judgers, the **IPs** would be most at
risk of confusion, anxiety, and conflict, for being introverts their
choice of the dominant would generally have been arrived at in
private, not, as is the case for their **EJ** peers, from the social
norms prevalent in their social context. Thus if the **IP** boy having
chosen **T** during later childhood, in adolescence will find himself
going along with the cultural current of expectation for his sex, and
so also for the girl **IFP**. Now, the type development theory would
predict, both will be inclined in adolescence to develop the extraverted perceptual auxiliary and should, thereby, be getting much
affirmative reinforcement from their environment, not only for
their previously established judgment, but also for their present
ventures into the exercise of extraversion.

But consider, in contrast, the situation of the **ITP** female and
IFP male: in addition to the conflict and anxiety surely attendant
on signals from the environment that they are behaving contrary to
the expectancies of their sexual peer group, these negative perceptions will surely inhibit, rather than reinforce efforts to exercise the
non-preferred extraversion and enhance a tendency toward role
diffusion rather than identity, and toward isolation rather than
intimacy. The situation for the **ETJ** girl and the **EFJ** boy is perhaps less difficult in adolescence for the emphasis on the exercising
of the introverted perception will by definition be private and hence

less subject to the scrutiny and pressure of the peer group, and the Es, furthermore, will be showing their best and third-best sides. A testable proposition is that cases that present as the more seriously dysfunctional will tend to be those with poorly differentiated dominants, especially those where the dominant is, in a manner of speech, also set against the cultural grain.

And remember, too, that these young Is will be showing, to the world, at their worst, in the case of the males, a primitive, savage, inhuman, frigid mockery of logic while the females will display feelings aggressively hostile, incredibly cold, savagely animalistic, all-or-none, and negative: "Teach me to feel!" screamed the suicidal, but type-sophisticated INTP young woman, a future Ivy League AM in philosophy, "God damn you! God DAMN YOU! You're supposed to be an INFP. Damn you to hell!! Teach me to FEEL!!!"

Psychological type has been shown to be useful, in the specific instance of identifying persons especially at risk for depression and suicide and helping them before the predisposing conditions spiral them into the maelstrom of personal and institutional crises, and catastrophes (Lacy, 1990). The collection of type data, comparable to the information now available on type and educational and career options, but relevant to conditions now vexing our campuses, such as the eating disorders, substance abuse, verbal and physical violence toward whomever is seen as "out" as well as between friends and acquaintances, etc., will be, I predict, an enormously useful aid in our response to these problems.

A principal benefit of serious study and research under any theory or system of developmental psychology is that all who drink from that fountain may gain some perspective on how the totality of a life, one's one and only trial as far as we know, may unfold. No guarantees, of course, but some notion of the odds. Teachers, counselors, and therapists should not, therefore, fail to initiate discussions about the *future's* implications and possibilities in the mutual deliberations about their students', clients', and patients' past and present concerns, for as Jung noted, ". . . in the last resort, we are conditioned not only by the past, but by the future, which is sketched out in us long beforehand and gradually evolves out of us" (1954, p.110).

96 COLLEGE STUDENT DEVELOPMENT

REFERENCES

Brownsword, A. W. (1987). *It Takes All Types!* San Anselmo, CA: Baytree Publication Co. for Human Resources Management Group.

Erikson, E. H. (1950). *Childhood and Society*, New York: W. W. Norton & Co., Inc.

Grant, W. H., Thompson, M. & Clarke, T. E. (1983). *From Image to Likeness.* Ramsey, NJ: Paulist Press.

Jaffé, A. (record. & ed.) (1963). *Memories, Dreams, Reflections by C. G. Jung*; (Richard & Clara Winston, trans.). New York: Vintage Books, a division of Random House.

Jeffries, W. C. (1991) *True to Type.* Norfolk, VA: Hampton Roads Publishing Co.

Jung, C. G. (1954). Analytical Psychology and Education, Lecture 2. In The Development of Personality (R. F. C. Hull, tr). In *The Collected Works of C. G. Jung*. H. Read, M. Fordham, G. Adler, & W. McGuire (Eds,). Vol. 17. Princeton, NJ: Princeton University Press

Jung, C. G. (1971). Psychological Types. (A rev. by R. F. C. Hull of H. C. Baynes's trans) In *The Collected Works of C. G. Jung*. H. Read, M. Fordham, G. Adler, & W. McGuire (eds.), Vol. 6. Princeton, NJ: Princeton University Press. (Original work published in 1921; English trans. by H. C. Baynes published in 1923.)

Kroeger, O. & Thuesen, J.M. (1988). *Type Talk: Or How to Determine Your Personality Type and Change Your Life.* New York: Delacorte Press.

Lacy, O. W. (1990) Nonthreatening, objective psychometric identification of students at risk for depression and/or suicidal behavior. Chap. 7 in *College Student Suicide*. L. C. Whitaker & R. E. Slimak (eds). New York: The Haworth Press, Inc.

Lacy, O. W., Frank, A. C., & Kirk, B. A. (1976). Number of counseling sessions, client personality, and reason for seeking counseling. *Journal of College Student Personnel, 17,* 405-409.

MacDaid, G. P., McCaulley, M. H., & Kainz, R. I. (1986, 1991). *Atlas of Type Tables*. Gainsville, FL: Center for the Applications of Psychological Type.

Myers, I. B. (1987) *Introduction to Type.* Palo Alto, CA: Consulting Psychologists Press.

Myers, I. B. & McCaulley, M. H. (1985). *Manual: A Guide to the Development and Use of the Myers-Briggs Type Indicator.* Palo Alto: Consulting Psychologists Press.

Myers, I. B with Myers, P. B. (1980) *Gifts Differing.* Palo Alto, CA: Consulting Psychologists Press.

Chapter 6

Applying Trans-Generational Family Theory and Therapy to College Student Psychotherapy

Kip C. Alishio

SUMMARY. While family systems theory and therapy have been integrated into psychological treatment in a wide variety of populations and settings, college therapists have been slow to find meaningful application to the treatment of students. Conflicting theoretical assumptions about the nature of the college student from the prevailing developmental model as opposed to the family theory model and the lack of an elaborated model for such application may be responsible. A model for applying trans-generational family interventions is proposed which includes (1) family-theory informed individual therapy; (2) Bowen family "coaching"; (3) families as consultants to individual counseling; and (4) on-going family sessions. Theoretical and practical issues are illustrated through case examples.

Family systems theories and their clinical application have gained rapid acceptance within the practice of counseling and psychotherapy in a wide variety of settings but have yet to find a legit-

Kip C. Alishio, PhD, is a clinical psychologist and Associate Director of the Student Counseling Service at Miami University, Oxford, OH 45056. The author gratefully acknowledges Roger Knudson for his wisdom, stimulation, and support in developing the ideas that underlie this project.

imate place in the treatment of late adolescents and young adults within the context of most university counseling centers. While most training programs now include at least one course, and often a sequence of courses, in theory and practice of family therapy, an extensive review of literature prior to 1990 revealed only 12 journal articles that explore the role of family dynamics in this population (Beit-Hallahmi and Colon, 1974; Babineau, 1975; Fulmer, Medalie and Lord, 1982; Lopez and Andrews, 1987; Whiting, Terry and Strom, 1984; Held and Bellows, 1983; Openlander and Searight, 1983; Lopez, 1986; Fulmer and Medalie, 1987; Okiishi, 1987; and Baron, 1988; Oles and Bronstein, 1989), and only five of these consider direct inclusion of family members in treatment. A recent special issue of the *Journal of College Student Psychotherapy* on bulimia among college students (Whitaker and Davis, 1989) included no articles on family influences and treatment of this disorder despite widespread acceptance in the psychiatric community of the importance of family influences in both etiology and treatment of eating disorders (Schwartz, Barret, and Saba, 1985; Sargent, Liebman and Silver, 1985; Selvini-Palazzoli, 1978; Bruch, 1978; and Minuchin, Rosman and Baker, 1978).

This paper explores two factors contributing to the slow integration of family therapy into the treatment of college students: (1) the predominance of a developmental view of college student psychology which most values separation from family as the mature outcome of the individuation process; and (2) the lack of elaborated models for such application, which results in idiosyncratic approaches that rely on application of techniques outside of a coherent conceptual framework for understanding what the therapy is attempting to change and how that change is to take place. A model identifying treatment options classified by theory and mode of intervention is offered along with case examples of several treatment options.

DEVELOPMENT
FROM AN "INDIVIDUAL" PERSPECTIVE

The prevailing model of college student psychology has its roots in, on one hand, a traditional psychoanalytic theory of intrapsychic development and, on the other hand, a humanistic approach which focuses on the here-and-now potential of human choice (Hanfmann, 1978). This view, represented for example in Chickering's (1981) edited volume *The Modern American College,* is defined by application of developmental principles to areas such as cognition, morality, capacity for peer relationships, academic capacity, identity processes, and intimacy. This definition presumes a basic separateness in the existence of the individual student. At its contextual best, this perspective places the student's needs, experiences, capacities, and constructions within the perspective of the larger individual life cycle and focuses on the relationship of each stage of the life cycle to the others (e.g., Erikson, 1950, 1968; and Chickering, 1969). Relational goals are described from an intragenerational perspective. These goals assume a basic independence from parents and other adults in contrast to the dependency of childhood and neglect further exploration of inter-generational bonds. When inter-generational bonds are addressed, as in some of Erikson's and Josselson's (1980) works, the focus is on the young adult's ambivalence regarding separation from the family, giving no consideration to prevailing family ambivalences or other transgenerational forces that create the interpersonal context in which the ambivalence of the young adult is developed and maintained. This view assumes that individuality exists "in" the young adult, that the goal of development is separation from the family, and that psychological intervention should facilitate this separation.

DEVELOPMENT
FROM A FAMILY SYSTEMS PERSPECTIVE

Family systems theories represent a fundamental shift in our understanding of the "individual." These theories hold that individuality can exist only in the context of a network of relationships with mutually-defining others in relation to whom one can "be" more or less of an individual (Lukes, 1973; Laing, 1969). The trans-generational family perspective, while not denying the existence of the individual, views the individual as a psychical system which exists within larger, defining relational systems which largely influence the limits of his/her behavior (Stierlin, 1981). Of these systems, the family is recognized as the most influential and therefore the preferred target of intervention.

It is within the family system that the individuality of each member is fundamentally confirmed as well as disconfirmed through relationship involvement. Confirmation occurs to the extent that children are related to as unique and valued individuals by other family members. Disconfirmation occurs to the extent that parents unconsciously encourage their children to assume functional roles in maintaining the parents' own unresolved emotional conflicts. These processes, called family projection (Scharff, 1989), result in family relational configurations which significantly restrict the identity development of the student. Three common configurations are parentification, in which the student essentially reverses roles with a needy and dependent parent to become the care provider; triangulation, in which the student plays the role of buffer and carrier of emotion between two family members, usually parents, who cannot tolerate direct exchange of emotion; and scapegoating, in which negative and intolerable family affect is projected onto and played out by one member of the family.

Three aspects of trans-generational family theory are particularly relevant to a discussion of late adolescent development: related individuation, loyalty processes, and the family life cycle.

Related individuation. A family perspective assumes that separation is a life-long, on-going process that is attained only to a relative degree. Rather than the breaking of parental ties, the mature family transactional mode is that of related individuation in which psychological separation of parents and children is ". . . accompanied by relatedness and [is] embedded in a continuing relationship" (Stierlin, 1981, p. 186).

Centripetal forces, which maintain binding and over-dependency, and centrifugal forces, which lead to expulsion or tenuous bonding, within a family inhibit the development of related individuation in adolescent-parent relationships. These forces may be present in more or less equal amounts, the intensity of each being small, moderate or high. The adolescent experiences a push to go out to fulfill needs and dreams which are largely family ones but which the student identifies with as one's own. Simultaneously, the student may feel a pull to stay close to the family and to fulfill more immediate family needs, such as providing emotional support to a parent. Stierlin calls this delegating. Delegated students typically display a limited and qualified autonomy in their level of identity development.

Loyalty implications. Boszormenyi-Nagy (Boszormenyi-Nagy and Spark, 1973; and Boszormenyi-Nagy and Krasner, 1988) observed that restraints on related individuation are not created within a two-generation nuclear family but are determined and maintained through a complicated and exacting ledger of invisible relational debts, entitlements, and loyalties transmitted from one generation to the next. Loyalty, which is "almost synonymous with family ties," is defined as "a preferential commitment to a relationship, based on indebtedness born of earned merit [or entitlement]" (1988, p. 15), such as that which a parent earns through parenting activity. Intense and unhealthy entitlement can accrue when, for example, parents, who sacrificed much of their childhoods or goals to satisfy their own parents in some way, pass those debts on to their children who are then expected to provide what the parents gave up or missed. If the children fulfill this debt of loyalty in a similarly self-sacrificing way, they will in turn become intensely entitled as young adults. These largely unconscious entitlements and loyalties then conflict with the young adult's developing commitments to peer and other adult relationships outside the family.

The young adult must find ways of acting and choosing which balance loyalty to family with loyalty to self and to peers that allow the child to maintain a relatively balanced "ledger" of relational debts. In this way movement toward related individuation is facilitated. These debts and loyalties may be expressed in a variety of ways in students' "choices." Career choice, for example, is often influenced by one's debts and need for maintaining loyalties. Often students are even quite conscious of this parental entitlement when they openly state that their choice of career direction is largely based on not wanting to "disappoint my parents." Identity development from this perspective becomes a matter of becoming attuned to what is communicated as "who we need you to be" and "what you owe us," and then finding ways of fulfilling those debts that do not leave one heavily entitled.

Treatment models which focus on the transference aspects of the therapeutic relationship typically ignore the meaning that such a relationship may have for the student's loyalties in the family. The development of a trusting relationship with a therapist may imply disloyalty to the family resulting from the student's own split loyalties between therapist and family. Family relationships are also potentially threatened by the possibility of growth in the student that increases existing indebtedness. The trans-generational approach emphasizes the necessity of considering the impact that change in student behavior will have within his/her network of significant relationships as well as identifying the forces that work against such change occurring. It then focuses on helping the student identify creative moves which facilitate individuation while simultaneously repaying family debts.

The family life cycle. The family model contrasts with individual developmental models of the life cycle in its focus upon the essential inter-connectedness of the adolescent's needs with the needs of each member of the nuclear and often extended family (Stierlin, 1981). The late adolescent's needs for autonomy, identity, separateness, and achievement–the traditional Eriksonian goals of adolescence–as well as for affiliation and responsibility outside the family can only be met in the context of other family members' needs and through a process of negotiation. In this negotiation process parental needs which are appropriately met in relationship with a pre-adolescent but inappropriately met in relationship with a late adolescent–for example, needs for closeness, inclusion, and care taking–must be redirected to allow for a structurally different parent-child relationship. Ackerman (1980) observed that the goal of adolescence is change in family relationships, including relationships among all family members. To the extent that these changes do not evolve, adolescence as a stage of life fails.

Families differ in the degree and rapidity with which such relational changes can be accommodated. A family system of relationships may be more or less flexible enough to accommodate changes without any member being unduly scapegoated or burdened. In such a family changes in the adolescing member are acknowledged by other members in ways that confirm not only the adolescent's uniqueness but also re-confirm the uniqueness of other family members. Parents, for example, are provided an opportunity to confront old pains and failures from their own adolescence and to resolve those conflicts anew within the context of their now mid-life status. By contrast, another family's relational bonds may be so inflexible that any attempt at change threatens the integrity of the system (Boszormenyi-Nagy, 1981). In this family the negotia-tion process is decidedly unilateral and the adolescent must plead for acknowledgement through, for example, development of an eating disorder or an attempted suicide. Ackerman states the para-dox that the family that is most stable is the one whose constituent attachments flex without breaking. Boszormenyi-Nagy further suggests that healthy functioning is reflected in the flexibility of the oscillation of the imbalances: the extent to which fairness and unfairness in the meeting of needs is rotated or shared by all family members. Dysfunction occurs when the imbalance becomes static, leading to scapegoating, parentification, triangulation and, ultimate-ly, symptom formation. Members of a healthy functioning family are capable of taking the perspectives of other members of the family and of participating in a multi-lateral rather than a uni-later-al or bi-lateral negotiation of needs.

FAMILY INTERVENTIONS WITH COLLEGE STUDENTS

Family-theory based interventions with university students must overcome not only the power of the prevailing model of college student psychology and the inertia of established practice but also the context of apparent separateness in which the student arrives on campus. These goals are best accomplished if interventions derive from an elaborated family theory which explicitly identifies the focus of change (e.g., family relationships) as well as the mecha-nisms of change and the role of the therapist. Such treatment op-tions, identified and classified in relationship to traditional treat-ment options, are presented in Figure 1. These classifications are based on the recognition that there are distinct differences between mode of intervention, i.e., who is actually participating in treat-ment through direct contact with the therapist, and the theory of change on which the intervention is based. Four treatment options

FIGURE 1

Treatment options as a function of mode and theory of intervention.

MODE

		Individual	Family/System	Group
Theory	Individual	Family Theory Informed	Traditional Family Consultation	Traditional/ Group Therapy
	Family/ System	Family Coaching	a) Planned Family/System Consultation; b) On-going Family Therapy	Family Coaching Support Group

are elaborated below with an emphasis on family coaching, planned family consultation, and on-going family therapy.

Family Theory-Informed Individual Therapy

The most common application of family theory with college students currently appears to be individual treatment in which the conceptualization of the student's troubles is informed in part by assessment and understanding of the student's larger family relational context. This understanding is then used to help the student develop insight into his/her current pattern of problems. This application to college student psychotherapy is described by Fulmer, Medalie and Lord (1982); it is more broadly elaborated for application to individual treatment by the Wachtel's in *Family Dynamics in Individual Psychotherapy* (1987). Family theory-informed individual therapy is probably the most common application because it is the easiest to accommodate: the practitioner does not have to significantly alter how one thinks about therapy or how one intervenes. It is still individual psychotherapy, albeit with greater sensitivity to the role the family has had and is playing in the student's struggles. Change is still conceptualized as taking place primarily inside the student and as resulting from the student-therapist relationship.

This approach, though, goes a step beyond traditional individual therapies in acknowledging that, as suggested by system theory, change in behavior of any member of a family will have an impact on other family members if the new behavior represents a structural change in the way that member relates to others in the family. For example, a bulimic student's decision to change her major against the wishes of her authoritarian father has no larger impact within the family system if she also enters into a pact with her overly-close mother to keep her decision a secret from father: no structural change has occurred in the relationships among the three. The current approach would instead explore with the student her ambivalences and fears of dialoguing with or confronting her father directly in the hope of de-triangulating her from the parents' relationship. However, it would attempt to resolve these ambivalences by focusing on ways in which those ambivalences are expressed in other relationships the student develops, especially that with the therapist. Once the student has made some progress with the therapist, the assumption is that she can now apply that change within her family relationships. While some attention is given to this component of treatment within this approach, actual change in family relationships often proves to be a more formidable and complex task than this approach is designed to accomplish. In these instances an approach that conceptualizes both the problem and potential solutions from a family theory perspective, and which includes contact with the family, is warranted. The three approaches that follow meet these criteria and as such are presented in more detail and with brief case examples.

Bowen Family "Coaching"

In contrast to doing individual psychotherapy informed by family theory is an approach described by Murray Bowen (1978) as family therapy with an individual client. This approach, called "coaching," views the individual client as the family's delegated emissary, and the presenting complaint is understood symbolically as a statement about the system as a whole. In order to shift from relating to clients as separate, decontextualized individuals, Bowen suggests imagining that the client comes into every session with an invisible family that forms the essential defining interpersonal context for that person. The goal of family coaching is an increase in the client's and the family's level of "differentiation of self," the proportion of life energy that is bound in family relationships as opposed to being available for intentional action by the individual (Kerr and Bowen, 1988). The primary action and locus of change in family coaching is the client's ongoing relationships with family members. The task of the practitioner is to first facilitate insight into triangles, multigenerational debts and loyalties, family projection processes, emotional cutoff, and other aspects of family emotional process and then to design interventions that the client can enact which will begin to change the client's ability to act in the context of these relational forces. Not only is the primary locus of change not between client and therapist, but Bowen advises the therapist to "stay out of the transference" to keep the emotional focus centered in the family relationships. Bowen and his colleagues make extensive use of the family genogram (see McGoldrick and Gerson, 1985) as a tool for aiding in the client's understanding of essential dynamics in the family. This intervention is well suited to therapy with college students because it mirrors the college student's life situation in that it explicitly acknowledges the student's attempts to achieve a new, "adult" status within the family but does so while acknowledging the student's fundamental connection to the family as an unattached young adult. The author is currently applying this approach within a group context in which students facilitate the coaching of other students. Results have been very promising. A brief individual case example follows. See Oles and Brostein (1989) for another case example.

Case Example of Family Coaching

"Casey," a junior, presented at intake a history of several years of moderate depression that included periodic suicidal ideation. A family genogram assessment revealed Casey, the youngest of three girls, to be stuck in a family role of "lost child." Her oldest sister, a chronic under-achiever, openly expressed bitterness toward her parents who in turn devalued her openly, while the self-absorbed and over-achieving middle daughter, cast as the fragile family "star," received most of the parental attention and concern, exemplified by a long-standing but ineffective focus on her eating disorder. Casey described the family, as well as her parents' marriage, as "very close" and as including "no conflict" except that between oldest sister and parents which was written off as "my sister's fault." Casey's struggle was framed in therapy as one of attempting to elicit appropriate parental concern and acknowledgement in a family context in which such concern is received through either self-destructive rebellion or symptom formation.

Following two initial attempts by Casey to express her feelings and neediness directly to parents, one scuttled by Casey's ambivalence and the other by parental denial, Casey again became depressed. However, instead of her usual internalizing and self-blaming, Casey this time told her "fragile" sister of her depression and disappointment at her parents's lack of responsiveness. The sister responded by calling the therapist in a panic to "do something" about Casey. The therapist, understanding this as an opportunity to not collude with the family rule that this daughter was incapable of giving of herself, chatted with the sister about her own experience of depression and encouraged her to apply this to helping Casey. The caller, predictably confused at being cast in the role of competent helper, ultimately rejected the therapist's suggestions and construed his refusal to call Casey as an indication of his "lack of caring." Later in consultation with the therapist, Casey developed a new perspective on her own–and her family's–assumption that this sister was incapable of supporting Casey or sharing of herself.

This series of events led Casey to understand her depression with greater clarity and to take responsibility for it in liberating ways. In subsequent sessions, she developed new insights into her relationships with her sisters: she identified and directly expressed her own anger at her star sister which helped her to then understand that sister's own limitations and family bindedness, and simultaneously developed a new empathy and compassion for her oldest sister that led to a budding friendship. A couple of sessions focusing on parental histories then led her to new understandings of her family's transgenerational role distribution. This helped Casey initiate several more focused talks with her mother in which her mother was able to acknowledge her own history as a child of a withholding, alcoholic father who developed a special relationship to Casey of which Mom was very resentful. Mom admitted that this made it difficult for her to express warm feelings to Casey. Casey drew much strength from these acknowledgments and experienced a release of energy that allowed her to plan and follow through with many more initiatives on the familial, peer, and career levels.

Families as Consultants to Individual Counseling

It can often be very helpful to include family members in ongoing individual treatment for single or multiple planned consultations when the individual treatment is conceptualized from a family theory perspective. Such consultations have traditionally been practiced from an individual perspective in which the goals are to inform and educate family members as to how to understand and "help" the identified client with their symptoms. These are clearly the goals of the interventions outlined, for example, in a special issue of the *Journal of College Student Psychotherapy* on "Parental Concerns in College Student Mental Health," (Whitaker, 1987) the very title of which assumes a fundamental separateness between parental and student mental health. When consultation is derived from family theory, family members are seen as key players in the problem which is now defined not as internal to the student but as embedded in the student-family relationships. The goals and purposes of these consultations depend upon the timing and needs of the on-going treatment.

One major purpose for family consultation is to aid in assessment, hypothesis testing, and treatment formulation by observing the student and family interact in vivo as opposed to relying solely on student report. Assessment done in this fashion often functions as a change mechanism in and of itself in that such discussions with a therapist have powerful emotional and cognitive effects on family relationships. These consultations are particularly salient as a part of crisis intervention, e.g., when a student comes to the attention of the center through a crisis such as suicidal behavior. However, such meetings can also be arranged to gain information later in the process. Informal reports from other family therapists confirm the author's experience that parents and families nearly universally respond affirmatively to a request from student clients to "come help me in my counseling." Not surprisingly, perhaps, the strongest resistance comes from the student and the practitioner. One of the most dramatic shifts in therapists' perspectives made possible by the family approach is in viewing members of the extended family as valuable resources for, rather than as obstacles to, the therapy process. Another opportunity for such assessment occurs when family members call the practitioner upon learning of their relative being in therapy with them. Traditionally these calls have been construed as intrusions, attempts to undermine the therapy, and breaches in confidentiality. From a family perspective, though, such "intrusions" are understood as often mis-guided attempts on the part of the family to achieve healthier functioning and provide fertile opportunity to assess dynamics in the family. At these times it is often beneficial to ask if the member would be willing to "join us," making clear the current limits that confidentiality imposes, and in so doing communicate a value of related individuation rather than of the disconnected independence which many family members fear to be the outcome of successful therapy.

A second change mechanism in family consultation is the assisting of students in gaining information from family members that will aid them in their current struggles, for example talking with parents about how they dealt with similar issues in their lives. Such consultations provide a safe, structured situation to open closed lines of communication and change the parent-child relationship from a unilateral one to a dialogic one around a key content area of conflict for the student.

A third change mechanism is direct and overt intervention in family relationships. These meetings are most effective when the focus of the intervention is specified and planned with the identified client (Beit Hallahmi and Colon, 1974). The goals should derive from the goals of the individual counseling as well as the assessed needs and condition of the family system. A brief case example involving all three change mechanisms follows.

Case Example of a Family System Consultation

"Bob," a 21-year old junior, presented with suicidal ideation, intense anxiety, and a semester-long pattern of class non-attendance. He responded well initially upon entering individual therapy but regressed quickly, leading to a suicide attempt of moderate lethality precipitated by disappointments in a romantic relationship. The therapist, having identified a pervasive self punitive tendency tied to Bob's perception of his father's view of him, shifted the treatment focus away from the client's pre-occupation with the rocky romantic involvement on to his family relationships. Bob responded with eagerness and fear, describing Dad as explosive, violent, and "someone who cannot be pleased." Bob refused to initiate discussions with his Dad on his own but agreed to ask his parents to come in "to help me." He had not told them of the depth of his depression or of his suicide attempt. The therapist enlisted the author to be consultant and co-therapist for the family session.

After an initial period of joining with parents and assessing the parents-child triad, the therapists turned the session over to Bob who had, in preparation with his therapist, identified a specific goal, to become able to tell his parents the extent of his struggles. Bob was remarkably present, focused, and anxious in this session–in contrast to his depressive demeanor in individual sessions–and effectively expressed himself to his parents, even telling of his suicide attempt. He was also able to express to Dad his fear of him and to confront him regarding some traumatic childhood events. With the facilitation of the consultant, Dad was able to express his feelings of distance and uncertainty in relation to Bob and shared details of his own experience as an undirected young adult with a bedridden father. He acknowledged covering up a deep sense of entitlement and lack of direction with bravado and "coming on too strong." The session ended with new closeness between father and son that proved fragile in the weeks ahead but formed the basis for very constructive and focused work in Bob's individual therapy. Suicide threat never reappeared for Bob while his treatment continued. At termination, Bob demonstrated a much clearer and more stable awareness of the distinctions between his own construction and demands of himself and those of him by his father. He was arguing more effectively with his father who in turn was more emotionally involved with his wife and less with his work.

On-Going Family Sessions

On-going family therapy including members of the family is a much under-used mode in this setting because of the apparent inconvenience and unavailability of family members. However, they are often much more available than therapists believe. The family can be regularly included when (1) the student identifies family issues as the central conflict and family members agree to be involved regularly after an initial consultation, or (2) the student is seriously suicidal or their physical health is in some other way at risk, e.g., serious eating disorder. Meetings for such treatment can be flexible with regard to frequency as this approach relies less on the development of transference to therapist through weekly meetings and more on facilitating interventions aimed at changing family relationships. It is not unusual for periods of a month or more between meetings to yield positive benefits, allowing interventions to take hold and spread among family relationships. While clearly impractical for students whose families live a great distance from the college, many families of students who attend large state universities live within an hour or two of the university. It may be necessary for the practitioner to be available for weekend or evening sessions. The following situation was treated through bi-weekly family sessions.

Case Example of On-Going Family Sessions

A professor called the counseling service concerned about his son who despite outstanding grades was experiencing paralysis and behaving irresponsibly regarding his career direction as the end of his undergraduate career approached. The father also reported his own grave concern about a flaring of a long-standing conflictual relationship between son and mother. Hypothesizing on the basis of this consultation that the relationships among the three were characterized by an enmeshment now exacerbated by the threat of son's impending next career move, the therapist recommended that the family come in to discuss these problems together. As the parents viewed these problems as belonging primarily to the son, the son was of course the most reluctant to participate. His willing participation was fostered in the first session as the therapist focused on assessment of current and past family relationships and re-framed the problem away from the description given by the parents as the son's negative attitude and lack of initiative toward a description that focused on the way the parents express their concern for their son. Quickly, positive alliances were formed between therapist and family members and the family agreed to meet bi-weekly for a period of five months. Significant issues of enmeshment and family projection in all three relationships were addressed in the process of assessing trans-generational family relationships. Particular effort was focused on helping the son free himself from his triangulated role in his parents' marriage in which he served both as a lightning rod for parental frustration related to their advancing age and as a surrogate for his mother's father for whom she continued to feel intense ambivalence. This de-triangulating was accomplished primarily by facilitating father's becoming more active and effective in helping his wife in her painful attempt to come to terms with her relationship with her dead father and secondarily by helping father come to terms with his own fears of his decreasing physical capacities. At termination the son was effectively applying to graduate schools in his chosen field, mother was renewing career interests long put aside for family needs, and father was talking openly about awareness of his own mortality brought on by recent operations. A follow-up session initiated by father 18 months later revealed the son was completing a master's degree, applying for doctoral work, and engaged to be married while mother was teaming with father on several professional projects.

CONCLUSION

This paper, through application of trans-generational family concepts to college student development, offers a supplement to the prevailing theory of college student development. It also suggests a framework to assist practitioners in determining how to apply interventions based on these concepts to college student psychotherapy. The addition of family oriented interventions to the university mental health unit increases the unit's range of responsiveness to vital student needs.

It is unclear what factors one need consider in matching student and/or family characteristics with form of intervention, but experience suggests that symptom severity, intensity of dependence between student and family, and student openness to family work are among the important variables. Geographical distance, financial considerations, and flexibility of parents' and therapists' schedules are among the practical considerations. More work is needed to specify these relationships.

A major barrier in implementing family-based interventions is the perception by administrators, if not by practitioners, that this treatment approach oversteps the center's responsibility to the individual student. Clearly where the limits of responsibility are drawn depends upon one's conceptualization of the person and of mental health in general. It can be argued from a family perspective that failure to include family in many cases is not only less effective, but uses more resources in terms of individual treatment hours in the long run.

REFERENCES

Ackerman, N.J. (1980). The family with adolescents. In E.A. Carter and M. McGoldrick (eds.), *The family life cycle: a framework for family therapy*. New York: Gardner Press.

Babineau, R. (1975). University mental health professionals and the avoidance of the family. *Journal of the American College Health Association*, 24, 2, 75-79.

Baron, J. (1988). Use of family psychotherapy techniques on the college campus. *Journal of College Student Psychotherapy*, 3, 1, 83-97.

Beit-Hallahmi, B. and Colon, F. (1974). Involving family members in student counseling. *Psychotherapy: Theory, Research and Practice*, 11, 3, 265-269.

Boszormenyi-Nagy, I. and Spark, G. (1973). *Invisible loyalties*. New York: Harper and Row, Pub. Inc.

Boszormenyi-Nagy, I. (1981). Contextual family therapy. In A.S. Gurman and D. P. Kniskern (eds.), *Handbook of family therapy*. New York: Brunner/Mazel, Inc.

Boszormenyi-Nagy, I. and Krasner, B. R. (1988). *Between give and take: A clinical guide to contextual therapy*. New York: Brunner/Mazel, Inc.

Bowen, M. (1978). *Family Therapy in Clinical Practice*. New York: Jason Aronson.

Bruch, H. (1978). *The golden cage: the enigma of anorexia nervosa and the person within*. Cambridge, MA: Harvard U. Press.

Chickering, A.W. (1969). *Education and identity*. New York: Jossey-Bass Inc. Publishers.

Chickering, A.W. (1981). *The modern American college*. New York: Jossey-Bass Inc. Publishers.

Cohler, B.J. and Geyer, S. (1982). Psychological autonomy and interdependence within the family. In F. Walsh (ed.), *Normal family processes*. New York: The Guilford Press.

Erikson, E.H. (1950). *Childhood and society*. New York: Norton.

Erikson, E.H. (1968). *Identity: Youth and culture*. New York: Norton.

Fulmer, R. and Medalie, J. (1987). Treating the male college student from a family systems perspective. In J. Coleman (ed.), *Working with troubled adolescents: A handbook.* London: Academic Press.

Fulmer, R., Medalie, J. and Lord, D. (1982). Life cycles in transition: A family systems perspective on counseling the college student. *Journal of Adolescence,* 5, 195-217.

Hanfmann, E. (1978). *Effective therapy for college students.* New York: Jossey-Bass Inc. Publishers.

Held, B. S. and Bellows, D. C. (1983). A family systems approach to crisis reactions in college students. *Journal of Marital and Family Therapy,* 9, 365-373.

Josselson, R. (1980). Ego development in adolescence. In J. Adelson (ed.), *Handbook of adolescent psychology.* New York: John Wiley & Sons.

Kerr, M. and Bowen, M. (1988). *Family evaluation.* New York: Jason Aronson.

Laing, R. D. (1969). *Self and others.* New York: Penguin Books.

Lopez, F. G. (1986). Family structure and depression: Implications for the counseling of depressed college students. *Journal of Counseling and Development,* 64, 508-511.

Lopez, F. G. and Andrews, S. (1987). Career indecision: a family systems perspective. *Journal of Counseling and Development,* 65, 304-306.

Lukes, S. (1973). *Individualism.* Oxford: Basil-Blackwell.

McGoldrick, M. and Gerson, R. (1985). *Genograms in family assessment.* New York: Norton.

Minuchin, S., Rosman, B. and Baker, L. (1978). *Psychosomatic families: Anorexia nervosa in context.* Cambridge, MA: Harvard U. Press.

Okiishi, R. W. (1987). The genogram as a tool in career counseling. *Journal of Counseling and Development,* 66, 139-143.

Oles, T. P. and Bronstein, L. R. (1989). Bringing the family "in": A family perspective on student adjustment to college. *Journal of College Student Psychotherapy,* 4, 2, 35-44.

Openlander, P. and Searight, H. R. (1983). Family therapy perspectives in the college counseling center. *Journal of College Student Personnel,* 24, 423-427.

Sargent, J. Liebman, R. and Silver, M. (1985). Family therapy for anorexia nervosa. In D. M. Garner and P. E. Garfinkel (eds.), *Handbook of psychotherapy for anorexia nervosa and bulimia.* New York: The Guilford Press.

Scharff, J.S. (1988). *Foundations of object relations family therapy.* Northvale, NJ.: Jason Aronson, Inc.

Schwartz, R. C., Barrett, M. J. and Saba, G (1985). Family therapy for bulimia. In D. M. Garner and P. E. Garfinkel (eds.), *Handbook of psychotherapy for anorexia nervosa and bulimia.* New York: The Guilford Press.

Selvini-Palazzoli, M. (1978). *Self-starvation.* New York: Jason Aronson.

Smith, R. L. (1991). Marital and family therapy: direction, theory and practice. *Counseling and Human Development,* 23, 7.

Stierlin, H. (1981). *Separating parents and adolescents.* New York: Jason Aronson.

Wachtel, E. F. and Wachtel, P. L. (1986). *Family dynamics in individual psychotherapy: A guide to clinical strategies.* New York: The Guilford Press.

Whitaker, L.C. (Ed.). (1987). Parental Concerns in College Student Mental Health. *Journal of College Student Psychotherapy,* 2, 1-2.

Whitaker, L.C. and Davis, W.N. (Eds.). (1989). The Bulimic College Student: Evaluation, Treatment and Prevention. *Journal of College Student Psychotherapy,* 3, 2-4.

Whiting, R. A., Terry, L. L., and Strom, H.H. (1984). From home to college, from college to home: an interactional approach to treating the symptomatic disabled college student. *Family Therapy Collections,* II, 30-43.

Chapter 7

Findings of the Survey
of Undergraduate Concerns:
Anxieties, Academics, and Ambitions

SUMMARY. Results of a survey among Princeton undergraduates on undergraduate concerns are reported. Areas found to be of greatest importance were concerns about wasting time and balancing academic and social activities. Academic concerns were considered of higher priority than social ones. Underclass students were more concerned than upperclass students about academic and social issues, males more concerned than females about drinking and drugs, and minority students more concerned than non-minority students about academic performance.

INTRODUCTION

From Shakespeare's play, "Romeo and Juliet," to Madonna's song, "Papa Don't Preach," adolescence has been portrayed as a time of struggle to establish independence and form identities. "Who am I?" adolescents ask themselves again and again as they formulate their attitudes, opinions, and goals in life. For students

Sarah D. Klagsbrun graduated from Princeton University in 1991 in the Department of Psychology. She is planning to attend medical school in the fall of 1993. Please address any correspondence to the author at: 941 Park Avenue, New York, NY 10028.

at a residential college like Princeton, who are living away from home and parental care, the tasks are even more difficult. Students need to decide on their own how to organize their time, when to go to bed, what foods to eat, which courses to take and what social groups to join. Over the course of their four college years, they must also choose a major area of study and eventually a career.

Most of the professional literature on adolescence has been created by theorists of human development who view adolescence as an important transition stage between childhood and adulthood. Erik Erikson, for example, describes conflicts that arise as adolescents try to establish continuity with their past in the midst of the changes they are experiencing (Erikson, 1950). Peter Blos emphasizes separation from parents as part of an adolescent's individuation process (Blos, 1979), while Harry Stack Sullivan focuses on the establishment of satisfying interpersonal relationships (Sullivan, 1953).

More specific studies about college students often build on these broad theories. Like Erikson and Blos, for example, Jane Loevinger and William Perry plot stages of development during which college students struggle with and resolve a number of personal and moral issues (Loevinger in Weathersby, 1981; Perry, 1981). Joanne Medalie uses Erikson's concept of adolescence as a time of "moratorium" (Erikson, 1950) and describes the college years as a period of consolidation in a young person's search for identity (Medalie, 1981).

Other research on college students has compared attitudes at a specific university in each of the college years (Giddan and Price, 1985; Komarovsky, 1985) or used large-scale surveys, such as those conducted by the Gallup Poll, the Carnegie Foundation, and the Cooperative Institutional Research Program (Boyer, 1987; Astin, Green, and Korn, 1988). No other studies have dealt specifically with the concerns of undergraduates in this survey form.

The purpose of the Survey of Undergraduate Concerns was to uncover areas of major concern to undergraduates and to see how, if at all, they change over the course of the college experience. In discussing the findings of that survey, this presentation seeks to answer the following questions: Are undergraduates most concerned with issues relating to identity formation, academic achievement, social life, or parental pressures? Are there differences between the concerns of underclass and upperclass students? Male and female students? Minority and non-minority students? And what do these differences signify? In addition, the author briefly examines how concerns expressed by college undergraduates in this survey correlate with the major theories and findings of other studies. In "Survey of Undergraduate Concerns: What do College Students Worry About the Most?" (Klagsbrun, 1990), I raised questions and formulated hypotheses that were based on those studies. Those questions and hypotheses will be referred to in this presentation.

METHOD

Subjects. The sample consisted of 225 Princeton undergraduates: 71 were freshmen; 61 sophomores; 41 juniors; and 52 seniors. Minority students numbered 49; non-minority 176. Fewer respondents were female (N = 81) than were male (N = 144), were children of alumni (N = 29) than were not (N = 196), and fewer were on scholarship or financial aid (N = 90) than were not (N = 135). [The lower number of women, minority students, and children of alumni represented in the final sample reflect their ratio within the complete undergraduate population at Princeton University.] The respondents were 78.4% of those contacted.

Procedure. A sample of 300 Princeton undergraduates was randomly selected. The survey was mailed to 287 students who could be reached. The day before the survey was placed in the mail, I called all subjects, explaining to them that they had been randomly chosen to participate in the survey and urging them to participate, to increase response rate as much as possible. I was open about the goals of the survey and explained as much about the survey as subjects wished to know. I also thanked all subjects *profusely* since there was no monetary or official compensation for their participation. Each survey form included my phone number in case subjects had future questions and the cover page noted a due date by which to complete and return it. Around the time of the due date, followup phone calls were made to remind subjects to complete and mail back the survey if they had not already done so. If subjects were not reached directly over the phone, messages were left with roommates or on answering machines.

At the time of the first follow-up phone calls, subjects who had not already sent in their survey were asked to call me as soon as they had placed their survey in campus mail. Follow-up phone calls were made to those subjects who had not notified me of the completion of their surveys. This type of follow-up continued for a month after the survey had first been mailed to insure that the final sample of subjects would be random and include all types of students at Princeton from the most efficient to the least. About ten students needed to be sent another copy of the survey because they or their roommates had lost or misplaced it. In one case, a subject's rabbit had chewed up the survey. I delivered additional copies to these subjects, who later returned them to me.

Survey. The survey was created by compiling a long list of college students' concerns, based on my own college experience as well as knowledge of other students' concerns. The first list, with a total of 30 concerns, was shortened to eliminate those that were too broad, such as "there is a void in my life" or too specific such as the statement "I am concerned about a political issue." Ten unofficial pilot subjects from all four years helped target and eliminate those concerns that were too broad, narrow, or double-barreled. Another group of twenty unofficial pilot students from all four years filled out the shortened version of the survey. Their feedback led to further refinements, such as adding the words "Everyone seems smarter than me" to the concern "I do not belong here academically," because some subjects were confused about the meaning of this concern. A group of 10 subjects filled out the final version, and their responses spanned the major areas of concern, indicating that no concerns seemed irrelevant to many subjects.

The final "Survey of Undergraduate Concerns" comprised 22 concerns covering academic, social, identity formation, and parental issues. The statement "I am not independent enough," for example, is considered an identity issue. I mixed up the order of the concerns so that, for example, all academic or social concerns were not listed together at the top or bottom of the list. All subjects were asked to rank this list of 22 concerns in order from 1 (their highest concern) to 22 (their lowest concern), using each number only once. On the second page of the survey, below the list of 22 concerns, subjects were asked to rank their level of happiness at Princeton from 1 (extremely happy) to 10 (extremely unhappy). On the third page of the survey, subjects were asked to include any additional concerns they had and to indicate whether these concerns are of primary importance (see Appendix A for copy of survey).

RESULTS

Of the 287 undergraduates mailed the survey, 62 did not return it in spite of follow-up phone calls. It seems unlikely that there were any major differences between this group and those who responded. Since some subjects reported never having received the survey and asked for duplicates, this may have been the case for those who did not respond. The surveys may have been lost in the mail or misplaced by roommates. Or, for those subjects who did not respond, it may have been that when messages were left with roommates or on answering machines the roommates erased them, forgot to relay the message, or simply were not effective in urging subjects to return the survey. Thus, differences may have existed in the willingness of the roommates of subjects to urge subjects to complete the survey but not in the subjects themselves.

Data analysis included finding the mean ranking for each of the 22 concerns in addition to the level-of-happiness-at-Princeton question. Two-tailed t-tests were also performed in order to investigate the effects that independent variables–such as class year, sex, and race–had on the ranking of each of the concerns and on the level of happiness question, and to investigate significant differences.

Subjects were asked to rank their concerns in descending order from 1 (top concern) to 22 (lowest concern), therefore *lower means* represent *concerns of high priority* to subjects. Likewise, the lower the mean of subjects' level of happiness at Princeton, the higher is their level of happiness.

The results of the survey are presented in four major parts. The overall findings for all subjects are presented first, followed by findings comparing the concerns of underclass and upperclass students; males and females; and minority students and non-minority students. A fifth section presents findings about levels of student happiness at Princeton University.

Overall Findings. The major finding is that wasting time and not being able to organize one's time adequately are primary concerns of undergraduates at Princeton. As shown in Table 1, the highest-priority concern, that with the lowest mean ($x = 6.72$), is "I waste too much time."

Another high priority concern ($x = 7.43$), with the second lowest mean, is "I have not achieved an adequate balance between my academic and social life." Organizing time is a measure of self-sufficiency and independence for college students who can no longer depend on parents or teachers to help them meet deadlines and balance their academic and social life. Related to these two concerns is the high-priority concern "I am not taking adequate care of my health" ($x = 7.84$). Eating well, sleeping enough, and caring for one's body are other aspects of independence, especially for students removed from parental guidance.

Because wasting time, adequately balancing one's academic and social life, and caring for one's health relate to matters of independence and control, it is somewhat surprising that the concerns "I do not have control over my life" and "I am not independent enough" were ranked much lower in importance ($x = 11.79$; $x = 12.17$, respectively) as shown in Table 1. The ranking of these concerns as less important might be explained by the fact that students are reluctant to make such global statements about themselves, although they recognize difficulties in the more specific areas of their lives such as being able to organize their time or care for their health. Or, students may view themselves as independent and in control of their lives simply because they are away from home and are forced to make many decisions on their own.

The second major finding is that Princeton undergraduates place concerns about academic matters above social concerns. Table 1 shows that "I am not doing well enough academically" ($x = 7.56$) and "I am not able to fulfill all my academic obligations" ($x = 9.60$) both appear above concerns about finding a lover, making close friends, and being physically attractive. These findings are

Table 1
*List of Concerns in order of their Mean Ranking from the Highest
Ranked Concern (lowest mean) to the Lowest Ranked Concern
(highest mean)*

Variable	x
I waste too much of my time	6.72
I have not achieved an adequate balance between my academic and social life	7.43
I am not doing well enough academically	7.56
I am not taking adequate care of my health	7.84
I will not be successful after I leave Princeton	7.90
I am not able to fulfill my academic obligations	9.60
I am not able to fing a lover/significant other at Princeton	9.90
I am not able to make enough close friends here	9.91
I am not physically attractive enough	11.72
I do not have control over my life	11.79
I am not independent enough	12.17
My parents expect more of me academically	12.38
I have taken on too many extracurricular activities	12.47
Something bad is happening to someone close to me	12.48
I do not belong here/most people seem smarter than me	13.35
I am not able to spend time with myself comfortably	13.97
The University does not pay enough attention to my needs	14.02

Table 1 (con't)

I may contract a Sexually Transmitted Disease or I may become pregnant/ get a woman pregnant	14.08
My parents would not approve of my social behavior	14.71
I drink or use drugs too much	16.00
I may be sexually assaulted	16.88

Note: N=225

surprising in that they differ from those of several other researchers (Giddan & Price, 1985; Boyer, 1987) who found that college students are more interested in social than academic life. The differences, discussed later, may reflect on the nature of Princeton students or the academic pressures of the University.

Academic concern may also be a reflection of the concerns of students about succeeding professionally after graduating from college. In Table 1, the concern "I will not be successful after I leave Princeton" ranks among the top concerns in importance (x = 7.90). This finding is consistent with the trend found by the Gallup organization toward increasing interest among college students of the 1980s in material success after graduation (Astin et al.; 1986) and for increasing interest in careers in business as opposed to liberal arts (Astin et al.; 1987).

Concerns About Parental Pressures. "my parents expect more of me academically" and "my parents would not approve of my social behavior" were ranked relatively low in importance (x = 12.38; x = 14.71, respectively). But, at least for academic issues, concerns about parental expectations may be subsumed under the larger concerns of not doing well enough academically or not being able to fulfill academic obligations.

Concerns of Underclass versus Upperclass Students. Although it might be expected that underclass students would show more concern about parental expectations and approval than upperclass students, no significant differences were found. Both rated the statements "my parents expect more of me academically" and "my parents would not approve of my social behavior" as having less importance to them than other items (Underclass students: x = 12.30, x = 15.11; Upperclass students: x = 12.50, x = 14.11, respectively).

Tables 2 and 3 show, however, that there are differences in the responses of underclass students and upperclass students to other items.

Table 2 shows a trend in the ranking of the concern "I waste too much time," with upperclass students giving it more weight (p = .055). As shown in Table 3, seniors give it greater priority than freshmen (p < .05). In fact, the means for this concern show a linear progression from freshmen (x = 7.30) to sophomores (x = 6.39) to juniors (x = 6.24) to seniors (x = 5.67). As students progress through college, and especially during senior year, they have less structured time and more time, for example, to work on their independent projects. Apparently, the concern about wasting time grows as more time becomes available to be organized on one's own.

As expected, concerns about academic achievement, on the other hand, are higher among underclass students than upperclass students. For example, Table 2 shows a significant difference between these two groups in the ranking of the concerns "I am not doing well enough academically" and "I do not belong here academically" (p < .01; p < .01). Table 3 shows freshmen rating these concerns as having greater importance to them than did seniors (p < .02; p < .02).

In spite of greater concerns among underclass students about academic performance, the concern "I have not achieved an adequate balance between my academic and social life" seems to remain a major concern among students throughout their college years. Table 2 shows no significant difference in the ranking of this concern by underclass and upperclass students, nor between the ranking of this concern by freshmen and seniors (Table 3).

My background paper on undergraduate concerns (Klagsbrun, 1990) raised the question of whether there would be differences in the response by class year to the item "I will not be successful after I leave Princeton" in view of the Gallup organization finding (March, 1986) that seniors are more confident than freshmen about

Table 2
Mean Ranking of Concerns of Underclass Versus Upperclass Students

Variable	Freshmen & Sophomores x	Juniors & Seniors x	t
I waste too much time	6.88	6.49	-0.62
I have not achieved an adequate balance between my academic and social life	6.95	8.11	1.65
I am not doing well enough academically	6.77	8.68	2.66***
I will not be successful after I leave Princeton	7.83	7.99	0.20
My parents expect more of me academically	12.30	12.50	0.25
Something bad is happening to someone close to me	13.27	11.37	-2.14*
I do not belong here academically (most people seem smarter than me)	12.49	14.57	2.71***
I may contract a Sexually Transmitted Disease or I may become pregnant /get a woman pregnant	14.93	12.88	1.24**
My parents would not approve of my social behavior	15.11	14.11	-1.44
I drink or use drugs too much	16.64	15.09	-1.93

Note: N=225
*p< .05   ** p<.02   ***p<.01   ****p<.001

Table 3
Mean Ranking of Concerns of Freshmen Versus Seniors

Variable	Freshmen x	Seniors x	t
I waste too much time	7.30	5.67	2.01*
I have not achieved an adequate balance between my academic and social life	6.68	7.81	-1.29
I am not doing well enough academically	7.04	10.38	-3.49***
I will not be successful after I leave Princeton	8.85	9.37	-0.47
I am not able to find a lover /significant other at Princeton	7.69	11.85	-3.52***
I am not able to make enough close friends here	8.56	11.13	-2.42**
I do not belong here academically (most people seem smarter than me)	12.59	15.15	-2.52**
I may contract a Sexually Transmitted Disease or I may become pregnant /get a woman pregnant	16.52	11.25	4.66****
I drink or use drugs too much	17.13	14.00	2.79***

Note N=123
*p< .05   **p<.02   ***p<.01   ****p<.001

the possibility of attaining good jobs after graduating from college. Class level differences were found, but not those expected. Although no significant differences were uncovered in the ranking of this concern by underclass and upperclass students, a significant difference was found in comparing freshmen and seniors to sophomores and juniors. Sophomores and juniors view this concern significantly greater in importance than freshmen and seniors (x = 6.49; x = 9.07, respectively, p < .001). While freshmen have not yet begun to think about post college activities, seniors may be more focused on completing their theses and not as much on life after Princeton; sophomores, and juniors too, are just beginning to make career decisions and are feeling uneasy about them.

The highly significant differences between freshmen and seniors, shown in Table 3, on the two items "I am not able to find a lover/significant other at Princeton" and "I am not able to make enough close friends here" (p < .02; p < .01, respectively) are easier to understand. The greater importance given by freshmen to these concerns reflects their newness to the college community and feelings of being outsiders, especially at Princeton, where eating clubs, the main centers of social activity, are least accessible to freshmen. Clearly, these concerns decrease in importance by senior year.

The concerns "I may contract a Sexually Transmitted Disease . . ." and "I drink or use drugs too much" were ranked relatively low in importance (x = 11.25; x = 14.00, respectively) in the overall mean ranking of all subjects, perhaps because students consider these concerns unimportant or they do not report their own problems in these areas (Gallup, December, 1984). Nevertheless, as Table 3 shows, each of these concerns is significantly more important to seniors than to freshmen (p < 001; p < .01, respectively). Table 2 shows a significant difference among underclass and upperclass students about contracting a Sexually Transmitted Disease (p < .02), suggesting greater sexual activity among upperclass students and/or greater knowledge of the potential hazards of sexual activity. It also shows a trend toward greater concern among the upperclass students about personal alcohol and other drug abuse (p = .055).

Finally, in the breakdown between upperclass and underclass students, Table 2 shows significantly greater importance given by upperclass students to the item "Something bad is happening to someone close to me" (p < .05), perhaps because older students know more people, are more aware of problems around them, or are more willing to take responsibility for others' problems. No differences were found in underclass and upperclass responses which included familial, peer, and academic problems.

Concerns of Male versus Female Students. Interesting discoveries were made when the responses of male students were compared to those of female students, and two findings are interesting because *no* significant differences were detected on concerns where differences might have been expected.

The significant difference in the rating of the concern "I am not able to find a lover/significant other at Princeton" ($p < .01$) as seen in Table 4 can probably be explained by the greater ratio of

Table 4
Mean Ranking of Concerns of Male Versus Female Students

Variable	Males x	Females x	t
I am not doing well enough academically	7.45	7.75	0.40
I will not be successful after I leave Princeton	8.23	7.31	-1.14
I am not able to find a lover /significant other at Princeton	8.80	11.86	3.33***
I am not physically attractive enough	12.00	11.23	-0.99
I do not belong here academically (most people seem smarter than me)	13.50	13.07	-0.53
The University does not pay enough attention to my needs	13.77	14.47	1.00
My parents would not approve of my social behavior	14.02	15.94	2.80***
I drink or use drugs too much	15.08	17.63	3.14***
I may be sexually assaulted	20.00	11.32	-14.36****

Note N=225
*p< .05   **p<.02   ***p<.01   ****p<.001

men to women at Princeton. It seems logical that this concern would be greater for Princeton men since fewer women are available to men for dating than vice-versa.

The greater importance given by men to the concern "My parents would not approve of my social behavior" may be related to the fact that they significantly rated the concern "I drink or use drugs too much" greater in importance than did women (p < .01). As Gallup found (December, 1984), college men tend to drink alcohol more frequently. Thus, men may be more concerned that their parents would not approve of their drinking behavior.

As expected, women are more concerned about the possibility of being sexually assaulted than are men (p < .001), a finding also supported by the Women's Needs Assessment Survey conducted at Princeton (Spring, 1989) which showed that women (78%) perceive sexual harassment as a much greater problem than do men (57%).

Another finding by the Women's Needs Assessment Survey, however, was, unexpectedly, not supported by the Survey of Undergraduate Concerns. The Assessment Survey found that women feel more strongly than men in their desires for Princeton to be "more accepting . . . sensitive, and welcoming than they . . . perceive it to be" (Assessment, 1989, p. 4). Table 4 shows that on the Survey of Undergraduate Concerns no significant difference was found on the rating of the concern "The University does not pay enough attention to my needs" by Princeton men and women. Perhaps the wording of this concern was too vague and had it reflected some of the feelings that came through in the Women's Needs Assessment Study, women would have rated it greater than did men. But the resources on the Princeton campus, such as the Women's Center, may make women feel that although problems exist, the University provides adequate resources.

No significant difference was found between Princeton men and women for the concern "I am not physically attractive enough." Both groups placed this concern toward the middle range (men: x = 12.00; women: x = 11.23) indicating, contrary to myth, that women–at least Princeton women–are not any more worried about their appearance than are men.

Concerns of Minority versus Non-minority Students. Minority students, like women, did not rate "The University does not pay enough attention to my needs" significantly greater than did non-minority students (Table 5), although minority students often verbally express dissatisfaction with the University. Perhaps, the University provides adequate resources such as the Special Services Counselor, to which minority students can turn when, for example, feelings of isolation arise.

All three academic concerns are of greater importance to minority than to non-minority students (Table 5): "I am not doing well enough academically"; "I do not belong here academically"; and

Table 5
Mean Ranking of Concerns of Minority Versus Non-minority Students

Variable	Minority Students x	Non-minority Students x	t
I am not doing well enough academically	6.00	7.99	2.32**
I am not able to find a steady lover /significant other at Princeton	9.40	10.05	0.58
I am not able to make enough close friends here	10.00	9.89	1.10
My parents expect more of me academically	10.49	12.91	2.74***
I do not belong here academically (most people seem smarter than me)	11.70	13.80	2.29**
The University does not pay enough attention to my needs	13.37	14.20	1.03
I drink or use drugs too much	18.08	15.41	-2.80***

Note N=225
*p< .05   **p<.025   ***p<.01   ****p<.001

"my parents expect more of me academically" ($p < .025$; $p < .025$; $p < .01$, respectively), perhaps reflecting the higher parental pressure on minority students to succeed and do well professionally after college (Hoffman, 1988).

Those high parental expectations and academic concerns may be part of the reason for the lesser rating minority students as a whole give to "I drink or use drugs too much" ($p < .01$). Since minority students seem most concerned about their academic success, they may spend less time socializing and more time studying, and since there are many more non-minority than minority students, the latter may feel less comfortable socializing at the eating clubs, the main social centers, where most campus drinking occurs.

The Level of Happiness of Princeton Undergraduates. The Survey asked students to rate their happiness at Princeton on a scale of 1 to 10 with 1 representing extreme happiness and 10 representing extreme unhappiness. The means were quite consistent among underclass and upperclass students, males and females, and minority and non-minority students (Table 6).

Table 6
Mean Ranking of Level of Happiness at Princeton

Variables	x	t
Underclass Student	3.54	
Upperclass Students	3.80	0.95
Male Students	3.60	
Female Students	3.73	0.46
Minority Students	3.94	
Non-minority Students	3.57	1.17
Children of Alumni	2.93	
Non-Alumni Children	3.76	-2.11*

Note N=225
*p< .05

The overall mean for all subjects was 3.65, reflecting a high level of happiness at Princeton. Children of alumni were happier than non-alumni children (p < .05). Perhaps children of alumni feel they belong at Princeton from the very beginnings of their undergraduate careers, having heard about or perhaps visited the University long before they even reached college age.

DISCUSSION

College students have much more freedom than high-school students to choose courses and manage time, and receive much less supervision from parents and teachers. As Perry (1981) and Medalie (1981) illustrate, among the tasks of college students are making decisions on their own and dealing with uncertainties. Learning to organize time and achieve a balance between work and play is an essential part of that task and an aspect of one's identity and taking control of one's own life. While Erikson (1950) and Blos (1979) regard young adulthood as a final stage of adolescence, when issues of individuation and identity are resolved, this survey suggests that the struggle of students to structure their lives and achieve balance is an integral part of the college years.

On the other hand, in keeping with the ideas of the developmental theorists, the lesser priority given to concerns about parental attitudes suggests that struggles for control and balance are internal. The main issue is not difficulty separating from parents, but, once separated, how to manage on one's own. (The statistical findings reported are reinforced by the 70 students who added their own concerns, about half referring to worries about making course and career decisions, arranging schedules, and choosing which eating club to join.)

The greater weight given to academic concerns over social ones by Princeton undergraduates, as opposed to those in other schools, may reflect the heavy academic demands made at Princeton, and/or the seriousness of Princeton students. However, the major studies, by Giddan and Price (1985) and King (1973), that showed social concerns ranking higher than academic ones among college students, were made during the 1970s. This decade characterized by student rebellion against established courses and curricula and as large surveys have shown (Astin et al., 1986), altruistic and philosophic student goals. The emphasis on careers and success after college among students of the 1980s might account for their greater interest in academics.

Notably, there are no significant differences between male and female students in academic concerns or concern about achieving success after leaving Princeton. As Mirra Komarovsky (1985) found in her study of Barnard women, the trend among college women today is increasing interest in having careers combined with family life. Princeton women, like those attending other universities, are as oriented toward academic and professional success as are men.

The strong academic concerns of minority students may result from the high expectations many experience from their parents and communities. Many minority students are the first in their families to attend college, and feel they must do well for their families as well as for themselves.

The lack of significant difference between minority and non-minority students in response to the concern "The University does not pay enough attention to my needs" deserves further thought. Of the 15 minority students who listed additional concerns on page three of the survey, 10 complained of feeling isolated and removed from the University, using terms such as "elitism," "separatism," and "discrimination" to describe the University atmosphere. Had this survey included more specific concerns about those feelings, minority student responses' might have been stronger.

In general, the majority of additional concerns students listed on page three of the survey related, as have concerns of students over the decades (Giddan and Price, 1985), to themselves rather than to political or societal matters. Although, overall, Princeton students like normal students studied by Daniel Offer (1984b), feel happy with their lives, they are concerned about issues of identity and about academic and social success.

REFERENCES

Astin, A. W., Green, K. C., & Korn, W. S. (1987). *The American freshman: Twenty year trends. 1966-1985.* Cooperative Institutional Research Program. Los Angeles: University of California.

Astin, A. W., Green, K. C., & Korn, W. S. (1988). *The American college student. 1985: National norms for 1981 and 1983 college freshmen.* Higher Education Research Institute. Los Angeles: University of California.

Astin, A. W. (1986). *1986 Freshman survey data.* Cooperative Institutional Program. Los Angeles: University of California.

Blos, P. (1979). *The Adolescent passage: Developmental issues.* New York: International Universities Press.

Boyer, E. L. (1987). *College: The undergraduate experience in America.* The Carnegie Foundation for the Advancement of Teaching. New York: Harper & Row, Pub., Inc.

Chickering, A. W. & Havighurst, R. J. (1981). The Life Cycle. In A. W. Chickering and Associates, *The Modern American college* (pp. 16-50). San Francisco: Jossey-Bass Inc., Publishers.

Clark, J. D. (1989). Women's Needs Assessment Survey, Spring 1989: Women's Views of their Experiences as Students at Princeton University. Unpublished.

Erikson, E. H. (1950). *Childhood and society.* New York: W. W. Norton & Co., Inc.

Erikson, E. H. (1968). *Identity: Youth and Crisis.* New York: W. W. Norton & Co., Inc.

Giddan, N. S. & Price, M. K. (1985). *Journey of Youth: Psychological Development During College.* Schenectady, New York: Character Research Press.

The Gallup Organization. (1984-1986). Selected surveys. Princeton: New Jersey.

Hoffman, F. (1989). Developmental Issues, College Students and the 1990s. *Journal of College Student Psychotherapy.* 4 (2), 3-12.

Klagsbrun, S. (1990). Survey of Undergraduate Concerns: What Do College Students Worry About Most? First Junior Paper, Princeton University, unpublished.

Komarovsky, Mirra (1985). *Women in College: Shaping New Feminine Identities.* New York: Basic Books, Inc.

Medalie, J. (1981). The College Years as a Mini-Life Cycle: Developmental Tasks and Adaptive Options. *The Journal of the American College Health Association.* 30 (2), 75-79.

Offer, D., Ostrov, E., & Howard, K. (1984a). The Self-Image of Normal Adolescents. In D. Offer, E. Ostrov, & K. Howard (Eds.), *Patterns of Adolescent Psychology* (pp. 5-17). Pergamon Press Inc.: New York.

Offer, D. & Sabshin, M. (1984b) Adolescence: Empirical Perspectives. In D. Offer, & M. Sabshin (Eds.), *Normality and the Life Cycle: A Critical Integration* (pp.76-107). Basic Books, Inc.: New York.

Perry, W. G. (1981). Cognitive and Ethical Growth: The Making of Meaning. In A. W. Chickering and Associates, *The Modern American College* (pp. 76-116). Jossey-Bass Inc., Publishers: San Francisco.

Sanford, N. (1962). *The American College: A Psychological and Social Interpretation of Higher Learning.* John Wiley & Sons: New York.

Sullivan, H. S. (1953). *The Interpersonal Theory of Psychiatry.* W. W. Norton & Co, Inc.: New York.

Van Hasselt, V. B. & Hersen, M. (1987). *Handbook of Adolescent Psychology.* Pergamon Press Inc.: New York.

Weathersby, R. P. (1981). Ego Development. In A. W. Chickering and Associates, *The Modern American College* (pp. 51-75). Jossey-Bass Inc., Publishers: San Francisco.

APPENDIX

    I am a junior in the Psychology Department and I am conducting a survey in order to determine what are the major issues that concern Princeton undergraduates today. You are one of the 300 undergraduates who have been randomly chosen to make up a representative sample of the entire undergraduate population at Princeton University. As a result, the accuracy of <u>the results of my survey and my Junior Paper depend on you</u>.

    All I ask is that you take a few minutes to rank this list of concerns from 1 to 22. (1 = the issue that you are concerned about the most and 22 = the issue you are concerned about the least.) Please do not use any number more than once even if you feel that it is difficult to decide which of two concerns is more significant for you. Just do the best you can. It may be easiest to fill in your top concern (#1) and your lowest concern (#22) first.

    When you've finished the survey, please insert it back into the yellow envelope and place it in campus mail by Monday February 26 or earlier. All you have to do is stick the adhesive with my address --look inside yellow envelope--on the outside of the envelope (over your address).

    Please do not put your name on this questionnaire in order to insure <u>anonymity</u>. Any questions, feel free to call me.

Thank you so much!!!
Sarah Klagsbrun
734-7168

<u>Please circle or fill in the blank</u>:

<u>Sex</u>:   male   female

<u>Class</u>:   '93   '92   '91   '90

<u>Major</u> (if known): _____

<u>Race</u> (optional): Latino Native-American Asian Black White Other

<u>Where are you from</u>?   South   Eastcoast   Midwest   West   Other

<u>Are you the son/daughter of an alumn</u>?   yes   no

<u>Are you on scholarship or financial aid</u>?   yes   no

Survey of Undergraduate Concerns

I am concerned that...

___I have not achieved an adequate balance between my academic and social life

___I drink or use drugs too much

___I may be sexually assaulted

___I will not be successful after I leave Princeton (i.e. getting a job, getting into a graduate or pre-professional school, etc.)

___I am not financially secure

___I am not doing well enough academically

___I am not able to make enough close friends here

___I have taken on too many extra-curricular activities

___I am not able to fulfill my academic obligations

___I am not independent enough

___I am not able to find a steady lover/significant other at Princeton

___My parents expect more of me academically

___I am not able to spend time with myself comfortably

___I am not physically attractive enough

___I waste too much of my time

___I may contract a Sexually Transmitted Disease (AIDS, Herpes, etc.) or I may become pregnant/get a woman pregnant

___I am not taking adequate care of my health (i.e.eating/ sleep/ exercise habits)

___I do not belong here academically (most people seem smarter than me)

___The University does not pay enough attention to my needs

___I do not have control over my life

___Something bad is happening to someone close to me (Please specify: _____)

___My parents would not approve of my social behavior

In general, how happy are you here at Princeton? (please circle)

1	2	3	4	5	6	7	8	9	10
extremely happy								extremely unhappy	

Are there any other issues of concern to you that were left out?
If so, please list them in order of importance to you (1-being the
highest). Also, indicate whether they are primary (you think about
them a lot) or non-primary to you.

                                                    (Please Circle One)

(1)_____   Primary   Non-Primary
_____
_____

(2)_____   Primary   Non-Primary
_____
_____

(3)_____   Primary   Non-Primary
_____
_____

(4)_____   Primary   Non-Primary
_____
_____

(5)_____   Primary   Non-Primary
_____
_____

Chapter 8

College Age Substance Abuse
as a Developmental Arrest

Timothy M. Rivinus

SUMMARY. Psychoactive chemical use, abuse, and dependence often serve as false detours or roadblocks to the development of college students. Chemical abuse consultation to the young person struggling with a normal developmental hurdle of late adolescence, or struggling with pathology brought to or occurring at that time, can be extremely rewarding. Not only can it prevent the development of short- or long-term chemical abuse but it also can be an ice breaker to a destructive development crisis. Knowledge of the individual and group psychodynamics of chemical abuse, and the developmental issues of late adolescence and early adulthood, is essential to providing such a consultation. Preparedness for the problems and crises of student substance abuse requires, in the college community, a set of attitudes, awareness, compassion, structure, support, and service systems that address substance use and abuse as an expected but uninformed and potentially destructive effort of a student to address a developmental challenge.

The miracle of adolescence and the first years of adult life is that anyone survives this period at all considering the unplanned, unsupervised, and high-risk rites of passage available to American youth of college age in the later 20th century. It is a period when

Timothy M. Rivinus, MD, is Assistant Professor of Psychiatry and Human Behavior, Brown University School of Medicine, 345 Blackstone Blvd., Providence, RI 02906.

The author gratefully wishes to acknowledge the assistance of Mary Larimer, PhD, Susan Lundgren and Mary Duquette in the preparation of this manuscript.

141

young men and women take or are exposed to extraordinary risks. Young males are often pressed into national service and/or sent off to war. For women in late adolescence and young adulthood, the risks of rape, unwanted pregnancy, and sexual oppression are manifestly abundant. For both sexes the rates of death resulting from automobile and other accidents, suicide, mental illness, HIV infection, and the onset of drug and alcohol abuse and addiction are higher than at any time in our history (Blum, 1987).

The main tasks of adolescence are to accept oneself and others and to prepare for adult life. Blos (1962) has pointed out that the heir of adolescence is the attitude towards the self. Late adolescents and young adults are no longer members of a nuclear family or fully financially and emotionally supported by the family and need to find a new and supportive peer group. Research in networking and risk suggests that when young adults and late adolescents get into trouble they usually do so in the company of peers or when they are abandoned by them. On the other hand, choices of peers and networks that support healthy development usually preclude high-risk-taking peer groups and high-risk activity.

Young men and women need work and play. Choices of action and vocation that support the emancipation tasks of late adolescence and early adult life depend on the development and sense of self-worth that goes with accomplishment, earning power, health, and safe leisure activities. Without a vocational option the young adult often chooses self-defeating action, including substance abuse. Patterns of play and recreation in adult life should promote health and well-being, not undermine or destroy them.

Choosing good people to love is important during late adolescence, and finding "the right one" of either sex is a crucial process. Relationships require work, trial and error. Heterosexual relationships are difficult enough; in our society a homosexual choice is even more difficult. In late adolescence a sense of one's own sexuality and a sense of acceptance and love of others helps the adolescent move beyond the family sphere and acquire a sense of spiritual acceptance. In late adolescence *eros* (sexual and physical passion and experience) begins to join with *agape* (altruistic love) and *thanatos* (spiritual awakenings and yearnings). If development is incomplete, these three types of love establish themselves as separate, remain unfulfilled or undeveloped.

Yearnings for relationship and sexual desire are intense during adolescence and early adulthood. Among the tasks of this period is to find someone with whom to share these feelings, to discover the essence of relationship, and a sense of humanistic and spiritual wonder that is greater than sexuality and sensuality alone. The intensity of this spiritual experience and the channeling of it turns the "adolescent philosopher" into someone with a philosophy of life and living (Kohlberg and Gilligan, 1972).

Mentors for the late adolescent and young adult must be dedicated and available. The provision of mentorship in a supportive setting *is* the function of the university. The adolescent or young adult who is helped by mentors and the university milieu to negotiate the struggles of the past and the transition process of the present, who is offered a framework for the social, psychological, and spiritual issues of this stage of growth and development, who is taught about the risks and strengths of certain kinds of affiliation, relationship, action, and thinking, gains advantages in withstanding the challenges and vicissitudes of the passage and indeed of the rest of life (Levinson, 1978). In the absence of mentorship and developmental assistance at moments of crisis and developmental challenge the temporary expedient of psychoactive chemical may be tempting to the adolescent when they are available. Indeed, in the 1990s, they are very available on college campuses.

With rare exception, psychoactive chemical use *disorder begins* sometime *during adolescence.* For the college student abusive chemical use has either become manifested in adolescents by college age, or a pattern of drug experimentation and expectations of drugs and/or alcohol begin in college that set the stage for later substance use disorder (Goldstein, Brown and Christiansen, 1985). In this context substance use disorder can be viewed as a disorder of development. The categories of developmental disorder are a useful meeting place for addiction theory and psychoanalytic and developmental theories (Brown, 1991; Rivinus, 1991). The concepts of developmental arrest and regression were proposed by the Group for the Advancement of Psychiatry (1966) to provide a diagnostic framework for the disorders of children and adolescents. The frameworks of growth and development still constitute the basis for research into the norms and disorders of childhood and adolescence (Offer & Offer, 1975; Loevinger, 1976; Kegan, 1982) and growth and developmental theory have been applied to the entire life cycle (Erikson, 1956 and 1965; Vaillant, 1977; Levinson, 1978).

The terms *developmental arrest, regression, or fixation* were derived from the psychoanalytic literature that suggested that intrapsychic conflicts arising from internal and external events in the development of the child (or adolescent) could set in motion pathological processes resulting in deviations or cessation of development. Despite the pathological implications of this framework there was also a therapeutic optimism expressed in these concepts which implied that in the process of diagnosis and treatment, the causes of the developmental deviation could be discovered, understood, unstuck, or re-routed.

Current diagnosis nosologies do not take the developmental model into account. Current nomenclatures tend to see psychiatric disorders as static, as either present or absent. Although useful for snapshot diagnoses, static models do not take pathogenesis or development into account. The field of addiction takes advantage of this viewpoint, however, by postulating that once you have the "disease" of addiction, you have it for life.

A stumbling block for many young people and their families first entering treatment for addiction to or abuse of a chemical, however, is that there is no easy answer to the questions, "How did this happen?" "What went wrong?" "What is the psychological cause of the addiction? How did it develop?" This may divert patient's or family's attention from the offending chemical and the destructive process of addiction itself and perpetuate the denial defense that is so central to the abuse and addiction process. The program of Alcoholics Anonymous (AA) has a corrective aphorism for this early psychological barrier. It exhorts the afflicted, "Don't ask *why* you drink [or use drugs], ask why you *drink* [use drugs]." For individuals to begin to grow again, to reverse the developmental arrest, deviation, or fixation, they must first, paradoxically, acknowledge powerlessness over the addictive process, acknowledge that they have a disease, and begin to regain control by forswearing the chemicals that retard development. At that point developmental understanding can begin.

Although an understanding of developmental causes may not be the beginning of treatment, it may signal the beginning of developmental growth that can follow the establishment of abstinence. AA has another well-known saying that describes post-abstinence development: "You are not responsible for your disease but you *are* responsible for your recovery." Therefore, after accepting the static process of "having the disease," AA shifts from a static framework to a developmental one. Once the primacy of diagnosis and the necessity of abstinence are established, the psychological mastery of recovery includes a reversal of the developmental stoppage or detour by steps towards new psychological growth (Brown, 1991). Growth is produced by change. Change results from the acknowledgement of arrested development. Arrested development results from unresolved issues for which the chemical at first provides a temporary solution.

This is the point at which addiction theory and psychoanalytic and developmental theory meet. The recovery process according to AA and Narcotics Anonymous (NA) necessitates returning to the level at which development is arrested and proceeding from there. It should come as no surprise, therefore, that the twelve steps of AA closely parallel the stages of growth according to a number of hierarchical theories of human development (see Table 1).

Three groups of college students with developmental deviations are most susceptible to substance use disorder. First, some students have already suffered developmental arrest by the time they reach college. They reach college by reason of their cognitive strengths, but emotionally they are painfully, often traumatically, arrested at preadolescent stages. Many of this group have already begun to use substances. Some are genetically predisposed to substance use disorder and/or have experienced the stress of growing up in dysfunctional, abusive, and/or chemically dependent families. They may begin to use, and then abuse, substances in attempts at mastery and to find relief from the pain that they bring to college.

A second group of students who develop substance use disorder may overlap with the first. These young people may be vulnerable because of the way they use alcohol or other drugs. They may associate with a heavy drinking peer group that fosters to substance use disorder. They choose chemicals that induce substance use disorder by their powerfully addictive effects. Most addictive chemicals including alcohol, cocaine, prescription sedatives, stimu-

TABLE 1
COMPARISON OF STAGE DEVELOPMENT THEORIES TO THE 12 STEPS OF ALCOHOLICS ANONYMOUS (AA)*

AA STEP (Adapted)	Erikson	Piaget	Loevinger	Kohlberg	Maslow
1. "We admitted we were powerless..."	Trust	Sensory-motor stage	Presocial	Surrender to authority	Survival orientation
2. Acceptance of higher power outside of the self	-	Preoperational thinking	Impulsive	Obedience orientation	Psychological satisfaction orientation
3. Surrender to others and idea of "higher power"	Autonomy	Concrete thinking	Opportunistic conformist	Instrumental orientation	Safety orientation
4. Self-evaluation and moral inventory	Initiative	Operational thinking	Conscientious	Instrumental orientation	-
5. Confession and sharing with another human being	-	-	-	Interpersonal orientation	Love and affection orientation
6 & 7. Beginning character and behavioral change	Industry	Formal operations	-	-	-
8 & 9. Apology to others and public commitment to change	Identity	-	-	Social orientation	Belonging
10. Commitment to broaden the scope of change to all life activities	-	-	Autonomous	Principles orientation	Esteem and self-esteem orientation
11. Spiritual commitment to change	Generativity	Post-formal dialectical	-	-	Self-actualization
12. Commitment to help others; altruistism	Acceptance	-	Altruistism	-	-

*Expanded and adapted from AA (1976), Loevinger (1976) and Kegan (1982) lants, steroids, and hallucinogens can induce a stress-related disorder in their own right. During the rapid neurological and cognitive growth in adolescence the nervous system is especially vulnerable to the biochemical influences of all psychoactive substances (Bean-Bayog, 1986). College students so exposed, even without prior developmental arrest, are extremely vulnerable to the chemical that can lead to pathological developmental deviation and arrest akin to post-traumatic stress disorder (PTSD).

The third group are students who are vulnerable because they struggle with current normal developmental tasks and who turn to psychoactive substances for a pseudoresolution of these issues. The developmental tasks of the college years prone to vulnerability include the following developmental steps of late adolescence and early adult-life:

1. *Adolescent turmoil: Yes or No?* Can adolescents and young adults negotiate adolescence as a stage of rapid developmental change and challenge successfully and without casualty? (Freud, A., 1958; Offer & Offer, 1975; Arnstein, 1984). Can they successfully master the developmental challenges and crises of the time (Settlage, 1990)?
2. *Separation-individuation:* Can adolescents and young adults master the issues of separation and individuation from family and place of origin and adjust to the college and young adult world (Blos, 1962, 1979)?
3. *The identity crisis:* Can adolescents negotiate identity issues and find themselves in their own and the adult world (Erikson, 1956, 1965; Ritvo, 1976)?
4. *Making healthy choices:* Can adolescents make healthy choices in terms of action and lifestyle, and adopt a healthy belief system (Mariman and Becker, 1974; Kleinot and Rogers, 1982; Gonzalez, 1988)?
5. *Healthy peer and network choices:* Can adolescents affiliate with others, make stable connections, and choose "good enough" people to be with (Gilligan, 1988)?
6. *Compromise with the normal (for adolescence) sense of invulnerability:* A sense of invulnerability is necessary for adolescents to sustain the bridge from childhood into young adult

life and contributes to the development of durability in the mature self. Invulnerability, if taken literally and not surrendered, however, can be an attitude preceding and dominating high-risk behavior. Can students move from the fantasy of invulnerability to a solid sense of confidence?

7. *Choice of interdependence over independence and dependence:* Can students accept interrelatedness as a principle rather than choose isolation or continue childlike dependence (Blos, 1954)?

8. *Resolution of vocational choice:* Can students plan a course of action for postcollege life?

Settlage (1990) has pointed out that the late adolescence brings a healthy drive towards resolution, growth, and maturity to the developmental crises of the period: (1) There is a strong biological and psychological "tension" towards crisis resolution and growth in late adolescence; (2) developmental challenges (for example, a new relationship, a loss, an experiment with drugs or alcohol) occur with great frequency during this time; (3) as a result of (1) and (2) a developmental crisis occurs reflecting the adolescent's uncertainty and anxiety over the prospect of success or failure in mastery of the challenge; (4) if there is mastery of the crisis, or developmental resolution occurs that leads to an integration of new skills, structures, and healthy attitudes towards the self, identity and self representation are met. Failure to resolve a crisis can result in a lack of confidence, disintegration, and a legacy of unresolved or negative attitudes towards the self.

Some shy, immature, or otherwise unready young people, may come from quite functional families and have a difficult time separating themselves from family. This group of students may feel liberated from their shyness and inexperience by psychoactive chemicals. Other young people from dysfunctional families have difficulties separating themselves from their families for different reasons. Children of alcoholic parents, children of divorcing parents, and children of neglectful or abusive parents often carry undue emotional baggage and are therefore unduly preoccupied with issues of separation and individuation from their earlier stressful family life. In troubled families the dysfunction of one family member may be compensated for by the high functioning of one or more others. Some children of alcoholic parents, for instance, have been heroes within their families before they escape to college (Wegscheider-Cruse, 1989). In the past they have taken care of their troubled parents and are the keepers of family integrity and intactness. When they separate from the family to go to college, they find themselves burdened with guilt and a strong pull to rejoin their troubled parents or siblings. This emotional baggage may not become apparent until the student has actually entered college and substance use provides a temporary escape.

> Aaron is a 21-year-old freshman who spent two years after high school at a college preparatory school, a time for him of (untreated) abstinence from psychoactive substances and academic success. His academic record in high school had been poor because of polysubstance use and family conflict. Since he has entered college his parents have decided to divorce and he has relapsed into drug use. His torment over his parents' divorce is temporarily lessened by regular use of large doses of marijuana, and alcohol. Substance use and a substance abusing peer group serve as a "transitional object" at a point when he feels he no longer has a home.

Young people struggling with identity issues, those struggling to find themselves, to identify their sexual orientation, to develop a sense of comfort with academic work or the opposite sex, those struggling with myriad choices during the college years, may find a pseudoresolution in the use of tranquilizing or stimulating chemicals.

> Bill is a 20-year-old sophomore struggling with a gender identity crisis. He has been physically attracted to males as long as he can remember. Socially, however, he prefers the company of women. To meet his physical needs and in accord with his sexual preference, he uses large amounts of alcohol, marijuana, and cocaine in company of similarly drug abusing males and becomes sexually involved with them. During his encounters he practices unprotected sexual contact. In the

aftermath of these encounters he is remorseful, questions his motives, and numbs himself with more substance use. He referred himself to the health service after having seen a videotape on human immunodeficiency virus (HIV) transmission in the young.

Young people who experiment with ways of behaving, choices of action, and ways of being that are new, daring, challenging, revolutionary, or "counterdependent" (which are often efforts to differentiate themselves from their families) often are at high risk for the development of psychoactive use disorder. For these young people the psychoactive substances are often chosen as "transitional objects" (Winnicott, 1953) that assist them in negotiating separation, individuation, and a sense of transitional identity. To choose a counterdependent habit that offers a psychological pseudoresolution to issues of identity, separation, individuation, and affiliation is a seductive psychological, social, and chemical reinforcing solution rolled into one neat package. The difficulty is not so much that the separation or identity stages are too much for the individual, but that the route of psychoactive substance use seems so much easier. By taking on a life of its own high risk activity such as substance abuse or unprotected sexual contact dictates future choices and actions.

Aliah is a 25-year-old African-American senior. She dropped out of college for three years to join affirmative action, voter, and civil rights efforts in a large metropolitan area. She has returned to college and has affiliated herself with a group that regularly uses marijuana and alcohol and plays music together. She is an accomplished singer. Her mother is a licensed practical nurse who has hoped that her daughter will go to medical school or at least follow her footsteps in registered nursing. Her father strongly hopes that she will go into business. In college she has followed a business track and has applied for business school but feels that a business career is contrary to her understanding of her African-American identity. Her career conflicts are temporarily resolved by her main leisure time activity, music and drugs. An unplanned and unexpected pregnancy brings her to counseling and to a painful and sudden life decision.

The choice of a peer group or network that predisposes itself to unhealthy, unhappy, or high risk-taking choices is another mode of initiation into psychoactive substance use disorder in the college years. Recent studies of college students show that choices of action are highly governed by association with individuals who make similar choices (Kandel, 1986). The initiation and affiliative rites of many college students involve alcohol and, in more recent years, drug experimentation and drug taking. This has become a culture now deeply rooted in college life.

Feelings of invulnerability are part of the transitional psychology of late adolescence. The invulnerability related to continued use of psychoactive chemicals without ill effects obvious to the user, particularly when reinforced by the sense of invulnerability bestowed by the effects of the chemicals themselves, is a particularly seductive and destructive phenomenon that is part of the addictive process. Ironically a sense of independence is a necessary developmental step for adolescents. Choices that confer a temporary sense of independence including the "right to drink and drug" have been defended as among those liberties expected by and for American youth. (After all it was resistance to a tax on a mildly addictive drug–tea–that heralded the American revolution. Political battles rejecting taxation and the restriction of access to liquor and drugs have been very much part of the independent ethos of this country.) The right to use liquor by the college student has been seen as basic to generations of former students. A major paradigm shift is needed if we are to change these strongly embedded cultural initiation rites to new-found knowledge about addiction and its potentially destructive consequences and progression.

Whether students can use college to prepare for vocational choice and a sustaining post-college occupation is of course developmentally crucial. Many gifted young people using psychoactive substances are unable to make the transition from college to a postgraduate plan despite previous college success and may enter into a state of prolonged adolescence (Blos, 1954). Some may need to do this; but if they use psychoactive substances to postpone or prolong the transition, they place themselves at risk for substance use disorder and a prolonged developmental arrest or problematic detour. Students even without the disruption of regular chemical use or abuse during college, who are unable to settle upon a post-graduate vocation or course of study meaningful to them may turn to substances in lieu of academic or vocational adaptations.

> Jennifer is a 22-year-old college senior. She has loved and experienced great successes in her college years but is unable to resolve the question of her next step. By the end of her senior year she has gravitated to isolated and group cocaine and alcohol use. She has chosen to take temporary work in her university town following college and remain with the drug using peer group, to whom she finds herself more and more strongly attached. "I have no idea what I want to do next" is the problem she articulates as she comes for her first interview.

IS EXPERIMENTATION
WITH PSYCHOACTIVE CHEMICALS ABNORMAL?

The answer is no. But this is a relative answer–relative to where the experimentation leads. It is also relative to the absence of relat-ed, concurrent or associated problems of behavior, thinking, and mood. A number of recent longitudinal studies have demonstrated that *some* experimentation with psychoactive chemicals is probably part of the typical developmental passage for many psychologically healthy American young people in the late 20th century (Jessor & Jessor, 1977; Jessor et al., 1980; Donovan et al., 1983; Kandel & Logan, 1984; Kandel et al., 1986; Newcomb and Bentler, 1988; Shedler and Block, 1990). In fact, some experimentation with alcohol and/or drugs without adverse consequences or concomitant problems is probably a sign of relative psychological health in the youth of our time. Total abstainers from drugs, in fact, may have more psychological problems than mild experimenters by a number of standard measures. *However,* for those young people with preex-isting problems, experimentation with substance use is: (a) likely to become problematic and disordered, and (b) move rapidly from stages of experimentation to substance abuse and dependence (Shedler and Block, 1990). This latter group would be significantly represented among students coming to a college counseling service.

Regular users of psychoactive substances are often young people who often struggle with long-standing issues of alienation, impulsivity, and subjective distress (Shedler and Block, 1990). Experimenters, who are likely later to give up psychoactive substances or eschew their regular use, usually do not show such features. A third group may use substances regularly or abusively for a time but give them up or do not become chronically or pathologically involved with their use and migrate from a peer group that uses chemicals to peers that do. Premorbid historical and family features, patterns of association and current diagnostic criteria for substance use disorder serve to distinguish the degree of risk and potential morbidity for a student (American Psychiatric Association, 1987; Rivinus, 1987).

Noting that research suggests that experimenters and frequent users and abusers of chemicals are different groups and that some students "mature out" of abusive use of substances in no way condones experimentation with psychoactive substances or suggests that chemical abuse is a normal transitional stage of adolescence. It merely emphasizes that, from an epidemiological point of view, some psychoactive substance experimentation appears to correspond with the normal rites (if not rights) of adolescent passage in late 20th century North American culture. Regular use, abuse, and dependence, however, does not (Donovan et al., 1983; Kandel et al., 1986; Shedler and Block, 1990).

Chemical Myopia

A further note of caution is warranted regarding the relationship of problem behaviors, thinking, and mood to youthful experimentation with psychoactive chemicals. *Any* psychological, behavioral, or academic problem can be exacerbated by psychoactive substance use. Even experimental use of a psychoactive substance produces for a period of time what has been called chemical "myopia" which ranges well beyond the period of intoxication alone (Steele and Josephs, 1990). Paradoxically, but not surprisingly, this chemical-related myopia serves as the underpinning for the desired, as well as the detrimental, effects of most psychoactive substances which are abused. Pain, worry, depressed mood, troubled thinking, or disordered behavior for example, are all commonly, and temporarily, relieved by psychoactive substance use. Following intoxication and brief relief, however, there comes a rebound exacerbation of mood, thinking, and behavior problems resulting from substance use that can have troubling psychological and adaptive consequences. For example, psychoactive substance abuse when superimposed on depressive mood in an adolescent is often sufficient to produce suicidal thinking and behavior (Levy and Deykin, 1989; Rivinus, 1990).

The Gateway Hypothesis and Age Effects

Longitudinal studies have also shown that an adolescent's age and prior drug use are related to the risks of initiation and continued use or discontinuation of drug use. For adolescents in the 1970s regular tobacco use usually begins at a mean age of 16; alcohol use at age 17; marijuana use at age 18 (Kandel & Logan, 1984). These mean ages have decreased in recent years but the original studies have given basic confirmation to a "gateway hypothesis" of drug initiation among youth (Johnson et al., 1987). *Not only do problems in adaptation precede regular chemical use but so does regular use of a more "accepted" chemical.*

Another implication of current research suggests that if college students are able to survive the college years without falling into regular use or abuse of psychoactive substances and have the capacity to develop healthy alternatives to drug use, the period of high risk for initiation into regular or abusive use of chemicals is largely over. For college students, who tend to be somewhat later in their initiation into the regular use and abuse of substances (Johnson et al., 1987), the college years are a critical period for the development of attitudes that perpetuate destructive use of substances or promote healthy lifestyle choices. Hence education on chemical use and promotion of healthy choices is critical and likely to have an impact during the college years (Robins et al., 1986; Gonzalez, 1988).

Network Effects, Prevention, and Intervention

Follow-up studies have demonstrated that the choice of whether to continue regular use of a psychoactive substance correlates with peer group choice. If peers use or abuse chemicals, then continuation of use is more likely. Young adults who have used or abused psychoactive chemicals and who discontinue experimentation or regular use correspondingly shift their peer group to a nonsubstance abusing peer group and value system (Jessor and Jessor, 1977; Kandel and Logan, 1984; Kandel et al., 1986).

Peer attitudes and behavior therefore, are critical. Education of peer groups and intervention by peers where necessary have proven to be extremely effective. However, this is not successful without clear, compassionate, and consistent assistance, mentorship, and sets of standards promoted by the college or university leadership and community. If acquiescence to the "right to drink and drug" is seen as part of the rites of independence of adolescents and is promoted by adults and the peer group, then drinking and taking drugs are likely to be more commonplace and the casualties more likely (Resnik, 1990). However, if the adult world and peers alike adopt a policy of promoting healthy lifestyle choices, provision of proactive mentorship and leadership, discouraging self-destructive acts and habit patterns, and intervening when these choices and patterns are out of control, then preventive efforts measures will have been maximally accomplished. The efforts of organizations such as Bacchus (Ryan, 1986; Gonzalez, 1988), the network of colleges and universities committed to the elimination of drug and alcohol abuse (Standards, 1987) and the work of Larimer and Marlatt (1991) to influence the Greek fraternities at the University of Washington (and on other campuses) represent innovative efforts to remodel old, ingrained and self-destructive lifestyle choices and traditions on campuses into healthy ones.

The implications of surveys of college student substance use are significant (Johnson et al., 1987). Primary prevention of alcohol use, considering that most college students (90%) have already experimented with alcohol, would not, therefore, be a cost-effective intervention in college. Many of these students drink alcohol regularly to the point of intoxication (45%), however, the inoculation of a healthy set of attitudes about excessive drinking, assistance with and provision of non-alcohol alternatives at student functions, and intervention policies in student groups who are already abusing alcohol, is clearly a more appropriate and specific intervention. For college students who have not yet chosen to experiment with drugs other than alcohol, primary prevention programs, of course, have much to recommend them and are a necessity on college campuses (Gonzalez, 1988).

How Can Booze and Drugs Be Taken Out of College Age Initiation Rites?

One of the problems of American culture (and of most industrialized countries) from the point of view of late adolescent development is the lack of initiation rites for men, women, and for the two sexes together. What initiation rites there are are usually improvised and invented by the young themselves, and are almost always aided, abetted, and fueled by alcohol and other drug experimentation, use, and abuse. As such these activities hardly initiate the young into a healthy adult life. Furthermore they blur and distort the experience of transition to adult life. Initiation to maturity by ceremonial drinking and drugging by unsupervised youth implies that the adult world does not understand the needs of the adolescent, does not really care to be joined by their youth, or to join them with compassion and interest as they become young adults. Without proactive programs to prevent, minimize, and provide attractive ceremonial alternatives to substance abuse on campus, intoxication, isolation, and escapism will be sanctioned, even promoted, as an acceptable mode of developmental passage.

David McClellan (1975) has done thought-provoking research into the rituals of power and affiliation in the young adult. Traditionally on North American college campuses the use of mind-altering chemicals has been incorporated into these rituals. College men have used alcohol, marijuana, and more recently cocaine, to enhance their sense of power and their abilities to affiliate. Closeness, connection, and affiliation have traditionally been seen as characteristically female traits and as relative weaknesses or capitulations of power in a male-oriented society. Therefore, for males alcohol and other drugs provide a useful lubricant that enhances closeness without the apparent sacrifice of power or loss of boundaries. Without the excuse, "we were drunk" or "wasted," American college men have difficulties with closeness without fear of boundary loss. Spokesmen for the current men's movement accurately observe that young men do not easily affiliate because they have not been initiated to a sense of safe and comfortable intimacy by older males, who themselves are uninitiated and threatened by younger men (Bly, 1990).

For North American college women, same sex affiliation has been more traditionally and more comfortably accepted by them than by their male counterparts and is less often associated with group intoxication than for males (Blos, 1980; Gilligan, 1982; 1988). However, as women reach for power in worlds of male dominance they tend to use male-oriented techniques to initiate themselves and have come to use tobacco, alcohol, and other psychoactive substances more commonly (Johnson et al., 1987). Power and invulnerability have become equated with experimental substance use for both sexes in late 20th century North America, and the rates of substance use disorder for both sexes have increased–because of more use (particularly by women) and by the greater availability of substances to the young.

In interactions between the sexes, young males often deal with their anxiety by the use of substances. Women are urged or expected to get "drunk" or "stoned" in the company of men as a way of establishing their submissiveness to male power, but do so also, paradoxically, to demonstrate their equality to them, and as an excuse to act sexually without relinquishing their status as "good" girls. As women grasp for more power they will certainly continue to use substances as a way of establishing their coequal status as users of these agents which are symbols of "power" and to achieve chic affiliation. What clearer example of the charade of initiation of power and affiliation could there be than the "animal house" stories of fraternities that we hear of periodically from various campuses throughout the land? Date rape, for example, is especially likely, as the boundaries are blurred, by intoxication, between "wanted" and "unwanted" advances. Suddenly, a casualty due to overdose or an intoxication-related accident or incident will shatter an event.

> The post-football game rites are about to take place. There is a victory or a loss. Young men gather together and celebrate the victory or drown the loss with intoxicants. A young woman among them is victimized by a gang rape. Or a date rape follows the party. One or more young men or women pass out or are so dangerously intoxicated they are taken to the college infirmary (or a local emergency room) for care. A motor vehicle accident occurs, tragedy strikes or is narrowly missed.

These are the initiation rites of the young. They almost always include alcohol and/or other chemicals in an attempt to master power or affiliation. Attempts at affiliation are distorted by intoxication, or become expressions of raw power or unbridled sexual drives. The adult world is neither present nor involved until after the fact. These rites sometimes result in tragedy. They are almost universally associated with intoxicating substances. They occur in the absence of sanctioned and supervised initiation rites to the culture of responsible adulthood.

Mixed Messages to Youth

The ambivalent situation due to the lack of enforcement of the legal drinking age and of the use of intoxicating substances in college communities presents a major problem for the young and for society at large. Youth who are initiated by use of intoxicating substances are also initiated to breach of the laws of the land. They are taught, as part of initiation, that intoxicated substances are acceptable social lubricants. They are taught that there are acceptable losses for this kind of initiation rite and that the laws of the land may be broken in the raw assertion of power and in the name of affiliation (Resnik, 1990). College students, so exposed, are taught the sanctioned abuse of power and absence of real affiliation by people in high places–currently a major national issue. These trends signal the subversion (or outright failure) of the true objectives of the university. These trends are a national problem that returns us to the attitude that we take toward our young people, their use of intoxicating substances, and the rites of adolescent initiation to a socially committed adult life. Our compassion for this human problem and our knowledge of the development of adolescent substance abuse requires that we do more.

Recommendations

1. The challenge for colleges at all levels is to bring the state of our knowledge of psychoactive chemicals and their effects on the human organism to all students, especially to those who are vulnerable. This information needs to be made part of the intellectual and moral atmosphere of our colleges of learning. How are we to bring the latest responsible information to college students about alcohol and other drug use and abuse, if we are not to consider this the purview of the university? It is important to recall that students have gotten most of the information and misinformation on this important topic from parents, peers and the advertising media. I and others have recommended that there be regular and routine orientation and course offerings on psychoactive chemicals and the development of the problems associated with them: intoxication, abuse, dependence, and other organic syndromes (Suchman and Broughton, 1988; Rivinus, 1990). It is not enough to say "boys will be boys and girls will be girls" with regard to alcohol and other psychoactive chemicals in these times.

2. Other courses for credit should include: semester-limited individual or group psychotherapy (with extensions available for credit), a course introducing coping skills, relaxation, self-defense and self-care skills, assertiveness training, and smoking cessation programs for smokers. Documented participation in mutual aid groups such as AA, NA, CA (Cocaine Anonymous), and COA (Children of Alcoholics) should also be counted for course credit (Duran & Brooklyn, 1988).

3. Students in crisis with psychoactive chemical abuse, and professors, deans, administrators, security personnel, campus police, counselors, and peers who interact with them, are permitted

crucial moments of human interaction. These are "teachable moments" in the course of a student's development (Rivinus, 1990). The message of these moments must convey that developmental crisis is rarely enhanced and almost always deepened by the use and abuse of psychoactive chemicals. All alcohol- or other drug-related incidents should be followed by mandatory time-limited counseling, mutual aid group attendance and nonpunitive probationary arrangements. Alternatives to substance use need to be taught and compassionately offered at these times. These include opportunities to share pain and reestablish connection with others, to prevent or minimize further trauma, to put the developmental crisis into perspective and to undertake the developmental steps necessary to unblock the arrest and reroute the detour along a healthier development path (Gonzales, 1988).

4. Alternatives to psychoactive substance use should be available at all activities of college life. Easy access to sporting facilities at odd hours (evenings, nights), use of relaxation and stress management centers, quality nonalcoholic beverage provision at all academic, social, and sporting events, counseling for dropped courses, and easy availability to time off (with assistance in time management during that time) should be available to students.

5. To create social functions and experiments that foster group bonding and affiliation with same and opposite sex in the company of responsible adult mentors and models *without the availability or "help" from intoxicating chemicals* is the challenge of the present and future on university campuses. Can sporting events and their success or defeat be disassociated from heavy alcohol use by undergraduates and alumni alike? Can "mixers" be chaperoned, modeled and conducted alcohol- and drug-free? Is there a future beyond the keg party? These are beginning questions that can produce creative answers and experiments of the kind that Larimer and Marlatt (1991) are currently performing in the Greek fraternities at the University of Washington. Can we take culturally evolutionary steps of this kind at this moment in history?

6. The double standard needs to be actively addressed (Resnik, 1990). Regional drinking age laws should be observed and enforced by the colleges and universities first at all events sponsored by colleges and taking place on college property. Ongoing debate and

dialogue should take place in colleges in which the rationale for law observance, the dangers of substance abuse, and the positive effects of alternate coping and recreational strategies are emphasized.

7. How are we to build an atmosphere of temperance and learning during the college years without tarnishing our credentials with the young by moralizing? How are we to limit the choices and opportunities for the illicit and often harmful use of psychoactive chemicals for pleasure, or pain or stress reduction without taking on the ills of prohibition and police action? The answers to these questions will not be easy. They should not oversimplify the challenge or the task; they should not be couched in denial or rigidity of a doctrinaire kind; they must not neglect the necessity of ongoing dialogue, the necessity of innovative programming, the importance of self-discovery facilitated by non-chemical means, and the basic need for a spiritual, mind-altering, or out-of-body experience and relief at all stages of life–starting during the college years when the remaining fantasies of childhood must be surrendered and the realities of the adult world faced for the first time without the direct assistance of family (Blos, 1979; Weil, 1982).

8. In this context our students need initiation rites that directly address the physical, psychological, and spiritual needs of the young. Every young person whose family pays tuition or who is granted a loan for higher education deserves to experience safe group and individual rites of passage, into adult life. Indeed this should be a national if not worldwide priority for youth. It would be a tragedy, as it has been in the past, to leave the initiation rites of college life to the young and to the available chemicals alone. Experience has taught us too much. The challenge for the college is to offer an initiation rite, created by the young and their mentors together, that is informed by knowledge, by example, and by healthy tradition (Bly, 1990).

CONCLUSIONS

Late adolescence and early adulthood is a time of great energy and yearning. After separation from family, the college student faces great expectations and possibilities. The brilliance of intellectual performance and the cognitive breakthrough possible to the late adolescent are nothing short of astonishing. The struggle and fervor of later adolescent love and emotional longing and yearning are memorable to all of us who have been through that period and have had the chance to observe those now passing through it. The surge of biological forces, of sexuality, of physical and mental prowess and performance produce envy and amazement in an older generation.

It is small wonder that alcohol and other drugs are used during these years. They are initiatory signals of that emancipation. They liberate, accentuate, and give sudden form to those strengths, longings, and urges–spiritual, intellectual, emotional, and biological. They given sudden relief or solace at a time when great strength is sometimes accompanied by great pain. They provide a lubricant and shape the rough edges of as yet unformed thought, unchanneled physical drives, and awkward, unskilled, unpracticed social and sexual urges and desires. Psychoactive chemicals, when first used, often seem magical to the young in their ability to galvanize or sedate powerful biological, psychological, social, and spiritual drives and forces. Furthermore, today psychoactive chemicals are available in great quantities to the college student with money or access.

The severe casualties in college of mild experimentation with drugs and alcohol during late adolescence are few relative to the total number of students, but the tragedies of their regular use and abuse are great. Approximately 70% to 80% of those students who suffer untimely accidental or suicidal death during the college years, for example, do so under the influence of alcohol or drugs (Rivinus, 1990). The vast majority of students who try alcohol or other drugs will discontinue experimental use and will mature out of an abuse pattern (although some will progress to abuse). But of those who experiment, some will not live long enough to "mature out." Those students regularly using chemicals or who have psychosocial conflicts before they arrive at college are likely to abuse chemicals (i.e., use repeatedly despite adverse circumstances resulting from use) during college. Of those who initiate psychoactive new chemical use during college, a small but significant percent will proceed to abuse or addiction status during college or later in their lives. To stretch towards the ideal of the university in our time we will need to continue to study and not deny this phenomenon, inform ourselves and our students further of the mechanisms and attendant risks of substance use, and offer them compassionate guidance and safer, and more developmentally sound alternatives and rites of passage during the college years.

REFERENCES

Alcoholics Anonymous (AA). (1976). *The Big Book,* New York: Alcoholics Anonymous World Services. American Psychiatric Association (1987). *Diagnostic and Statistical Manual, III–Revised,* pp. 165-186, Washington, DC: Author.

Arnstein, R. L. (1984). Developmental issues for college students. *Psychiatric Annals,* 14(9), 647-651.

Bean-Bayog, M. (1986). Psychopathology produced by alcoholism. In R. E. Meyer (Ed.), *Psychopathology and addictive disorders,* pp. 334-345, New York: The Guilford Press.

Blos, P. (1962). *Adolescence: A psychoanalytic interpretation.* New York: The Free Press.

Blos, P. (1954). Prolonged adolescence: The formulation of a syndrome and its therapeutic implications. *Am. J. Orthopsychiatry,* 24, 733-742.

Blos, P. (1967). The second individuation process of adolescence. *Psychoanalytic Study of the Child,* 22, 162-186.

Blos, P. (1979). *The Adolescent passage.* New York: International Universities Press.

Blos, P. (1980). Modifications in the traditional psychoanalytic theory of female adolescent development. In S. C. Feinsten, P. L. Giovacchini, J. G. Looney et al. (Eds.), *Adolescent psychiatry,* (pp. 8-24), Chicago: University of Chicago Press.

Blum, R. (1987). Contemporary threats to adolescent health in the United States, *JAMA,* 257, 3390-3395.

Bly, R. (1990). *Iron John: A book about men,* (pp. 180-206). Reading, MA: Addison-Wesley Pub. Co., Inc.

Brown, S. (1991). Children of chemically dependent parents: A theoretical crossroads. In T. M. Rivinus (Ed.), *Children of chemically dependent parents: Multiperspectives from the cutting edge,* (pp. 103-130). New York: Brunner/Mazel Inc.

Donovan, J., Jessor, R., & Jessor, S. (1983). Problem drinking in adolescence and young adulthood: A follow-up study. *J. Stud. Alcohol,* 44, 109-137.

Duran, H., & Brooklyn, J. (1988). Inherent problems in substance abuse education on university campuses: Student perspectives. In T. M. Rivinus (Ed.), *Alcoholism/chemical dependency and the college student*, pp. 63-88. New York: The Haworth Press, Inc.

Erikson, E. H. (1956). The problem of ego identity. *J Am Psychoanalytic Assoc.* 4, 56-122.

Erikson, E. H. (1965). *Identity: Youth and crisis*, New York: W. W. Norton & Co., Inc.

Freud, A. (1958). Adolescence. *Psychoanalytic Stud. Child*, 13, 255-278.

Gilligan, C. (1982). *In a different voice: Psychological theory and women's development*. Cambridge, MA: Harvard University Press.

Gilligan, C. (1988). Adolescent development reconsidered. In Carol Gilligan, Jamie Victoria Ward, & Jim McKenn Tayen (Eds.), *Remapping the moral domain: New images of self in relationship*. (pp. vii-xxxviii) Cambridge, MA: Harvard University Press.

Goldman, M. S., Brown, S. A., & Christiansen, B. A. (1987). Expectancy theory: Thinking about drinking. In Howard T. Blane, & Kenneth E. Leonard, (Eds.) *Psychological theories of drinking and alcoholism* (pp. 181-226). New York: The Guilford Press.

Gonzales, E. V. (1988). Integrated treatment approach with the chemically dependent young adult. In T. M. Rivinus (Ed.), *Alcoholism/chemical dependency and the college student* (pp. 147-175). New York: The Haworth Press, Inc.

Group for the Advancement of Psychiatry (1966). *Psychopathological disorders in childhood: Theoretical considerations and a proposed classification*, Vol. VI, Report No. 62 (pp. 83-195). New York: Author.

Jessor, R., & Jessor, S. L. (1977). *Problem behavior and psychosocial development: A longitudinal study of youth*. New York: Academic Press.

Jessor, R., Chase, J. A., & Donovan, J. E. (1980). Psychological correlates of marijuana use and problem drinking in a national sample of adolescents. *Am. J. Public Health*, 70, 604-613.

Johnson, L., O'Malley, D., & Bachman, J. (1987). *National trends in drug use and related factors among American high school students and young adults*, 1975-1986, DHHS Publ. No. (ADM) 87-1535, Washington, D.C.: U.S. Government Printing Office.

Kandel, D. B., & Logan, J. A. (1984). Patterns of drug use from adolescence to young adulthood: Periods of risk for initiation, continued use and discontinuation. *American Journal of Public Health*, 74, 660-666.

Kandel, D. B., Davies, M., Karus, D. et al., (1986). The consequences in young adulthood of adolescent drug involvement. *Arch. Gen. Psychiatry*, 43, 746-754.

Kegan, R. (1982). *The evolving self: Problems and process in human development*, (pp. 86-87) Cambridge, MA: Harvard University Press.

Kleinot, M. C., & Rogers, R. N. (1982). Identifying effective components of alcohol abuse prevention programs. *J. Stud. Alcohol*, 43, 802-811.

Kohlberg, L., & Gilligan, C. (1972). The adolescent as a philosopher. In J. Kagan & R. Coles (Eds.), *Twelve to sixteen: Early adolescence*. New York: Norton.

Larimer, M. E., & Marlatt, G. A. (1991). *Booze, sex, and the Greek system: Examining community reinforcement of high-risk behaviors.* Paper presented at the 25th Annual AABT Convention, Nov. 21-24, New York.

Levinson, D. J. (1977). *The Seasons of a Man's Life.* New York: Knopf.

Levy, J. C., Deykin, E. Y. (1989). Suicidality, depression, and substance abuse in adolescence. *American Psychiatric Association,* pp. 1462-1467.

Loevinger, J. (1976). *Ego development: conceptions and theories,* San Francisco: Jossey-Bass Inc., Publishers.

Mariman, L. A., & Becker, M. H. (1974). The health belief model: Origins and correlates in psychological theory. *Health Education Monographs,* 2, 336-353.

McClellan, D. C. (1975). *Power: The inner experience,* New York: Irving.

Newcomb, M. D. & Bentler, P. M. (1988). *Consequences of adolescent drug use: Impact on the lives of young adults.* Newbury Park, Calif.: Sage Publications Inc.

Offer, D., & Offer, J. (1975). *From teenager to young manhood,* New York: Basic Books, Inc.

Resnik, H. (Ed.) (1990). *Youth and drugs: Society's mixed messages,* OSAP Prevention Monograph-6 Washington, DC: U. S. Department of Health and Human Services.

Ritvo, S. (1976). Adolescent to woman. *J. Am Psychoanalytic Assoc,* 24 (suppl), 127-139.

Rivinus, T. M. (1987). Alcohol and drug abuse in college students. *J. Coll. Stud. Psychotherapy,* 1(4), 5-31.

Rivinus, T. M. (1990). The deadly embrace: The suicidal impulse and substance use and abuse in the college student. *J. Coll. Stud. Psychotherapy* 4, 45-77.

Rivinus, T. M. (1991). Psychoanalytic theory and children of chemically dependent parents: Ships passing in the night? In T. M. Rivinus (Ed.) *Children of chemically dependent parents: Multiperspectives from the cutting edge* (pp. 103-130) New York: Brunner/Mazel, Inc.

Robins, L., Helzer, J., & Przybeck, T. (1986). Substance abuse in the general population. In J. Barrett and R. Rose (Eds.) *The Family therapy of drug abuse and addiction,* New York: The Guilford Press.

Ryan, J. W. (1986). Conference keynote address. Proceedings of the first national conference on campus alcohol policy initiatives (pp. 77-80). Denver, CO: BACCHUS of the U.S., Inc.

Settlage, C. F. (1990). Childhood to adulthood: Structural change in development toward independence and autonomy. In R. A. Nemiroff and C. A. Colarusso (Eds.) *New dimensions in adult development* (pp. 26-46) New York: Basic Books Inc.

Shedler, J. & Block, J. (1990). Adolescent drug use and psychological health: A longitudinal inquiry. *American Psychologist,* 45 (5), 612-630.

Network Planning Group (1987). *Standards of the network of colleges and universities committed to the elimination of drug and alcohol abuse.* Network Planning Group Meeting, September 21-22. Revised at a Meeting of College Presidents, December 9, 1987, Revised at a Meeting of the Higher Education

Secretariat January 5, 1988, and Revised at the Network Planning Group Meeting, February 2, 1988.

Steele, C. M., & Josephs, R. A. (1990). Alcohol myopia: Its prized and dangerous effects. *American Psychologist,* 45 (8), 921-933.

Suchman, D., & Broughton, E. (1988). Treatment alternatives for university students with substance use/abuse problems. In T. M. Rivinus (Ed.), *Alcoholism/chemical dependency and the college student* (pp. 131-136). New York: The Haworth Press, Inc.

Vaillant, G. (1977). *Adaptation to life.* Boston: Little, Brown & Co.

Wegscheider-Cruse, S. (1989). *Another chance: Hope and help for the alcoholic family* (pp. 104-115). Palo Alto, CA: Science and Behavior Books.

Weil, A. (1982). *The natural mind: An investigation of drugs and the higher consciousness.* Boston: Houghton Mifflin Co.

Winnicott, D. W. (1953). Transitional objects and transitional phenomena. Published in the *International Journal of Psycho-Analysis,* 34 (2) (1953) pp. 89-97.

Chapter 9

College Student Development:
African Americans Reconsidered

Harold E. Cheatham
Linda Berg-Cross

SUMMARY. In this chapter we briefly discuss the history of United States higher education and college student development theory, identify some deficiencies and provide perspectives on the concepts of Eurocentricity and Africentricity. We then set forth a rationale and proposed intervention model for the intentional and systematic intellective and psychosocial development of the African American college student.

HISTORICAL PERSPECTIVE

The ostensible purpose of education in America has been students' development. Education, as originally conceived, was focused on students' moral development; social usefulness was later adopted as an equally important educational goal. Education in America also reflected cleavages along social class, regional (i.e., north/south), and political-"racial" lines. Children of the rich

Harold E. Cheatham, PhD, NCC, is Professor of Education and Coordinator, College Student Personnel Option in Counselor Education program at The Pennsylvania State University, 311 CEDAR Building, University Park, PA 16802-3110. Linda Berg-Cross, PhD, ABPP, is Professor of Psychology and Director of Clinical Training in the Psychology Department, Howard University, Washington, DC 20059.

received a qualitatively different education than those of the poor who, if educated at all, "were prepared solely for their limited stations in life" (Hofstadter, Miller, & Aaron 1959; p. 111). The origin and perpetuation of the two class system of education in the United States is epitomized in a quote attributed by Hofstadter et al. to a liberal minister who "bluntly distinguished the abilities of the base-born and the well-born" averring that: "Their bodies are *human*, but they are *brute* all beside . . . Those of lower class can go but a little ways into their inquiries into the natural and moral constitution of the world" (Hofstadter et al. 1959, p. 111) (emphases in original text).

Without religion as a strong organizing force or motive to create interest in learning, educational developments in the south generally lagged behind those in the northern colonies. Some basic *instruction* was provided for children of the poor but *education* was reserved for the children of the rich (Hofstadter et al.; 1959). The cleavages are perhaps even more dramatic when one considers the legal prohibition of education for African Americans and the belated and grudging post-"Civil" War establishment of separate educational opportunities for young men and women of African descent. Penn School (now Penn Center) established by the Quakers at St. Helena, South Carolina in 1862, and termed by its current director as ". . . symbolic of the inequities that still exist between the races in this nation" (Schneider, 1991; p. 22), and Ashmun Institute (now Lincoln University, Pennsylvania) founded in 1854 as America's first institution with an international design and with meager and limited support (Harris, Figgures, & Carter, 1975) exemplify America's educational legacy to African Americans.

Education was regarded more as a necessity than as an ornament in theocratic, colonial America. In the eighteenth century, the introduction of secular subjects modified but did not replace the religious emphasis prevalent in seventeenth century education. "Nurseries" for ministers, as Harvard College was termed at its founding in 1636, were intended to instill "right conduct" and ensure students' moral development (Hofstadter et al.; 1959).

In the nations' earliest educational institutions commitment to students' development was enunciated as the legal concept *in loco parentis* and implemented through rather rigidly enforced behavioral norms. Throughout the nineteenth and the early twentieth century an emphasis on moral development prevailed. Empowered to act in behalf of parents and in the best interest of students, institutional representatives were neither obliged nor disposed to consult with their preadolescent and adolescent charges about how to best serve students' development.

In loco parentis, which Moore and Upcraft have termed the "original student development theory" (1990, p. 4) met its demise during the 1960s "student revolution." However, it was first to yield to modifications promoting attention both to students' intellectual *and* social development. These modifications were enunciated in such documents as the 1937 and 1949 Student Personnel Point of View which focused on "the unique and peculiar characteristics of programs that help college adolescents to achieve self-development" (Williamson, 1961, p. 20). This position statement elevated students to the status of co-participants in their own development while the institution was to continue to provide the requisite environs and opportunities. The 1949 Student Personnel Point of View sharpened the focus to specifically address the importance of collegiate instruction and complementary and specific student personnel programming that promotes socialization and development to prepare the individual for full growth and maximum service in the society.

Importantly, these events were taking place at a time when postwar U.S. society was being obliged to move toward more liberal and inclusive policies. This occurred in the "Truman era" when desegregation of the U.S. Armed Forces had been initiated by presidential directive and when U.S. higher education had been implored by The President's Commission on Higher Education (1947) to appraise and clarify its aims and societal role. Asserting that a goal of education is ". . . to ensure equal liberty and equal opportunity to differing individuals and groups, . . ." (p. 5), the Commission noted that: "Perhaps [education's] most important role is to serve as an instrument of social transition, and its responsibilities are defined in terms of the kind of civilization society hopes to build" (p. 6).

THEORIES OF COLLEGE STUDENT DEVELOPMENT

Student development theory is a specific psychology derived from theories of human development with a special focus on developmental changes occurring throughout the phase of the life cycle of one termed "student."

Poised to offer equal liberty and opportunity to diverse individuals and groups, postwar U. S. higher education needed to move radically beyond its elitist and class-bound traditions to effect understanding of the characteristics and functioning of students whose ranks increasingly comprised veterans and other non-traditional matriculants.

The early 1960s have been noted as a period of significant scholarship addressing college students' growth and development and, more specifically, the relationship between that development and intellectual, social, environmental, and relational influences (Moore, & Upcraft, 1990). Specific foci on the role of culture and gender are missing from the early theories and developmental models; rather the models and theories have been advanced and empirically validated as if culture and gender were constants.

Partly out of: ". . . exasperation at the tendency of many academicians to treat the student as a kind of "blackbox" Astin developed a theory of student involvement (1984, p. 299). He described traditional pedagogical theories, which he termed (a) subject matter theory, (b) resource theory, and (c) individualized or eclectic theory, respectively as assigning students a passive role in the learning process; being unproductively competitive for a limited resource (i.e., bright students); and expensive to implement as well as difficult to define with precision. Citing such behavioral terms as attachment, commitment, devotion, engagement, and participation, Astin (1984) explicated involvement theory in five basic postulates: (1) Involvement refers to the investment of physical and psychological energy in various general as well as specific objects; (2) Involvement occurs along a continuum; (3) Involvement has both quantitative and qualitative features; (4) The amount of student development and personal learning associated with any educational program is directly proportional to the quality and quantity of student involvement; and (5) The effectiveness of any educational policy or practice is directly related to the capacity of that policy or practice to increase student involvement. Astin suggested that the final two postulates are key, in that, embedded in them are clues for designing more educational programs. Assaying the elegance of his theory, Astin averred that Involvement theory, concerned as it is with behavioral processes, is more directly observable and measurable than is the concept of motivation and that the theory subtly encourages educators to focus more on students' behavioral actions than on the effects of their own interventions.

Another widely used theory of student development was advanced by Chickering (1969; 1981) who proposed that student development is an *intentional* intervention that promotes such capacities as clear values, integrity, communication skills, critical thinking and synthesis, a sense of tolerance and interdependence, empathy, understanding and cooperation, and a capacity for intimacy that goes beyond mere competence and tolerance. In postulations similar to Astin's, Chickering proposed that the student's basic personal identity development would be facilitated through appropriate programmatic interventions. He conceptualized collegiate institutions as developmental communities, and recognized that students are not homogeneous but developmentally different from one another. Chickering posed the question of the consequence of taking this human development as the unifying purpose of higher education; as well as the consequences that accrue to the individual and the society when there is greater awareness of the interactions between self and system.

Chickering's model is interactive; it contains seven vectors: (a) developing competence, (b) managing emotions, (c) developing autonomy, (d) establishing identity, (e) freeing interpersonal relationships, (f) clarifying purposes, and (g) developing integrity. The collegiate environment then is postulated as providing the conditions which facilitate students' development along the vectors. Among the experiences postulated as focusing and nurturing behavior that, in turn, provokes introspection and growth are: (a) clarity and consistency of objectives; (b) redundancy which occurs as a function of institutional size; (c) choice and flexibility in curriculum, teaching and evaluation; (d) residence hall arrangements which foster interpersonal relationships; (e) positive faculty-student and student administration interactions; and (f) a student culture which complements a positive academic environment (Knefelkamp, Widick, & Parker, 1978).

Throughout the 60s and early 70s African American scholars increasingly criticized existing and emerging theories and models that did not address the specific sociocultural experiences of ethnic minority persons and women. That challenge, joined by other ethnic minority scholars and women, has been comprehensive and effective and is now commonplace. Yet much of current human development theory does not reflect the reality of a multicultural society. Astin (1982; 1984) seems to have recognized the limitations of existing theories in asserting that a likely reason for the notable failure of attempts at extending educational opportunities to "underprepared students" (a euphemism used then and now to refer primarily to ethnic minorities) was the continued adherence by most faculty members to the subject matter theory of learning (i.e., students' development depended primarily upon exposure to the right subject matter). Similar assent accompanies Chickering's (1969) note that students are developmentally different, not homogeneous. Neither of these widely used theories of student development specifically accommodates ethnic, gender or cultural differences as they relate to engagement in and completion of developmental tasks.

The Student Developmental Task and Lifestyle Inventory (SDTLI; Winston, Miller, & Prince, 1987) and its predecessor, Student Developmental Task Inventory (Winston, Miller & Prince, 1979) are the most widely used instruments to assess Chickering's theory of psychosocial development of college students. Citing numerous researchers, Miller and Winston and reported that the SDTLI provides ". . . considerable evidence to support the contention that college students *as a group* [italics added] share common challenges and that development is coherent and predictable" (1990, p. 102). Despite that claim, there exists little evidence that the identity development of African American, and other ethnic minority students is accounted for in the aggregate research data.

A significant problem is that U.S. higher education has not really changed with time. Despite some accommodation following from 60s protest movements for curricula of relevance, curricula remain traditional and "relevant" courses remain peripheral to rather than incorporated in the educational enterprise. Or they are implemented in ways that still permit students to complete baccalaureate degree study without having come to terms with the substance of the protests, let alone with immersion in "diversity options" recently invented on U.S. campuses and recently challenged by traditionalists as capitulation to "political correctness." Similarly, students in training in mental health and related human services are being credentialed without comprehension of cultural diversity and alternates to traditional, Eurocentric models of intervention.

The real and yet unfulfilled purpose of education is to humanize, to free citizens, a convention which requires curricular structure and contour in conformance with student development and related social and behavioral evidence/research findings.

PERSPECTIVES
ON AFRICAN AMERICAN COLLEGE STUDENTS

African American student development is arguably distinct from student development in general and hence development of this cohort is not adequately accommodated in existing theories and models of college student development. Over the recent decade attempts have been made to extend theories and models to incorporate and explain gender and ethnic/cultural differences (Baldwin, 1981; 1984; Baldwin, Duncan, & Bell, 1987; Cheatham, 1990; Cross, 1971; Helms, 1984; Parham, 1989).

Developmental differences have been reported in studies using the SDTLI to assess African American students. Cheatham, Slaney, and Coleman (1990); and Jordan-Cox (1987) reported gender differences not reported in studies of White students. Jordan-Cox (1987) found African American women preceding their male counterparts in interpersonal relationships, autonomy, and life purpose. Further, she noted that first year students differed on 9 of 12 variables while seniors differed from each other on only three variables—all in the area termed interpersonal relationships. In Jordan-Cox's conclusions there is the suggestion that characteristics in the collegiate environs may have effected the differences noted. That notion, is consistent with the nurturing experiences postulated by Chickering (cited in Knefelkamp et al., 1978).

Cheatham et al. (1990), found seniors, whether attending the historically Black collegiate (HBC) or predominantly White institution (PWI), ahead of other students on SDTLI indices of Educational Involvement, Career Planning and Life Management. Differences also were reported for Cultural Participation and Emotional Autonomy. The results of the Salubrious Lifestyle (i.e., sense of well-being) favored students at the HBC's. The role of ethnic and cultural influences in psychosocial development was not clear in that study. However, it is clear that the characteristics that distinguish ethnic minority students from their counterparts must be taken into account in concepts and programs designed to promote students' development.

INSTITUTIONAL ROLE IN STUDENTS' DEVELOPMENT

College students undergo rapid and profound developmental changes as they mature from teenagers into young adults. During the journey through college, reasoning abilities are sharpened, political consciousness is raised, intimacy skills are cultivated, careers are chosen, and identities are chiseled with a renewed and deepened vigor. A successful college experience is one that transforms and enriches the lives of the students through a series of challenging, developmental tasks.

African American students must rally to these developmental challenges while at the same time struggling with additional developmental concerns related to their racial and cultural identity. They must find a way to be part of the majority culture without either compromising or abandoning their ethnic heritage; to endorse the values of their collegiate institution without endorsing historic and/or "new racism"; to fashion an acceptable American dream without accepting a second class image. To examine the course of African American college student development requires that the reader first have a national perspective on the problems faced by ethnic minorities, in general, in U. S. higher education. Before discussing the more psychological aspects of racial identity and personal growth, it is imperative to develop comprehension of the developmental issues of such students at a systemic, institutional level. Only within this cultural context can the dynamics of psychological development be appreciated and appropriate interventions designed and implemented.

At a systemic level, college student development occurs in three phases: (a) enrollment; (b) persistence in college once they start attending; and (c) attainment of a specific degree certifying all college requirements have been met. Higher education has failed African Americans at each institutional stage.

Among U. S. high school graduates 26% of African Americans enroll in college compared to a 34% rate for Caucasian students (National Center for Education Statistics, 1988). Further, considering that over 25% of African American high school students drop out before graduation (American Council of Education, 1988), it is even more imperative to increase the number of students who enter college, persist, and graduate in a timely manner.

Persistence in college is another problem that African American students face. The rate at which these students leave college before earning the first degree has increased between 1972 and 1986. The oft quoted statistic that enumerates more African American males incarcerated in the U. S. penal system than on college campuses attests to the seriousness of the problem of the unaddressed educational needs of this cohort. The two most prevalent factors associated with college attrition are low social-economic status (SES) and low academic abilities. Only 23% of low SES students complete a four year degree in less than six years. Only 14% of students with low academic ability complete the requirements for a four year degree in less than six years. Among high academic ability African American students, 47% drop out of public colleges and a more disturbing 60% drop out of private colleges.

Reschooling students to prepare them for college work was initiated as early as the 1840s for poorly educated farm boys (Nevins, cited in Fenske; 1981). Utilization of that early convention is even more important today as part of the mission of all institutions of higher learning that proclaim their commitment to increased minority enrollment and graduation. Helping low socio-economic students pay for college was, at one point, a priority of the national government. There is evidence that, for students who come from poor families to succeed in college, financial support is critical The National Institute of Intercollegiate Colleges and Universities (NIICU) analysis revealed that among all students who were given federal grants, 90% return for a second semester. Without federal grants, only 75% of the students return. The really dramatic figure occurs for African Americans who are not given a federal grant–only 30% return for a second semester. The NIICU data are particularly striking when it is noted that their analysis is only of grants in federal aid (i.e., students who received aid from the institution or other sources were not deleted from the "no funding" group.) This procedure undoubtedly results in an underestimate of the number of African American students who leave school because of burdening debt or inability to pay.

Motivation and goals of the students are other variables that have been shown to predict academic performance of African Americans (Clark & Plotkin, 1964). Considerable research effort has been directed toward assessing how well standardized test scores and grade point averages predict success for African Americans. Overall, the results indicate these standardized indices are far more likely to predict the success of White than of African American students (Sowa, Thomas, & Bennett, 1989).

The most important question for collegiate institutions to ponder may be, "How successful are we at getting African American students to graduate?" Historically, colleges on the whole have graduated only 50-55% of each freshman class over a four year period, regardless of race. Currently the overall rate of graduation for all students, six years after freshman matriculation is 41%; for African Americans and Hispanics that rate drops to 25% and 30%, respectively.

Social class and academic ability are important factors associated with persistence in college and attainment of a degree, but are factors that universities cannot affect directly. Many factors within the institution's control have been linked to academic success but only a few have been subjected to systematic and rigorous study. Intercollegiate athletic participation has long been postulated to have a positive impact on interpersonal and social skills and the motivation to complete one's degree. Some empirical support for this comes from a study by Pascarella and Smart (1981) who found that African American athletes were more likely than their non-athletic counterparts to obtain a high status job early in their careers.

Another factor repeatedly associated with persistence and success in attaining a degree is the extent to which students identify with and feel comfortable with the institution they are attending. Because of the perceived and/or real racism that exists on many predominantly White campuses, it has been concluded that African American students would prosper more in traditionally African American institutions (cf., Baldwin, 1987; Fleming, 1984). Yet, research on this point remains inconclusive (Cheatham, Slaney & Coleman, 1990).

African Americans constitute only 10% of the nation's college students and 73% of that cohort attend predominantly White institutions (PWI) (National Center for Education Statistics, 1988). Fifty-one percent of the baccalaureate degrees however are granted to African Americans who attend historically Black colleges and universities (HBC). That is, an African American student is twice as likely to graduate from an HBC than from a predominantly White university (American Council of Education, 1985). Caution is required with this observation since contradictory data have been reported over a nine year period by Astin (1982) who reported that nationwide 67% of African American students who enroll in PWIs graduate compared with 65% who attend HBCs.

Is there some "magic bullet" offered by the Black colleges and universities? Do predominantly White colleges have toxic factors that disproportionately affect African American students? Is there a difference in motivation or academic preparedness between students who choose to go to the two different types of institutions?

There is general agreement that many African American students feel conflict and isolation at White institutions (Fleming, 1984). Yet, there is some evidence that the advising process and/or compliance with the advising process may dramatically differ between the two institutions. Williams and Leonard (1988) found that many African American students take "easy" courses outside their major requirements while dropping more difficult courses within their majors. While they may appear to have adequate grade point aver-

ages, they fail to graduate because they do not fulfill course requirements in their selected major. Also, many of the majors that
may be most attractive to African Americans are closed to them
because of low scores on the Scholastic Aptitude Test (SAT). Thus,
students may end up majoring in a field that has not truly captured
their interest although results from standardized tests suggest that the
"forced" academic major is consistent with the student's ability.

AMERICAN STUDENT DEVELOPMENT
AND CURRICULAR INTERVENTION

African American students frequently characterize the predominantly White collegiate environment as rejecting or only superficially accommodating to their interests. What they are suggesting
in such evaluations is that the western values, ethos, beliefs and
sociocultural traditions predominate; that little evidence exists to
suggest that other world views and values are appreciated and taken
into account in dominant societal institutions. A cursory look at an
institution's published student activities calendar can quickly and
unfailingly inform one of the cultural perspective through which the
curriculum and co-curriculum have been derived.

A western world view values competition more than cooperation,
individuation more than interdependence, mastery over nature more
than harmony or complementarity with nature, and theoretically, at
least, it emphasizes rigid adherence to time. Eurocentrism assumes
cultural homogeneity or ". . . belief in the comparative superiority
of Anglo-American culture in particular and Euro-American culture
in general" (Jackson, 1986; p. 32). As such, students from other
cultures often find their culture, and its various forms and components diminished or excepted. A recent example serves the intended
point. African American students in a church-related Chicago high
school elected to have a separate prom despite alleged threats of
expulsion for doing so after reputedly having had their input regarding the prom music for the "all-school" prom rejected. National news reports suggested that White students felt hurt and
abandoned by those students who wouldn't accede to the majority

will; that is, to the will of the dominant culture to have a Euro-centric prom.

African Americans are not a monolith although they share a common sociocultural history and experience based upon negative attribution to color and ethnicity, and to some extent on the slavery experience. The concept Africentrism argues that despite enforced isolation, denied education and other insidious aspects of slavery, an ethos that has a sturdy base in African form and tradition survived and is manifested in values, beliefs, and ethos that are the legacy of African Americans.

Africentrism, in contrast with Eurocentrism, places emphasis on interdependence rather than on individualism and stresses affiliation, collectivity, respect for elders and obedience to authority. Boykin (1983) identified a set of values retained from an African belief system that characterize contemporary African American culture. The most discernible and important include: (1) a rhythmic-music-involvement orientation; (2) an emphasis on affect; (3) communalism; (4) expressive individualism (i.e., self-assured in personal esthetics); (5) a social time perspective; (6) orality, and person-to-person orientation (p. 342). Collegiate environments that do not acknowledge and incorporate the cultural value of African American and other ethnic minority students retard rather than promote these students' psychosocial development.

In an effort to fulfill the mission of higher education, universities and colleges are entering the 90s with an emphasis on diversifying the traditional curriculum to include the contributions of minority members. All students learn more quickly and more in depth when they feel the material being presented is personally relevant. However, the diversification of curricula should best be viewed as a developmental process, in itself. There are simple and more advanced levels of diversification. An ideal college experience would foster the intellectual development of the student in tandem with the student's political consciousness. There are at least five different levels of diversification possible in liberal arts curricula.

Level I includes all the special "topic" courses that expose students to their own ancestry. Many students still graduate high school without even a minimal understanding of their racial and cultural history. For these students, an Africentric curriculum is one that helps them claim their cultural heritage through history, stories, art, music, philosophy, and the study of contemporary issues. An Africentric curriculum is available at many institutions across the country where African and African American Studies Programs exist. Such programs must be at the very foundation of a diversified curriculum because a strong, well developed conceptual understanding of oneself presages the capacity to empathize with and find commonalties with one's fellow beings.

As students mature in their understanding of the curriculum the nature, goals, and subject matter of the curriculum also mature. Level I is the nurturing level at which information is literally fed into the hungry, receptive mind. They should be available without any prior prerequisites.

At the next level are courses that integrate the history and culture of people of color into the standard curricula. A course in psychology would include the work of relevant minority psychologists. Level II curricula are more demanding for the teacher, but not for the student. Texts and teaching materials are still not readily available in most subject areas and so the teacher/scholar researcher has to methodically devise course syllabi to reflect the contributions of ethnic minority scholars to particular academic disciplines.

The student who has mastered the material in Levels I and II has the vocabulary and background experiences prerequisite to Level III instruction. Level III is the level of empathic understanding and is based on understanding material from the perspective of the scholar who produced it. At the simplest level, this might involve being exposed to scholars who have studied intelligence and "intelligence" testing from a strictly Eurocentric perspective and those who have studied it from different perspectives. Here students are not just being exposed to "contributing scholars who are people of color." They are being exposed to the life blood of innovation–a conceptual understanding of critical events based on the life perspective of the scholar. It is at this level that the spiritual/intellectual links between personal reality and culture are created, forged, and maintained.

The most advanced level of instruction involves fostering transcultural understanding. Empathic understanding is but one step on the path to human understanding. It is an important, vital, inescapable step. However, once a student has mastered Level III, a diversified curriculum takes the spotlight off the two cultures being contrasted in Level III and beams it on a multiple cultural/multi constituency perspective. The student who develops the capacity to apprehend "bystander interventions" from a White and Black perspective, can begin to understand it from an Asian perspective, or Republican perspective or young person's perspective. The reality of multiple realities becomes a pressing intellectual puzzle and students who hear information at this level will ask the critical question, "But what are the implications of this policy (product, idea, etc.) from the perspective of the other people who will be affected?" Clearly, some courses are organized such that all four levels of understanding are in constant interplay. For faculty attempting to reorganize their curricula, a developmental approach may make the task more manageable.

When students are exposed to all four levels, each of which has been amply complemental by co-curricular programs and emphases on African and African American culture, form, beliefs and ethics, we have a well educated individual with a thorough grounding in the realities relevant for intelligent living in the twenty-first century.

INSTITUTIONAL INTERVENTIONS

What seems to be generally true is that many African American students on many predominantly White college campuses have a deep sense of alienation. This alienation is an additional burden and has been hypothesized to contribute to these students' disproportionate dropout rate. Yet, researchers acknowledge that there is enormous diversity among African American students, particularly in relation to how comfortable and/or alienated they are from the majority of students on campus.

Nettles and Johnson (1987) concluded that African American and White students have different developmental needs regarding peer group relations, academic integration and satisfaction with the collegiate experience, and thus that differential approaches are necessary in collegiate institutions addressing ethnic group members' socialization needs.

One factor that appears critical in facilitating retention rates among African Americans is the availability of mentors and role models (DeFour, 1991). Blackwell (1981) reported that the number of African American faculty was the most important predictor of first year African American student enrollment as well as the total number of African American students graduated. Students generally, and particularly many ethnic minority and first-generation college-going students, need someone to assist them in attending to their academic interests, cutting through red tape and gaining inside information (i.e., to provide "legibility") (c.f., Trippi & Cheatham, 1991). The lack of appropriate ethnic/professional role models on campus hinders the African American student because mentors tend to seek out proteges who are perceived to be similar to themselves (Kanter, 1977). When cross-race, mentor-protege relationships are developed, they are often not as supportive or beneficial as same-race mentor-protege relationships (Sanders, 1991). Faculty who are committed to mentoring African American students must go out of their way to let the student know that they believe in them, respect them, and want them to succeed. Miville (1991) suggested that, in support of students' development, faculty give interested students encouragement in coauthoring papers, presenting at professional meetings, and that they introduce students to other professionals who can assist their career development.

Several writers have provided evidence that African American students are responsive to a variety of interventions and particularly to those which authenticate the student's sense of self and which provide the students with a sense of genuine community on White campuses (cf., Carroll, 1988; Cheatham, Tomlinson & Ward, 1990; Jones, 1985; Locke & Zimmerman, 1987). Locke and Zimmerman (1987) reported that a program predicated on a theory of human development promoted significant growth in ego development in African American students. Those student volunteers trained as peer counselors to their counterparts registered positive gains in moral reasoning. Locke and Zimmerman (1987) noted that counseling about racial issues triggered more intense responses among peer counselors and resulted in less objective levels of reasoning. That effect noted, they concluded that psychological growth among African American students may be a key to enhancing these students' success on White campuses. From the aggregate research it seems safe to conclude that ethnic minority students face different developmental tasks, engage in these in different orders and with differing intensities. Identity development looms as a specific task faced by ethnic minority students and as such ought to be incorporated into stage development theory.

Yet another factor influencing the degree of alienation African Americans report on predominantly White campuses is how much pre-college interracial experience the student has. The sparse research on this point is at first puzzling. Some surveys have shown that the more interracial experiences a student has before college, the less alienated they will feel when they arrive at a predominantly White campus (Pascarella & Terenzini, 1991). Others have shown (Allen, 1985) that prior interracial experiences are unrelated to feelings of social isolation. Such contradictions are to be expected unless the quality of prior interracial experiences is controlled for in these studies.

Without regard to the attitude with which students enter a campus, interracial friendships are more likely to blossom if the campus environment emphasizes cooperative, interactive, multicultural programs and activities. Scant research on the effects of interracial friendship in college supports this assertion but there is an important body of research on the factors that promote interracial friendships in the elementary school years. Repeatedly, these studies show that classroom climates that encourage interaction create stable interracial friendships (Hansell & Slavin, 1981; Hallihan & Williams, 1987). At the college level, diversification workshops and so-termed "politically correct" course readings ultimately may do much less for the promotion of exuberant, genuine, interracial friendships than might genuinely integrated dorm rooms, social activities, and working subgroups within classrooms, laboratory courses, and discussion sections. The intended inference is that there will be an inverse relationship between genuine interracial friendships and the sense of alienation that an African American student generally experiences on a predominantly White campus.

This assertion does not diminish the critical role of Africentric organizations in providing social supports and an ethnic "home-ground." Rather, it argues that the option to affiliate also in familiar environs and contexts is a critical complement to the collegiate social experiences that alleviate one's sense of alienation.

Data are needed on the role of quality interracial friendships. Observations and reports of students suggest that on most campuses such friendships are exceptional rather than ordinary. If we are correct in positing that interracial friendships would lead to decreased alienation and increased success at college, we would expect to find successful African American seniors more likely to have such interracial friendships. A study that examined this issue, albeit indirectly (Steard, Jackson, & Jackson, 1990) found that successful African American seniors at predominantly White universities tended to be loners (the study didn't examine the extent of intra and inter racial friendships). The students did not report high needs for affiliation or affection and valued their peers primarily for their information value. Within this group of seniors, the greater the expressed desire for affection and support from their White classmates, the greater was the likelihood for these students to report feeling alienated.

Fulfilling affiliation needs has been posited as one of the nine developmental tasks of African American students (McEwen, Roper, Bryant, & Langa, 1990). When students choose to fulfill those needs by interracial dating, other developmental tasks are likely to be differentially affected as well (e.g., developing racial and ethnic identity, interacting with the dominant culture and developing identity).

There is virtually no current literature on interracial dating on today's college campuses. The only reported survey in the past ten years was reported in 1986 (Clark, Windley, Jones, & Ellis, 1986). Clark et al. found in two largely White Southern universities that more African American men than African American women preferred to date interracially, but very few African American men or women were involved in such dating. Our telephone conversations with the counseling centers of several large universities confirm that interracial dating does exist to some small extent on college campuses, more often between international students and White students but occasionally between African Americans and Whites. In the latter instance, the most common interracial dating pattern is between African American men and White women. This pattern is still very prevalent in high schools around the country.

It has been suggested that popular, athletic African American men gain increased prestige by dating White women and that White women date a higher status African American men than they could successfully compete for among White men. Examining this notion, Murstein, Merighi and Malloy (1989) reported that, among interracial courting couples, the African American member was judged to be significantly more physically attractive than the White member. Skin color operated as an exchange variable in the relationships, and as racial prejudice weakened so did the relevance of skin color.

While the dominant behavioral pattern is for African American men to date White women, Korolewicz and Korolewicz (1985) found, contrary to Clark et al. (1986), that among African Americans, the women were more apt to prefer interracial dating while, among the whites, men preferred interracial dating. It is unclear if this is a spurious result or if there is a real dichotomy between dominant interracial dating preferences and dominant interracial behavior patterns within each group. Indeed, among professionals, many African American women are dating White men due, reportedly, to the paucity of African American men of a similar occupational status.

Other factors potentially effective in modulating feelings of alienation on a predominantly White campus and increasing academic success include career orientation, athletic involvement, involvement in campus social activities, degree of affiliation with the minority community on campus and off campus, and individual factors such as introversion/extraversion and stability/instability.

IMPLICATIONS

1. Universities must help African American students face the universal developmental tasks of identity formation, intimacy skills,

career skills, etc. These tasks have long been recognized as important educational goals.

2. Universities must also help those African American students who have academic deficits with academic skills development. However, they must not stigmatize those students who are not in need of such services by implying or asserting that their success depends on utilizing and/or valuing such services. The art of offering the right service to the right client rests on a careful, thorough assessment of each student.

3. Collegiate institutions simply cannot successfully educate without assisting African American students in dealing with the concomitant task of emerging both as an adult and as an ethnic minority.

4. Success in college has been related to successful mentoring relationships. All students and particularly many African American and other ethnic minority students need the opportunity to develop comfortable mentor relationships within the university. There are not enough African American faculty to mentor all the undergraduates who desire and/or need this relationship. Indeed, such mentoring should not be a task solely of minority faculty although there is evidence that same race mentoring experiences are often the most valuable for minority students. Counselors can be very effective in creating mentoring pyramids so that each African American freshman is assigned an upper class (i.e., junior or senior) minority mentor, who could meet as a group with a minority faculty or staff member (for example, see Locke & Zimmerman, 1987).

5. Success in college depends upon feeling "at home" socially. Great diversity exists among African American students as to the importance each personally attaches to ethnicity, how difficult it is to move between the two cultures and how psychologically invested they are in each culture. Counselors must assess each African American student on each of these three dimensions (importance of ethnicity, degree of biculturation, and level of immersion). The questions to ask freshmen are simple and straight-forward and will help construct appropriate programs. For example, a Likert-type questionnaire (on a seven point scale with 1 = not at all important; 4 = moderately important, and 7 = of the utmost importance)

similar to the following could be administered at freshmen orientations:

a. How important for you is it to learn more about your heritage and ancestry while you are at college?
b. How important for you is it to be spiritually close to your ethnic peers at the university?
c. How important for you is it to learn more about the heritage and ancestry of other ethnic groups while you are at college?
d. How important for you is it to you to develop close friendships with people of a different ethnic group than your own?
e. How easy is it for you to make friends within your own ethnic group?
f. How easy is it for you to make friends with individuals from other ethnic groups?

Students who express a need and desire to be integrated into the wider university context should be nurtured in that direction. Students who express a need and desire to have the support and comfort of a peer ethnic group should be nurtured in that direction. Most students will likely need nurturing in both areas. However, in an era of limited resources, programs should be geared to meet the most pressing needs of the study body. Counselors need to assist African American students attending predominantly white collegiate institutions to have both their ethnic support systems and an integrated college experience.

6. Minority students should have the opportunity to get vocational testing early during their freshman year. Their program should be monitored to ensure that they are meeting their major requirements in a timely, normative manner.

7. Students should have an identified person in the counseling office who attends to financial problems. Often students need emotional support and problem solving strategies to deal with loans, budgets, and family financial pressures. Many who would never go to see a therapist would venture into a less portentous "SOS Money Ship."

8. Campuses need to develop rituals that link the university with the student and their cultural references groups. Everything from

homecoming to foods served in the cafeteria to "sayings" and inclusionary messages on sweatshirts need to be broadened to appeal to students who otherwise will become disenfranchised.

9. Counselors need to address racial concerns in the very beginning of counseling. Goals in integration and ethnic identity development need to be explored as viable, valuable goals.

10. Counselors need to monitor the extent of alienation that exists on their campuses. Assessment of alienation would include monitoring reported feelings of isolation, lack of comfort in class and in social activities, and reported incidents of racist individual as well as institutional policies and practices. Counselors need to work with students to develop specific action agendas that will reduce alienation without creating discriminatory, isolationist policies and practices.

REFERENCES

Allen, W. R. (1985). Black student, White campus: Structurally interpersonal, and psychological correlations of success. *Journal of Negro Education, 54,* 134-147.

American Council on Education (1988). *Minorities in higher education.* (Seventh Annual Status Report). Washington, D.C., Author.

Astin, A. W. (1982). *Minorities in American higher education.* San Francisco: Jossey-Bass Inc., Publishers.

Astin, A. W. (1984). Student involvement: A developmental theory for higher education. *Journal of College Student Personnel, 25,* 297-308.

Baldwin, J. A. (1981). Notes on an Afrocentric theory of personality. *The Western Journal of Black Studies, 5,* 172-179.

Baldwin, J. A. (1984). African self-consciousness and the mental health of African-Americans. *Journal of Black Studies, 15,* 174-194.

Baldwin, J. A. (1987). African psychology and Black personality testing. *The Negro Educational Review, 38,* 56-65.

Baldwin, J. A., Duncan, J. A. & Bell, Y. (1987). Assessment of African self-consciousness among Black students from two college environments. *The Journal of Black Psychology, 13,* 27-41.

Blackwell, J. E. (1981). *Mainstreaming outsiders: The production of Black professionals.* Bayside: General Hall.

Boykin, A.W. (1983). The academic performance of Afro-American children. In J. T. Spence (Ed.), *Achievement and achievement motives: Psychological and sociological approaches* (pp. 321-371). San Francisco: W. W. Freeman.

Carroll, J. (1988). Freshman retention and attrition factors at a predominantly

Black urban community college. *Journal of College Student Development, 29,* 52-59.

Cheatham, H. E. (1990). Africentricity and career development of African Americans. *Career Development Quarterly, 38,* 334-346.

Cheatham, H. E., Slaney, R. B., & Coleman, N. C. (1990). Institutional effects on the psychosocial development of African-American college students. *Journal of Counseling Psychology, 37,* 453-458.

Cheatham, H. E., Tomlinson, S. M., & Ward, T. J. (1990). The African self-consciousness construct and African American students. *Journal of College Student Development, 31,* 492-499.

Chickering, A. (1969). *Education and identity.* San Francisco: Jossey-Bass Inc., Publishers.

Chickering, A. W., & Havighurst, R. J. (1981). The life cycle. In A. W. Chickering & Associates (Eds.), *The modern American college* (pp.16-50). San Francisco: Jossey-Bass Inc., Publishers.

Clark, K. B., & Plotkin, L. (1964). *The Negro student at integrated colleges.* New York: National Scholarship Service and Fund for Negro students.

Clark, M., Windley, L., Jones, L., & Ellis, S. (1986). Dating patterns of Black students on White Southern campuses. *Journal of Multicultural Counseling and Development, 14,* 85-93.

Cross, W. E., Jr. (1971). The Negro-to-Black conversion experience: Toward a psychology of Black liberation. *Black World, 20,* 13-27.

DeFour, D. (1991). Issues in mentoring ethnic minority students. *Focus, 5,* 1-2.

Fenske, R. H. (1981). Historical foundations. In U. Delworth & G. Hanson & Associates (Eds.), *Student services: A Handbook for the Profession.* (pp. 3-24). San Francisco: Jossey-Bass Inc., Publishers.

Fleming, J. (1984). *Blacks in College.* San Francisco: Jossey-Bass Inc., Publishers.

Hallinan, M., & Williams, R. A. (1987). Interracial friendship choices in secondary schools. *American Sociological Review, 54,* 67-78.

Hansell, S. & Slavin, R. E. (1981). Cooperative learning and the structure of interracial friendships. Sociology of Education, 54, 98-106.

Harris, J. J., Figgures, C, and Carter, D. G. (1975). A historical perspective of the emergence of higher education in Black colleges. *Journal of Black Studies, 6,* 55-68.

Helms, J. E. (1984). Toward a theoretical explanation of the effects of race on counseling: A Black and White model. *The Counseling Psychologist, 12,* 153-165.

Hofstadter, R., Miller, W., & Aaron, D. (1959). *The American Republic* (Vol.1). Englewood Cliffs, NJ: Prentice-Hall Inc.

Jackson, G. (1986). Conceptualizing Afrocentric and Eurocentric mental health training. In H. P. Lefley & P. B. Pedersen (Eds.), *Cross cultural training for the mental health professions* (pp. 131-146). Springfield, IL: Charles C Thomas.

Jones, E. (1985). Psychotherapy and counseling with Black students. In P. Pedersen (Ed.). *Handbook of cross-cultural counseling and therapy.* Westport, CT: Greenwood Press.

Jordan-Cox, C. A. (1987). Psychosocial development of students in traditionally Black institutions. *Journal of College Student Personnel, 28,* 504-511.

Kanter, R. M. (1977). *Men and women of the corporation.* New York: Basic Books, Inc.

Knefelkamp, L., Widick, C., & Parker, C. A. (Eds.) (1978). *Applying new developmental findings* (New directions for student services No.4). San Francisco: Jossey-Bass Inc., Publishers.

Korolewicz, M., & Korolewicz, A. (1985). Effects of sex and race on interracial dating preferences. *Psychological Reports, 57,* 1291-1296.

Locke, D. C. & Zimmerman, N. A. (1987). Effects of peer-counseling training on psychological maturity of Black students. *Journal of College Student Personnel, 28,* 525-532.

McEwen, M., Roper, L., Bryant, D., & Langa, M. (1990). Incorporating the development of African American students into psychosocial theories of student development. *Journal of College Student Development, 31,* 429-436.

Miller, T. K., & Winston, R. B., Jr. (1990). Assessing development from a psychosocial perspective. In D. G. Creamer and Associates (Eds.), *College student development: Theory and practice for the 1990s* (pp. 99-126). Washington, D. C.: American College Personnel Association Media Publication No. 49.

Miville, M. (1991). Personal and professional perspectives on mentoring and the VREG graduate student. *Focus, 5,* 14.

Moore, L. V. and Upcraft. M. L. (1990). Theories in student affairs: Evolving perspectives. In. L. V. Moore (Ed.), *Evolving Theoretical Perspectives on Students* (pp. 3-23). San Francisco: Jossey-Bass Inc., Publishers.

Murstein, B., Merighi, J., Malloy, T. (1989). Physical attractiveness and exchange theory in interracial dating. *Journal of Social Psychology, 129,* 325-334.

National Center for Educational Statistics (1988). *Digest of educational statistics.* Washington, D.C. U. S. Government Printing Office.

Nettles, M., T., & Johnson, J. R. (1987). Race sex, and other factors as determinants of college students' socialization. *Journal of College Student Personnel, 28,* 512-524.

Parham, T. A. (1989). Cycles of psychological Nigrescence. *The Counseling Psychologist, 17,* 187-226.

Pascarella, E. T. & Smart, J. C. (1991). Impact of intercollegiate athletic participation of African American and Caucasian men: Some further evidence. *Journal of College Student Development, 32,* 123-130.

Pascarella, E. & Terenzini, P. (1991). *How college affects students.* San Francisco, CA: Jossey-Bass Inc., Publishers.

Sanders, D. (1991). Minority issues in mentor protege relationships. *Focus* (APA Newsletter), *5,* 13.

Schneider, K. A historic district in South Carolina struggles to preserve Black history. *The New York Times* (Nation) Sunday, 5/16/91, p. 22.

Sowa, C, Thomas, M., & Bennett, C. (1989). Prediction and improvement of academic performances for high risk Black college students. *Journal of Multicultural Counseling and Development, 17,* 12-22.

Steard, R., Jackson, M., & Jackson, D. (1990). Alienation and interactional styles in a predominantly White environment: A study of successful Black students. *Journal of College Student Development, 31,* 509-515.

The President's Commission on Higher Education (1947). Establishing the goals (Volume 1). *Higher Education for American Democracy,* Washington, D.C.: U. S. Government Printing Office.

Trippi, J. & Cheatham, H. E. (1991). Counseling effects on African American college student graduation. *Journal of College Student Development, 32,* 342-349.

Williams, T. M., & Leonard, M. M. (1988). Graduating Black undergraduates: The step beyond retention. *Journal of College Student Development, 29,* 69-75.

Williamson, E. G. (1961). *Student personnel services in colleges and universities* (pp. 3-35). New York: McGraw-Hill Inc.

Winston, R. B., Jr., Miller, T. K. & Prince, J. S. (1979). *The student developmental task inventory.* Athens GA: Student Development Associates.

Winston, R. B., Jr., Miller, T. K., & Prince, J. S. (1987). *Student developmental task and lifestyle inventory manual.* Athens, GA: Student Development Associates.

Chapter 10

Gender Paradoxes
in College Student Development

Frances L. Hoffmann

SUMMARY. This chapter is an exploration of gender and the contemporary college student, with particular attention to points of tension and contradiction in emerging analyses of gender relations on college campuses. Evidence of considerable convergence in men's and women's aspirations, attitudes, sex-role stereotypes, alcohol and other drug use, and personality and cognitive abilities inform models arguing for an appreciation of essential similarities between the sexes. On the other hand, differences perspectives call attention to persistent patterns of gender differentiation in interaction styles, appearance norms, eating disorders, sexual coercion, and other arenas of campus life. College policy and practice affecting gender issues need to strike a careful balance between recognizing the legitimate points of contention and arenas for misunderstanding between the sexes without exaggerating their claims of difference.

There have been moments in history of relative clarity in defining the origins and consequences of gender distinctions. This is not one of them. The past twenty years have witnessed the publication of literally hundreds of articles and books exploring what differenc-

Frances L. Hoffmann, PhD, is Visiting Associate Professor of Sociology at the University of Missouri-St. Louis, 8001 Natural Bridge Road, St. Louis, MO 63121 and Research Fellow at Four Winds-Saratoga Hospital, 30 Crescent Avenue, Saratoga Springs, NY 12866. Reprint requests should be addressed c/o Department of Sociology, University of Missouri-St. Louis.

es, if any, distinguish the sexes and what consequences, if any, those differences imply. Paradoxes abound. While there is general agreement that definitions of masculinity and femininity are socially constructed in the context of changing cultural and social structural imperatives, considerable debate remains about the current status of gender relations. Competing gender paradigms coexist in contemporary society, the legacy of the challenges to traditional sex role models of the post World War II era. This chapter is an exploration of gender and the contemporary college student, with particular attention to points of tension and contradiction in emerging analyses of gender relations on college campuses. It makes no effort to be a comprehensive review of the literature. Rather, representative research has been selected to illustrate the issues and controversies.

THE PARADOXES

Jacklin (1990, 121) characterizes the effort to study the socialization of gender as the study of a "moving target"—the very processes one seeks to identify and understand change before one's eyes. Indeed, the now widely-cited feminist analyses of female development (the best known of which include Miller, 1976, 1984; Chodorow, 1978; Gilligan, 1982; Belenky, 1986; Josselson, 1988) have been framed and modified through a period of intense transformation in gender ideology and structure in the culture at large. Arising in response to models of development descriptive, at best, of male development, feminist theories explored the "pathways to identity in women" (Josselson, 1988) at the very moment in history when those pathways were multiplying and the models of male development they opposed were themselves being challenged (see e.g., Kimmel, 1987; Whitaker, 1987; May, 1988; Kimmel & Messner,1989; Dickstein et al., 1991). The resultant mix of theory and research is, depending on one's perspective, a confused muddle or a rich and challenging collection of disparate perspectives and findings in need of synthesis.

The strands running through this collection are found in the chronology of thinking about gender relations of the past few decades. Traditional sex role models, dominant in the 1950s and 1960s, posed fundamental differences between the sexes in temperament, aptitude, and interests. Sex roles were seen as distinct, but complementary–whatever structural disadvantages women experienced resulted from the limitations imposed by women's "nature" rather than institutionalized discrimination. The Women's Movement challenged this model, arguing instead for models of fundamental equality between the sexes–whatever men could do, women could do as well, assuming a social structure and culture supportive of full integration of women into the labor force and political life. The ensuing years witnessed profound changes in women's lives (and to a lesser degree in men's lives) as their educational and occupational aspirations were transformed. Yet persistent patterns in gender differentiation remained. Feminist research and theory of the past few years as well as the emerging men's studies scholarship have revisited the question of differences between the sexes to explore a new set of questions: How do we account for the persistence of gender differentiation in some arenas and its significant reduction in others? How are we to resolve the tensions between traditional and emerging models of femininity and masculinity? Are there "male" and "female" paths to identity and, if so, what are their consequences for relations between the sexes? What new issues emerge when race, sexual preference, class are added to the analysis? These are important questions for theory and research; they are critical questions for students as they negotiate the shifting sands of gender identity and relations.

On college campuses, dating and intimate relationships, sexual harassment, acquaintance rape and other forms of sexual coercion, and rates of eating disorders, suicide, and depression are all differentiated by gender. The literature explaining the etiology and prevalence of these phenomena makes much of differences between the sexes in socialization patterns and social statuses. On the other hand, college men and women have converged significantly in many areas, among them, job, family, and educational aspirations, expressed life objectives, and drug and alcohol use patterns. These similarities are underscored by a body of literature, predominantly from psychology, which finds few personality or behavioral variables which consistently distinguish the sexes.

Taken together, the similarities and differences perspectives, and their variations, provide considerable challenge to campus counseling and student affairs staff interested in developing program and policy which respond to, but do not exacerbate, gender conflicts in campus life. In this era of campus preoccupation with issues of *differences*, the degree to which the sexes are divided by temperament, demeanor, aspirations and behavior are frequently exaggerated. On the other hand, sex differences in social behavior and psychopathology persist, requiring continued effort to understand the contemporary mix of social and cultural conditions which underlie them.

THE SIMILARITIES

The essential arguments of the similarities perspective are that men and women share more in common as human beings than divide them by sex, that differences within gender categories far exceed those between, and that the history of the past twenty years has been a history of impressive convergence in sex roles and expectations. Emerging as a challenge to the exaggerated claims of sex differences of the post-World War II era, the similarities perspective predominated in the early days of the Women's Movement. While the ensuing decades have witnessed both feminist and anti-feminist challenges to this perspective, its essential assumptions are supported in several areas of inquiry.

Aspirations, Political and Social Attitudes. The Astin surveys of entering American freshmen (Astin, A.), conducted annually under the auspices of the American Council on Education and the University of California at Los Angeles, offer compelling evidence of significant convergence in college men's and women's aspirations, attitudes and occupational choices over the past two decades (see also Komarovsky, 1982). Men's and women's educational goals have clearly converged: in 1972, 30.3% of entering men and 16.1% of entering females reported aspiring to a Ph.D. or other professional degree, a difference of 14.2%. By 1986, that gap had closed to 1.5%, with 21.6% of the men and 20.1% of the women reporting a goal of Ph.D. or its equivalent. Men's and women's ratings of objectives considered essential or very important have converged as well: as Table 1 indicates, the average percentage difference between men's and women's responses to 17 items included on both the 1972 and 1990 Astin surveys has declined from 9.0 to 6.0. Only three items, "influencing social values," "helping others in difficulty," and "becoming successful in own business," differentiated the sexes by more than 8% in 1990, whereas six did in 1972.

With few exceptions, social and political attitudes are converging as well. Table 2 presents the proportion of male and female freshman agreeing with a series of attitude items which were asked both in 1982 and 1990. Responses to these items converged in all cases except two: "Marijuana should be legalized" (in 1982, 6.1 percentage points separated men's from women's responses to this item, in 1990 the difference had increased to 10.1) and "It is important to have laws prohibiting homosexual relationships" (differences in responses to this item increased from 19.4 in 1982 to 21.5 in 1990). Overall, the average difference between the proportion of men and women agreeing with the attitude items dropped from 12.2 in 1972 to 9.0 in 1990.

Finally, occupational aspirations have become similar (see Astin; Jacobs, 1989). Over the past two decades, young women's occupational goals have increasingly moved toward male-dominated occupations and away from female-dominated occupations and their occupational aspirations have shown increasing diversity; these patterns are particularly true of women planning to complete college degrees (Jacobs, 1989, 73). Young men's occupational choices have not changed as dramatically and are concentrated among fewer rather than more occupational categories. Taken together, these changes produce significant reduction in dissimilarities between men's and women's career choices. As Table 1 indicates, men and women report a similarly strong commitment to combining family and work roles, although women are more likely to see family roles as conflicting with work roles than are men (DiBenedetto & Tittle, 1990).

Alcohol and Other Drug Trends. The National Institute on Drug Abuse has been conducting nationwide annual surveys of high school and college drug and alcohol use patterns since 1975, offer-

TABLE 1. Objectives Considered Essential or Very Important, By Sex, 1972 and 1990

	1972			1990		
	%M	%F	(M-F)	%M	%F	(M-F)
achieve in performing art	10.1	13.8	-3.7	10.3	11.2	-.9
be authority in field	64.8	55.7	9.1	67.4	63.6	3.8
obtain recognition from peers	41.2	31.9	9.3	56.0	54.0	2.0
influence political structure	18.7	12.2	6.5	22.9	18.6	4.3
influence social values	29.0	32.0	-3.0	36.3	48.4	-12.1
raise a family	62.2	67.8	-5.6	68.2	70.6	-2.4
be administratively resp.	29.7	17.6	12.2	44.2	41.8	2.4
be very well-off financially	50.6	30.2	20.4	77.7	70.3	7.4
help others in difficulty	59.4	75.1	-15.7	50.9	71.4	-20.5
contribute to scientific theory	13.6	7.2	6.4	20.3	14.5	5.8
keep up with political affairs	50.6	46.6	4.0	46.5	38.9	7.6
succeed in own business	55.2	32.5	22.7	49.5	38.0	11.5
help clean up environment	45.5	43.6	1.9	33.5	34.3	-.8
develop philosophy of life	67.3	75.0	-7.7	41.8	44.3	-2.5
participate in commun. action	26.6	31.9	-5.3	22.1	29.1	-7.0

Source: "The American Freshman: National Norms for Fall 1972, 1990" by Alexander Astin. Published by ACE and UCLA.

198

TABLE 2. Agree Strongly or Somewhat, By Sex, 1982 and 1990

	1982			1990		
	%M	%F	(M-F)	%M	%F	(M-F)
gov't not protecting consumer	64.4	73.1	-8.7	64.7	71.6	-6.9
gov't not controlling pollution	74.9	82.2	-7.3	87.0	88.7	-1.7
fed. milit. spending increased	47.9	29.9	18.0	29.0	21.8	7.2
too many rights for criminals	74.3	65.5	8.8	69.8	63.2	6.6
should abolish death penalty	23.1	33.5	-10.4	18.5	24.1	-5.6
abortion should be legalized	53.7	55.9	-2.2	65.0	64.8	.2
married women's act's. best in home	33.6	17.6	16.0	30.6	20.5	10.1
sex OK if people like each other	64.0	32.8	31.2	66.3	37.9	28.4
marijuana should be legalized	32.5	26.4	6.1	30.6	20.5	10.1
busing OK to achieve balance	43.8	49.8	-6.0	56.4	57.1	-.7
prohibit homosexual relations	57.0	37.6	19.4	56.0	34.5	21.5
students help evaluate faculty	69.9	70.0	-.1	74.9	75.0	-.1

Source: "The American Freshman: National Norms for Fall, 1982, 1990" by Alexander Astin. Published by ACE and UCLA.

ing now a rich data base for exploring gender issues in this area (Johnston et al., 1989). Overall, significant declines in the proportion of college student use of any illicit drug have been registered through the 1980s. In addition, while men reported using marijuana, cocaine, methaqualone, and stimulants at higher rates than women in the early 1980s, by 1988 usage patterns had become virtually identical. Alcohol use patterns have been more stable through the decade, with convergences between the sexes in terms of reports of daily and 30-day prevalence rates (prevalence is defined as percent reporting using within the given time frame). Reports of heavy drinking (defined as having 5 or more drinks in a row within the past two weeks) have converged since the mid-1980s. However, significant differences between the sexes for this behavior persist, with approximately 15% more college men reporting episodes of heavy drinking than college women (Johnston et al., 1989, p. 301).

Gender Stereotypes and Evaluation. Feminist scholarship of the early 1970s documented widespread public agreement about what characteristics differentiated the sexes, and found that characteristics associated with women were consistently devalued. Confirmation of these findings came from many quarters. The oft-cited Broverman et al. (1972) research revealed that both male and female clinicians were more likely to attribute negative characteristics to women than to men. Similar findings were reported through the 1970s as researchers found, for example, that students were more likely to evaluate women teachers negatively; workers reported preferences for male supervisors; patients for male physicians. More recent research finds striking change in these patterns. For example, Eagly and Mladinic (1989), surveying 203 students at Purdue University, find attitudes and stereotypes about women to be more favorable than those about men. In a follow-up to the Broverman research, Kaplan et al. (1990) fail to find significant differences in psychiatrists' ratings of optimal mental health for females and males, with two exceptions: female psychiatrists were more likely to rate masculine traits as optimal for females; male psychiatrists were more likely to choose traits representing low levels of masculinity and femininity as optimal for both sexes.

Both the content and evaluation of gender stereotypes are more complicated today than 20 years ago. Stereotypes about women have become less negative, in part because traditional female attributes (nurturance, connectedness with others, sensitivity) have been reevaluated more positively, and in part because women have come to be seen as possessing what were traditionally masculine attributes (competence, career commitment, assertiveness). Correspondingly, some traditional masculine stereotypes (dominance, competitiveness, aggression) have been devalued and men have been increasingly seen as capable of what were traditionally feminine attributes (nurturance, sensitivity, caring).

Personality Characteristics and Cognitive Abilities. Maccoby and Jacklin's (1974) *The Psychology of Sex Differences,* the groundbreaking review of over 1400 studies of sex differences in cognitive skills, temperament and social behavior, found consistent support for only four differences between the sexes: male superiority in mathematical and visual/spatial functioning; female superiority in verbal abilities; and greater aggressiveness in males. Their work encouraged a spate of research throughout the 1970s to extend the search for sex differences to a range of relatively unresearched cognitive and interpersonal arenas. Deaux (1984), Jacklin (1989), and Maccoby (1990) provide reviews of these more recent investigations. Summarizing the major research undertaken since 1974, the majority of it on college students, they report *reductions* in sex differences in verbal abilities and no consistent pattern of gender differences in mathematical or spatial functioning, except that males outscore females on the highest end of the mathematics continuum (Jacklin, 1989, p. 114).

Findings of sex differences in personality traits are similarly sparse and/or inconsistent. Further, even when sex differences are found, the proportion of the variation in behavior accounted for is very small. Deaux (1984) reports that sex differences found in, for example, studies of influenceability, aggression, and attribution account for no more than 5% of the overall variance. Studies of sex differences outside of the laboratory find even less variation. For example, Hollander (in press), reviewing leadership studies, finds few differences between men and women leaders. Taken together, this research leads to the conclusion that men and women draw upon similar behavioral, intellectual and emotional repertoires in their day-to-day lives. In Maccoby's terms:

> In general . . . personality traits measured as characteristics of individuals do not appear to differ systematically by sex. This no doubt reflects in part the fact that male and female persons really are much alike, and their lives are governed mainly by the attributes that all persons in a given culture have in common. (Maccoby, 1990, p. 513)

While it may be true that men and women share common repertoires of personality and cognitive traits, it is also true that men and women differ significantly in terms of what characteristic patterns of behavior and interpersonal styles are likely to be elicited from these repertoires. We know, for example, that approaches to friendship and intimate relationships vary by sex, that men are more likely to be sexual aggressors than women, that women are more likely to experience eating disorders than men. How are these patterns explicable without a model which poses fundamental personality differences between the sexes? To answer this question, the focus in contemporary gender research has shifted from an interest in finding enduring and consistent sex differences in personality and aptitude[1] to exploring the ways in which gender differences emerge, and wax and wane, in the changing *contexts* of social interaction. We all participate in groups, in social structures, and in a set of cultural values and expectations–what we do and how we think about ourselves are shaped in these contexts. To one degree or another, researchers interested in exploring the range of issues which are clearly gender differentiated look to structural and cultural contexts for explanatory frameworks. Contemporary differences models contrast with their earlier forebears by recognizing the fluidity of gender-differentiated behaviors and their responsiveness to changing structural and cultural conditions.

THE DIFFERENCES

The Significance of Context. If the search for enduring and consistent differences between the sexes has yielded inconclusive results, interest in contextual effects has born more fruit. Significant among contextual effects are the nature of the task being investigated, the sex of the researcher (affecting both interpretation of results and behavior of research subjects), and the gender composition of groups (Deaux, 1984; Maccoby, 1990). The last is of particular salience on campuses because many of gender-based conflicts confronted by counseling and student affairs staff are group, rather than individual, phenomena. Harassment of women at fraternity social events is but one example. Gender differences in behavior within single- versus mixed-sex groups appear very early in life.

There is a voluminous child development literature focussing on the effects of gender on behavior, interactive styles and group effectiveness in mixed- versus same-sex play groups and classroom settings. Maccoby (1990, p. 514) summarizes its major findings: sex segregation throughout childhood is widespread, and preferred playmates (in situations where choice is possible) are overwhelmingly the same sex and remain so regardless of the activity. Further, children's interactive styles, their influenceability and their ability to influence, are affected strongly by the sex of their partners or the gender composition of their group. Early on, boys' and girls' responsiveness to suggestion differentiates on the basis of the sex of the person doing the suggesting: Boys respond to other males but not to girls; girls are more responsive than boys both to other girls and to boys (Serbin et al., 1984). Overall, this research lays a foundation for understanding gender-differentiated behavior in the college years. Sex differences in verbal styles, the forms and expression of friendships, sharing of confidences, concern for rules, patterns of dominance, use of jokes and boasts, and other behaviors which emerge in the context of same-sex interactions of childhood, are reinforced in broader social and cultural structures, and underlie many of the patterns of cross-sex interactions observed on contemporary campuses. This research helps to frame recent work examining emerging trends in dating relationships and friendships among college students, especially that which focusses on arenas for miscommunication between men and women as they negotiate sexuality and intimacy.

Dating, Sexual Intimacy, Romance. Describing contemporary dating norms on college campuses is a little like describing the proverbial half-empty (or half-full) bottle: traditional mores are very much in evidence even though student surveys reveal strong support for alternative dating patterns. In this arena, as in so many others, the structural changes which have so dramatically expanded career options for women have outpaced cultural norms and values which affect intimate relationships. As we've seen, college men and women expect to combine careers and families, have similar educational aspirations and espouse egalitarian relationships as a goal. The Boston Couples Study (Peplau & Campbell, 1989) finds virtually universal agreement among the 231 college age couples surveyed that both partners should have equal say in a relationship. But patterns of traditional sex role interactions persist among a significant minority of the couples. While 49% of the women and 42% of the men described their relationship as egalitarian, 35% of the women and 45% of the men reported that the man had more say. Only 17% of the women and 13% of the men reported the woman had more say. Allgeier and Royster (1991) reported shifting patterns in rules for courtship and mate selection toward a desire on both partners' parts for more equality, intimacy and openness with one another and away from more traditional gender-based values. On the other hand, research by Rose and Frieze (1989), in which a sample of 97 college students were asked to write a script for men's and women's activities on a first date, finds strong evidence of traditional gender/power relationships. Student scripts described women's activities in preparing for a first date in terms of the private, personal and interpersonal sphere–concern for appearance, maintaining conversation, controlling (restricting) sexuality. Men's activities were described in more instrumental, public-sphere terms: initiating, planning and paying for the date, and orchestrating the activities of the evening, including sexuality. Interestingly, students with more dating experience were *more* likely to write gender based scripts (descriptions of hypothetical events which may or may not conform to students' behavior.) But actual dating behavior may depart from this pattern. Allgeier and Royster (1991) summarize research which shows, in fact, women are actively engaged in the selection of a dating partner, usually, though not exclusively, through indirect means, and frequently share the cost of the date. However, once a dating pattern is initiated, the balance of power shifts and their research finds that men are more likely to attempt to move the relationship to greater sexual intimacy.

Two forms of gender differentiated behavior recur as major themes in this body of research: females' greater preoccupation with appe/arance and male dominance in sexual negotiation. The former is implicated in the prevalence of eating disorders among college women; the latter in the prevalence of sexually coercive behavior on the part of college men. These two arenas of gender differentiated behavior are paradigmatic cases of the difficulties faced by some students when processes of gender development are in conflict with major social and cultural changes in gender relations.

Appearance Norms, Eating Disorders, and Autonomy. Peplau and Campbell (1989) have identified factors affecting the balance of power in relationships: social norms (favoring men), imbalance in the involvement of either partner in the relationship, and resources outside of the relationship. The latter is especially important for women, for a woman's relative power in a relationship increases as her educational and career aspirations increase, whereas men's relative power is independent of career and educational aspirations. In the absence of strong career aspirations on the part of women, appearance norms loom large in the balance of power, a finding supported by the research cited above and constituting the central theme of Holland and Eisenhart's (1990) important ethnography, *Educated in Romance.*

Educated in Romance is an analysis of the effects of peer culture on women students' experiences and aspirations in two southern colleges, one predominantly white, the other predominantly black. A sample of 23 students, all freshmen in 1979, participated in intensive interviews and observation by the researchers over a two year period, and were re-interviewed at the time of graduation and again in 1987. Interested in exploring the mechanisms through which career and relationship decisions were formed and revised, Holland and Eisenhart's research confirms what student affairs and counseling staff have long recognized, namely, that the formal curriculum and cocurriculum have distressingly little impact on student growth and development. They summarize the results of their research:

For gender, agemates are more virulent purveyors of gender privilege than school authorities or school materials. As we followed the women's experiences . . . we found that the peer system promoted and propelled the women into a world of romance in which their attractiveness to men counted most . . . In the shadow of the peer society, academics commanded only limited attention. (Holland & Eisenhart, 1990, p. 8)

Holland and Eisenhart found student cultures on both campuses in which questions of who was dating whom, who was more attractive and why predominated in conversation among women students. All of the women faced considerable peer pressure to participate in what some subjects called "the sexual auction block." Responses to these pressures were not uniform: some complained but adapted, some struggled to reconcile conflicting values, some opted out of the sexual marketplace through a variety of strategies, including settling into a less than desirable relationship in order to avoid the open competition. Discouraging for those of us long involved in organized activities on behalf of women is the fact that few of Holland and Eisenhart's subjects, even those expressing the strongest opposition to the norms governing feminine attractiveness and the culture of romance, found collective means to express their dissatisfaction. Women on college campuses are faced with strong, and competing, pressures toward success in the relationship marketplace, on the one hand, and autonomy, independence and success in the career marketplace, on the other. Appearance norms loom large in both arenas. Reconciliation of these pressures takes many forms, some adaptive, some life-threatening.

Appearance norms, particularly cultural preoccupation with youthfulness and slenderness, are clearly implicated in the etiology and prevalence of eating disorders among adolescent women in America. It is beyond the scope of this review to summarize the now-extensive literature exploring the psychodynamic and sociocultural sources of eating disorders [see, e.g., Brumberg (1988) for an in-depth historical analysis of the disorders; *The Bulimic College Student: Evaluation, Treatment and Prevention*, also published as a special triple issue of the *Journal of College Student Psychotherapy* (Whitaker & Davis, 1988/1989) for analyses of bulimia and its relationship to the collegiate environment; Rastam & Goldberg

(1991) for discussion of familial influences on eating disorders; and Lucas et al. (1991) for incidence trends]. For the purposes of this review, I'd like to highlight emerging research and theory which places the prevalence of bulimia and anorexia nervosa on college campuses in the context of competing gender paradigms confronting today's young women in the transition to adulthood. Early psychodynamic models of eating disorders couched them in terms of a desire to retain the dependency of childhood and to avoid the autonomy and independence of adulthood. More recent research has challenged this interpretation, arguing instead that eating disorders result from an over-identification with emerging cultural norms for women promoting success, independence, and control (Steiner-Adair, 1989; Steiner-Adair, 1988/89; Wurman, 1988/89).

This research draws directly upon Chodorow's, Miller's, and Gilligan's reformulations of processes of identity development in women. According to these theorists, women's identity is formed through the establishment and maintenance of relationships–the self emerges in interaction with, rather than opposition to, the voices and experiences of others. The developmental risk for women, given greater orientation to the perceptions of others in their identity development, is an underdeveloped inner voice or core self. Psychodynamic conflicts which arise from an over-identification with approval from others are exacerbated in the contemporary cultural context which increasingly values individual initiative, control, and autonomy for women. Because much of young men's sense of self has been defined through *contrasting* self with other, the movement to autonomy and independence is consistent with earlier developmental processes. In contrast, socialization experiences and cultural expectations are in conflict for some young women, particularly those whose early family relationships jeopardized the development of an individuated self with which to negotiate the new expectations for female adulthood. For Steiner-Adair (1988/89; 1989) and Wurman (1988/89), the contemporary prevalence of bulimia among young women is attributable to this cultural double bind. It represents a dramatic effort to present the new public persona of a self-made, in-control, needing-nobody autonomy masking an absence of self, an inability to define an identity without the approval of an external audience.

Support for this model is suggested by Steiner-Adair's research (1989), in which she conducted in-depth interviews with 32 girls at a private high school, asking them to describe their perceptions of cultural standards for women and their aspirations for themselves. The girls were assessed for eating-disordered behavior in an effort to find relationships between their perceptions of societal standards affecting women, the standards to which they held themselves, and their eating habits. Two groups emerged, "Wise Women" and "Super Women," distinguished by their relative abilities to recognize and choose among the array of contemporary standards of female behavior those which were most meaningful for themselves. Wise Women accurately identified the competing cultural images of women and talked in terms of which images they saw as appropriate for themselves. Recognizing both relationship and achievement pressures on women, they felt confident in their own ability to decide for themselves how to effect a balance. Super Women, significantly more likely to report preoccupation with ideal body weight and appearance concerns, had no "self" to place in dialogue with the societal ideal–for them, the fast track, slim, attractive, independent super-woman of magazine cover fame *was* their ideal. For Super Women the resolution of the autonomy versus connectedness dichotomy was a drastic splitting of public and private selves, conforming on the surface to cultural ideals, privately battling selves experienced as both needy and greedy. Self destructive eating patterns become for some the battleground for this conflict between externally imposed standards of achievement and beauty and internally felt needs for care and connectedness.

The autonomy-relatedness dualism informs recent thinking about eating disorders and remains the central problem for contemporary developmental theorists and for those seeking to counsel women caught in an historical moment in which its tensions remain unresolved (see Hare-Mustin & Marecek, 1986). Feminist efforts to develop new models of women's development which avoid the false dichotomies of traditional formulations have inevitably affected analyses of men's roles as well.

Sexual Coercion and the Contradictions of Modern Masculinity. Susan Brownmiller's (1975) now-classic work firmly located the phenomenon of rape in the social structure, redefining it as a form of social control embedded in patriarchal societies, imposed on women by men. Subsequent feminist analyses have elaborated this formulation, drawing an increasingly wide net around behaviors once taken-for-granted as natural expressions (or prerogatives) of male sexuality and recasting them as socially constructed forms of domination. Scholarly and media attention (with frequent flights of hyperbole) have focussed on the prevalence and consequences of what are now all defined as forms of "sexually coercive behavior": sexual harassment in the workplace and classroom; peer harassment; spouse abuse; date/acquaintance rape; and gang rape (see, e.g., Ehrhardt & Sandler, 1985; Hoffmann, 1986; Muehlenhand & Linton, 1987; Martin & Hummer, 1989; Amada, 1989; McKinney & Maroules, 1991; Lyman, 1991). There are common themes to these analyses: sexual coercion of women by men is ubiquitous, embedded in the normative framework of American masculinity, reinforced in the socializing experiences of male groups (especially fraternities and team sports), and a mechanism through which male privilege and control are maintained and perpetuated. Forms of sexual coercion range from the linguistic (sexist jokes, catcalls, verbal persuasion, verbal threats), to the structural (misuse of authority), to the physical (use of force, violence). Efforts to understand the etiology of sexual coercion have focussed on those aspects of masculine culture and social norms which reinforce, if not encourage, sexual domination and on studies of the types of men most likely to engage in such behavior (Bernard et al., 1985; Murstein et al., 1989; Lisak, 1991).

Burkhart and Fromuth (1991) offer a conceptual schema for an understanding of the prevalence of male sexual domination and female victimization in modern society. Differential patterns of socialization in childhood lead to differences in interactive styles between the sexes. When reinforced with the misogynist imagery and beliefs widely promoted in American culture, these interactional differences lead to patterns of heterosexual interaction in which masculinity is associated with the pursuit of sex, femininity with limiting it. In support of this model, Burkhart and Fromuth review a wide variety of studies documenting sex differences in the attribution of responsibility for sexual encounters, in defining what constitutes sexual behavior, and in norms for the timing of sexual interactions. They conclude that the prevalence of sexually coercive behaviors is a not-surprising outcome of "normative and interactional misunderstanding" (1991, p. 85).

Feminist analyses of the commonalities among the range of behaviors now defined as sexual coercion have called needed attention to their sources in normative patterns of male-female interactions, their serious consequences for the lives and psychological well-being of their victims, and their role in maintaining gender inequality throughout the fabric of American society. Law and policy have been significantly affected by these new formulations of sexual coercion, reflecting a measure of support for the new perspective on gender relations which they represent. But significant disagreement remains about what is below the surface of these issues. There is considerable disagreement among college students about what behaviors can be reasonably seen as constituting sexual coercion and about who bears responsibility for them.

In a sample of 351 undergraduates, 23% reported having received or initiated at least one violent act during a date. Both men and women saw themselves as co-involved in the behavior and neither saw the behavior as particularly problematic (Matthews, 1984). Further, emphasis on the degree to which sexual coercion is part of the normative gender landscape neglects the fact that most men *don't* rape or harass women. Koss et al.'s national survey of 6159 students finds 75% of the males reported *no* involvement in sexually aggressive (including verbal) behavior. Correspondingly, while women report high rates of being subjected to forms of sexual harassment or abuse, what is lost in many of these reports is that most women report coping effectively with the behavior and see themselves as agents in a process in which they exert both influence and responsibility.

The extremes in differences of opinion in defining sexual coercion are illustrated in Lisak's (1991) studies of "unreported rapists." His research revealed a not-insignificant number of college men, who, by their own description, engaged in behavior classifiable by others as rape but who did not define it as outside of normal ranges of consensual sexual interaction. Studies of incarcerated rapists find similar denial of the degree of coerciveness in sexual encounters–see Koss et al., 1987, 169). Estrich's (1987) *Real Rape* is an analysis of why many women subjected to what the law would consider to be rape do not see it that way themselves. When is rape rape (not to mention, when is a sexist joke sexual coercion) is a question answered with certitude by some, ambivalence by many others.

These findings reveal deep divisions in definitions of what constitutes sexual coercion and who bears responsibility for it. Emerging and traditional sexual scripts are competing for the moral terrain, with the risk of self-righteous polemic generating defensive backlash. There is a need to read the various surveys on sexual coercion and to listen to our students very carefully. We can exacerbate the already-existing tensions between the sexes by policy and practice which ascribe offender status to men in general and victim status to women in general. These difficulties are addressed only through the search for new modes of interaction and communication which find common ground between the sexes. Allgeier and Royster (1991) and Lyman (1987) provide impressive beginnings in this search.

CONCLUSION

The task ahead is to join the similarities and differences perspectives in deepening our understanding of the ways in which gender does, and does not, affect patterns of interaction, forms of psychopathology, and social roles and relationships. College students today confront a bewildering array of competing values and cultural expectations. Many of their problems are manifestation of mutual misunderstandings, mixed feelings, and profound disagreement about their rights and responsibilities as men and women. We serve our students best by inviting them, with us, to explore the complexities and tensions inherent in a society profoundly affected by gender, but a society in which the differences which divide us are addressable with due attention to our common humanity and our common repertoire of hopes, aspirations, and capacity for empathy.

NOTE

1. Indeed, the rapidity with which changes in measured sex differences in such areas as verbal abilities has occurred led one research team to conclude, "we can say that whatever the reason, in these studies females appear to be gaining in

cognitive skill relative to males rather faster than the gene can travel!'' (Rosenthal
& Rubin, quoted in Jacklin, 1989, p. 114)

REFERENCES

Astin, A. (1972, 1986, 1988, 1990). The American freshman: national norms for
    fall _____. Higher Education Research Institute, UCLA:ACE.
Allgeier, E. & Royster, B. (1991). New approaches to dating and sexuality. In
    E. Grauerholz & M. Koralewski (Eds.) *Sexual Coercion* (pp. 133-148). Lex-
    ington, MA: Lexington Books.
Amada, G. (1989). Date rape on the college campus: the college psychotherapist
    as activist. *Journal of College Student Psychotherapy*, 4(2), 89-93.
Belenky, M., Clinchy, B., Goldberger, N., Tarule, J. (1986). *Women's Ways of
    Knowing*. New York: Basic Books, Inc.
Bernard, J.L., Bernard, S.L., & Bernard, M.L. (1985). Courtship violence and
    sex typing. *Family Relations–Journal of Applied Family and Child Studies*,
    34(4), 573-576.
Broverman, I.K., Broverman, D.M. & Clarkson, F.E. (1970). Sex role stereo-
    types and clinical judgments of mental health. *Journal of Consulting and Clini-
    cal Psychology*, 34,1-7.
Brumberg, J.J. (1988). *Fasting Girls*. Cambridge, MA: Harvard Univ. Press.
Burkhart, B. & Fromuth, M.E. (1991). Individual psychological and social psy-
    chological understandings of sexual coercion. In E. Grauerholz & M.A.
    Koralewski (Eds.) *Sexual Coercion* (pp. 75-90). Lexington, MA: Lexington
    Books.
Chodorow, N. (1978). *The Reproduction of Mothering*. Berkeley, CA: University
    of California Press.
Deaux, K. (1984). From individual differences to social categories: analysis of
    a decade's research on gender. *American Psychologist*, 39, 105-116.
DiBenedetto, B. & Tittle, C. (1990). Gender and adult roles: role commitment
    of women and men in a job-family trade-off context. *Journal of Counseling
    Psychology*, 37(1), 41-48.
Dickstein, L. (1984). Psychiatric issues of women college students today. *Psychi-
    atric Annals*, 14(9), 653-660.
Dickstein, L; Stein, T; Pleck, J; Myers, M; Lewis, R; Duncan, S; Brod, H.
    (1991). Men's changing social roles in the 1990s: emerging issues in the psychi-
    atric treatment of men. *Hospital & Community Psychiatry*, 42(7), 701-704.
Eagly, A. & Mladinic, A. (1989). Gender stereotypes and attitudes toward wom-
    en and men. *Personality and Social Psychology Bulletin*, 1(4), 543-558.
Ehrhardt, J.K. & Sandler, B.Q. (1985). Campus gang rape: party games? Ameri-
    can Association of Colleges, Washington, D.C.
Estrich, S. (1987). *Real Rape*. Cambridge, MA: Harvard Univ. Press.
Gilligan, C. (1982). *In A Different Voice*. Cambridge, MA: Harvard University
    Press.

Hare-Mustin, R.T. & Marecek, J. (1986). Autonomy and gender: some questions for therapists. *Psychotherapy*, 23(2), 205-212.

Hoffmann, F. (1986). Sexual harassment in academia: feminist theory and institutional practice. *Harvard Educational Review*, 56(2), 105-120.

Holland, P.C. & Eisenhart, M.A. (1990). *Educated in Romance: Women, Achievement and College Culture*. Chicago: Univ. of Chicago Press.

Hollander, E.P. (in press). Leadership and power. In G. Lindzey & E. Aronson (Eds.). *Handbook of Social Psychology*, 3rd Ed. Reading, MA: Addison-Wesley Pub. Co., Inc.

Jacklin, C.N. (1990). Female and male: issues of gender. In S. Chess & M. Hertzig (Eds.) *Annual Progress in Child Psychiatry and Child Development* (pp. 111-126). NY: Brunner/Mazel, Inc.

Jacobs, J.A. (1989). *Revolving Doors: Sex Segregation and Women's Careers*. Stanford, CA: Stanford Univ. Press.

Johnston, L.D., O'Malley, P.M. & Bachman, J.G. (1989). Drug Use, Drinking, and Smoking: National Survey Results from High School, College and Young Adults Populations, 1975-1988. USDHHS: National Institute on Drug Abuse, DHHS Publication # ADM89-1638.

Josselson, R. (1988). *Finding Herself: Pathways to Identity Development in Women*. San Francisco: Jossey-Bass Inc., Publishers.

Kaplan, M.J., Winget, C., & Free, N. (1990). Psychiatrists' beliefs about gender appropriate behavior. *American Journal of Psychiatry*, 147(7), 910-912.

Komarovsky, M. (1982). Female freshmen view their futures: career salience and its correlates. *Sex Roles*, 8(3), 299-314.

Koss, M., Gidycz, C., & Wisniewski, N. (1987). The scope of rape: incidence and prevalence of sexual aggression and victimization in a national sample of higher education students. *Journal of Consulting and Clinical Psychology*, 2(2), 162-170.

Lucas, A., Beard, M., O'Fallon, M, & Kurland, L. (1991) 50-Year trends in the incidence of anorexia nervosa in Rochester, MN. *American Journal of Psychiatry*, 148(7), 917-922.

Lyman, P. (1987). The fraternal bond as a joking relationship. In M.S. Kimmel (Ed.) *Changing Men* (pp. 148-164). Newbury Park, CA: Sage Publications Inc.

Kimmel, M. (1987). *Changing Men: New Directions in Research on Men and Masculinity*. Newbury Park, CA: Sage Publications Inc.

Kimmel, M. & Messner, M.A. (1989). *Men's Lives*. Newbury Park, CA: Sage Publications Inc.

Maccoby, E. (1990). Gender relationships: a developmental account. *American Psychologist*, 45(4), 513-520.

Maccoby, E. & Jacklin, C.N. (1974). *The Psychology of Sex Differences*. Stanford, CA: Stanford Univ. Press.

Martin, P. & Hummer, R. (1989). Fraternities and rape on campus. *Gender & Society*, 3(4), 457-473.

Matthews, W. (1984). Violence in the college years. *College Student Journal*, 18(2), 150-158.

May, R. (1988) The developmental journey of the male college student. *New Directions for Student Services,* 42, 5-18.

McKinney, K. & Maroules, N. (1991) Sexual harassment. In E. Grauerholz & M. Koralewski (Eds.) *Sexual Coercion* (pp. 29-44). Lexington, MA: Lexington Books.

Miller, J.B. (1976). *Toward a New Psychology of Women.* Boston: Beacon Press.

Miller, J.B. (1984). The development of a woman's sense of self. In *Work in Progress.* Wellesley, MA: Stone Center for Developmental Services and Studies.

Mishkind, M., Rodin, J., Silberstein, L., & Striegel-Moore, R. (1987). The embodiment of masculinity. In M.S. Kimmel, (Ed.) *Changing Men* (pp. 37-52). Newbury Park, CA: Sage Publications Inc.

Muehlenhand, C.L. & Linton, M.A. (1987). Date rape and sexual aggression in dating situations. *Journal of Counseling Psychology,* 34, 186-196.

Murstein, B.I., Chalpin, M.J., Heard, K.V., & Vyse, S.A. (1989). Sexual behavior, drugs and relationship patterns on a college campus over thirteen years. *Adolescence,* 24(93), 125-139.

Peplau, L.T. & Campbell, S.M. (1989). The balance of power in dating and marriage. In J. Freeman (Ed.) *Women: A Feminist Perspective,* 4th Ed. (pp. 121-137) Palo Alto, CA: Mayfield Publishing.

Rose, S. & Frieze, I.H. (1989). Young singles' scripts for a first date. *Gender & Society,* 3(2), 256-268.

Rastam, M. & Gillberg, C. (1991). The family background in anorexia nervosa: a population based study. *Journal of American Academy of Child and Adolescent Psychiatry,* 30(2), 283-289.

Serbin, L.A., Sprafkin, C., Elman, M., Doyle, A. (1984). The early development of sex differentiated patterns of social influence. *Canadian Journal of Social Science,* 14, 350-363.

Steiner-Adair, C. (1988/89). Developing the voice of the wise-woman: college students and bulimia. In L.C. Whitaker & W.N. Davis (Eds.). *The Bulimic College Student: Evaluation, Treatment and Prevention* (pp. 151-165). New York: The Haworth Press Inc.

Steiner-Adair, C. (1989). The body politic. In C. Gilligan, N. Lyons & T. Hanmer. (Eds.) *Making Connections* (pp.162-182). Troy, NY: Emma Willard School.

Thompson, E.H. & Pleck, J.H. (1987). The structure of male role norms. In M.S. Kimmel (Ed.) *Changing Men* (pp. 25-36). Newbury Park, CA: Sage Publications Inc.

Whitaker, L.C. (1987). Macho and morbidity: the emotional need versus fear dilemma in men. *Journal of College Student Psychotherapy,* 1(4), 33-47.

Whitaker, L.C. & Davis, W.N., Eds. (1988/89). *The Bulimic College Student: Evaluation, Treatment, and Prevention.* New York: The Haworth Press Inc.

Wurman, V. (1988/89). A feminist interpretation of college student bulimia. In L.C. Whitaker & W.N. Davis (Eds.) *The Bulimic College Student: Evaluation, Treatment, and Prevention* (pp. 167-180). New York: The Haworth Press Inc.

Chapter 11

The Influence of Gender Identity on Separation Related Depressive Phenomena in College Men and Women

Thomas D. Mann

SUMMARY. The chapter examines the effects of gender identity formation on the depressive configurations of men and women. It is proposed that the separation-individuation processes in males and females differ significantly and, in conjunction with gender identity development, contribute to dramatic differences in males' and females' orientations toward relatedness, autonomy, separation, and their internal and external object worlds. Clinical vignettes are included as a means of illustrating the contrasting manifestations of men's and women's struggles with separation-individuation.

Depression affects all aspects of a student's life, including academic functioning, social, family and intimate relationships, internal representations of self and other, and the type of help-seeking behavior that the individual employs. The present chapter is aimed at examining the influence of gender identity formation on separation related depressive phenomena in college men and women. The psychodynamics and manifestation of the depressive experiences of men and women, as well as how these dynamics are likely to be

---

Thomas D. Mann, PhD, is Clinical Psychologist at The Devereux Foundation, Mapleton Center, 19 South Waterloo Road, Devon, PA 19333.

triggered and present themselves in the college setting will also be explored.

EPIDEMIOLOGY OF DEPRESSION

First, it is important to briefly reexamine the well documented findings from epidemiological studies which indicate that the prevalence of depression in women as compared to men is roughly 2:1. A variety of explanations have been forwarded with regard to whether these striking demographics do in fact reflect a true preponderance of women who suffer from depression. Differences in neuroendocrine functioning (Gold and Pottash, 1983), side effects of oral contraceptives (Parry and Rush, 1979), hormonal changes during pregnancy (Pitt, 1982), the postpartum period, and premenstrual phase (Halbreich, Endicott, and Nee, 1978; Pitt, 1982), and a state of learned helplessness created by women's internalization of traditional sex-role expectations (Weissman and Klerman, 1977), to name a few, have all been offered as explanations for the reported greater incidence of depression in women. However, the most significant determinant may simply be women's greater willingness to express their emotional distress and also seek treatment (Boyd and Weissman, 1981; Clayton, 1983).

MALES' VERSUS FEMALES' UTILIZATION
OF PSYCHOTHERAPEUTIC SERVICES

It is interesting to note that while roughly twice as many women utilize outpatient college psychotherapeutic services (Whitaker, 1987), twice as many men require psychiatric hospitalization (D'Andrea and Martinez, 1989; Whitaker, 1990). In addition, three times as many women make suicide gestures/attempts, but twice as many men actually commit suicide (Schwartz, 1990). The question must then be asked: How do males attempt to cope with their emotional conflicts and turmoil, if not by seeking out others and communicating their distress?

There is more than sufficient research and clinical evidence that males frequently display their depressive experiences in the form of depressive equivalents, such as alcoholism, drug abuse, and antisocial behavior. These, and various other acting out behaviors, have been found to be more common in depressed males than depressed females (Johnson, O'Malley, and Bachman, 1988; Clayton, 1983; Kovacs, Feinberg, Crouse-Novak, Paulauskas, and Finkelstein, 1984). Moreover, there is evidence that when such avenues for acting out are blocked, the incidence of depression in males and females is equal. Egeland and Hostetter (1983), and Egeland, Hostetter, and Eshleman (1983) examined the prevalence of affective disorders among the Amish (who possess strong prohibitions against the use of alcohol and antisocial behavior) and found that the ratio of females to males diagnosed as possessing a Major Depressive Disorder, according to the SADS/RDC criteria, was roughly 1:1.

THE DEPRESSIVE CONFIGURATIONS OF MEN VERSUS WOMEN

When males and females do exhibit or communicate their depressive experiences more directly, their symptomatic presentations have been shown to differ significantly. Blatt and his colleagues found that females' depressive experiences are more likely to be manifested in anaclitic configurations. That is, their concerns tend to revolve around feelings of dependency, loneliness, helplessness, rejection, the wish to be close to others, a fear of abandonment, and difficulty expressing anger for fear of alienating and losing loved ones. Males' depressive experiences are more likely to be manifested in introjective configurations, revolving around issues of guilt, self-criticism, self-blame, feelings that one has not lived up to standards, hopelessness, and an ambivalence about self and others. Thus, women's symptomatic preoccupations reveal a greater relational focus as compared to men's, whose depressive concerns more typically revolve around issues associated with achievement, competency, and autonomy. These gender differences have been found to be significant in both clinically depressed inpatients and outpatients (Blatt, Quinlan, Chevron, McDonald, and Zuroff,

1982) and in a general college population (Chevron, Quinlan, and Blatt, 1978).

Blatt's original theoretical formulations appear to have been guided by Mahler (1968), who linked the fear of loss of the object (fear of abandonment) with the symbiotic and early separation-individuations subphases. Fear of the loss of the object's love and approval, on the other hand, was associated with the later separation-individuation subphases. In anaclitic depression, primary concerns were theorized to revolve around the need-gratifying relationship with the maternal object. Object relationships were asserted to be at the symbiotic level to beginning subphases of the separation-individuation stage. At this level, differentiation between self and object is incomplete, with object representations being defined in functional terms and sensorimotor schemas. Thus, Blatt postulated that in anaclitic depression objects are defined primarily in terms of the gratification or frustration they provide. The failure of the object to provide nurturance and gratification was theorized to lead to the experience of helplessness and abandonment. A sense of well being is achieved only from a continual supply of love and nurturance. "The representations of the object [in anaclitic depression] express a preoccupation with frustration and gratification . . . but there is relatively little internalization of the experiences of gratification or of the object providing the satisfaction" (Blatt, 1974; p. 117).

In contrast, Blatt postulated that in introjective depression objects are not defined in terms of their ability to provide need gratification, but rather as a source of approval and acceptance. Although self- and object-representations were theorized to be more differentiated than in anaclitic depression, they were believed to be fragmented, polarized, and ambivalent. Object relations in introjective depression were hypothesized to be at the later subphases of the separation-individuation stage of development. However, these object relationships are highly ambivalent and the person is unable to resolve and integrate contradictory feelings. As a result, "depression develops at this stage, not from abandonment and neglect, but rather from markedly ambivalent, demanding, depreciatory, and hostile [internalized] parent-child relationships" (Blatt, 1974; p. 118). Blatt posited that, in introjective depression, guilt could arise from the hostile and aggressive feelings toward the object, and/or from a harsh and punitive superego. Because of the higher level of object representation and object constancy that was theorized to underlie this type of depression, it was believed that the threat of object loss could be tolerated to a greater degree than in anaclitic depression.

Given Blatt's original developmental postulates, along with Blatt et al.'s (1982) and Chevron et al.'s (1978) findings that females more typically express their depressive concerns in anaclitic configurations, one might err in concluding that females' depressive experiences reflect more primitive developmental issues and concerns. Neither clinical nor empirical evidence supports this. While investigating the depressive experiences of college males and females, Mann (1988) and Blatt, Wein, Chevron, and Quinlan (1979) found no significant gender differences with regard to level of conceptual object representation in spite of these apparent gender differences with regard to depressive preoccupations. The ostensible finding that females' depressive concerns are developmentally more primitive than males appears to be related to the following phenomena. The separation-individuation processes in males and females differ significantly and, in conjunction with gender identity formation, contribute to dramatic differences in men's and women's orientations toward relatedness, autonomy, and their internal and external object worlds.

GENDER IDENTITY AND ITS INFLUENCE ON THE DEPRESSIVE PREOCCUPATIONS OF MEN AND WOMEN

Of particular interest is the relational focus of women's symptomatic configurations in contrast to men's presentation, which often reveals an ostensible interpersonal disconnection and separateness that is maladaptive in response to their emotional needs. In order to understand these symptomatic orientations, one must examine the development of gender identity in males versus females, and how this differentially affects the separation-individuation process.

Chodorow (1974, 1978) argued that although females struggle

Chodorow (1974, 1978) argued that although females struggle with separation-individuation in a qualitatively different way than males, this does not mean that females are developmentally less advanced, or less healthy psychologically. Rather, she postulated that because the primary caretaker during the first three years of life is typically the mother, the early processes of gender identity formation differ significantly for males and females, differentially affecting the separation-individuation process. Central to Chodorow's argument was the observation that the developmental processes of gender identity formation and separation-individuation unfold simultaneously. She argued that because female gender identity develops within the close emotional relationship with the primary caretaker–the mother–girls are more prone toward fusing the experience of attachment and closeness with the formation of feminine identity. She postulated that, as a result, female identity is rooted in a relational and interdependent context. Conversely, the process of separation-individuation is enhanced by the unfolding of gender identity formation in males, since identification with the father facilitates separation from the primary caretaker. Moreover, separation from the primary caretaker is essential for identification with the father to occur.

> Girls emerge from this period [of gender identity formation] with a basis for "empathy" built into their primary definition of self in a way that boys do not . . . Girls emerge with a stronger basis for experiencing another's needs or feelings as one's own . . . Furthermore, girls do not define themselves in terms of the denial of preoedipal relational modes to the same extent as do boys. Therefore, regression to these modes tends not to feel as much of a basic threat to their ego. From very early, then, because they are parented by a person of the same gender . . . girls come to experience themselves as less differentiated than boys, as more continuous with and related to the external object-world, and as differently oriented to their inner object-world as well. (Chodorow, 1978, p. 167)

Thus, Chodorow argued that for boys, the formation of gender identity is critically tied to separation and independence, since separation from the primary caretaker is essential for identification with the father. Conversely, she postulated that because female identity is rooted in attachment with the primary caretaker, "feminine personality comes to define itself in relation to other people more than masculine personality does" (1974, pp. 43-44).

It seems clear that when Chodorow states that females "experience themselves as less differentiated" than males, she is not conceptualizing this psychological phenomenon in hierarchial terms. Rather, she is noting the qualitatively different relationship that females develop with their internal and external object worlds. These gender orientations exert profound effects. Chodorow proposed that, as a result of these differences, male identity is more threatened by intimacy while female identity is more threatened by separation. She argued that this is why males, on the whole, tend to experience more problems in the area of relatedness and intimacy, while females struggle more with individuation and autonomy.

Gilligan (1982) similarly argued that males' exaggerated autonomy and separateness impair their capacity for intimacy. Because the development of masculinity is dependent on such exaggerated separateness and autonomy, intimacy is particularly threatening, arousing unconscious fears of merger and a loss of self.

Fox-Keller (1985) argued that autonomy, in its extreme, can connote a radical separateness from others to the extent that it creates a disconnection from others. She noted that there is the tendency to equate and, therefore, confuse the term autonomy with separation and independence. Increased autonomy, however, when equated with an exaggerated and isolating separateness does not enhance one's sense of self if it curtails one's relational capacities.

The perspectives espoused by these theorists provide an alternative view of development. That is, the direction of healthy development is not exclusively toward greater separation and severing of preoedipal ties. It is also a process of growth with regard to interpersonal relatedness. Fox-Keller describes healthy autonomy as a psychological phenomenon which need not choose between independence and intimacy, and separation and relatedness. She asserts that healthy autonomy "reflects a sense of self . . . as both differentiated from and related to others, and a sense of others as subjects with whom one shares enough to allow for a recognition of their independent interests and feelings, in short a recognition of them as other subjects. It develops not simply out of the experience of competence, of being able to affect others and one's environment in ways that feel satisfying, but also, and essentially, out of the experience of continuity and reciprocity of feeling in the relation between infant and mother" (p. 99).

Thus, healthy separation and autonomy would appear to be a sort of psychological balancing act in which relatedness and separation-individuation are integrated. Similarly, the fear of loneliness and disconnection is balanced with the fear of merging and loss of boundaries. These views implicitly assume that the exaggerated attempt to delineate absolutely between self and other represents a miscarriage of development in the sense that it fosters alienation through a defensive type of separateness.

From the preceding theoretical formulation, we can more critically examine the separation-related experiences and manifestations of depression in college men and women. Due to feminine gender orientation, women are likely to manifest and communicate their separation-related depressive experiences in different ways than men. However, whether women are more vulnerable to the development of depression and its associated symptoms at the time of such a major separation as leaving home to enter college is less straightforward.

Chodorow, Gilligan, and Fox-Keller suggest that men and women struggle in opposite directions with regard to separation-individuation. That is, women "experience themselves as less differentiated . . . [and] more continuous with and related to the external object world," while men are more disconnected from their internal and external object worlds due to their exaggerated separation and "denial of preoedipal relational modes" (Chodorow, 1978; p. 167). However, as the clinical vignettes presented later in this chapter will illustrate, men's and women's relationships to their object worlds are more complex than men simply being independent from, or less cathected to their preoedipal object world, and women being at the anaclitic developmental level of object relations because of their inability to separate and individuate. Both men and women possess strong ties to their preoedipal object world. However, men do appear to defend against the regressive pull of these experiences more rigidly. Consequently, men may appear more separate and less interpersonally cathected, though they also struggle with emotional separation.

Nonetheless, one cannot ignore the predominance of obvious separation related depressive presenting problems associated with relational concerns on the part of women who seek help in college counseling centers. Psychotherapists in college counseling centers are familiar with the common presenting complaints of women: The breakup of an intimate relationship or friendship; loss/death of a friend or intimate other; family conflict; abortion; and eating disorders. The separation-related focus is often obvious for women but not for men.

Consistent with these observations, Lopez, Campbell, and Watkins (1986) found that the depressive experiences of college women were associated with greater concerns over separation and autonomy than college men's. Mann (1988) studied mildly depressed college men and women who possessed equivalent levels of object representation and found that depressed women displayed a significantly stronger relational orientation, placing greater emphasis on the relational components of their lives than men. Moreover, as women's level of depression increased, their relational concerns also increased.

Support for these differences in gender orientation and depressive preoccupations has also come from research on subliminal perception, which is an effective means of testing genetic and dynamic propositions under systematic and controlled laboratory conditions. The subliminal psychodynamic activation method (Silverman, 1983) was designed to activate unconscious fantasies, wishes, and anxieties. Since stimuli are presented below (conscious) perceptual thresholds, they are considered at an unconscious level. One such subliminal stimulus that has been researched extensively has been the written message "mommy and I are one." Silverman hypothesized that the activation of unconscious fantasies of oneness with the good mother of early childhood would produce ameliorative effects by gratifying unconscious dependency needs (see Silverman, 1983, for a review of supporting research). To this end, Mann (1988) found that the subliminal message "mommy and I are one" significantly reduced levels of depression and anxiety, and increased self-evaluations in mildly depressed college women.

This had no ameliorative effects in men, who displayed equivalent levels of object representation.

Together, these studies support the postulate that feminine identity is rooted in a relational context which affords females greater access to their preoedipal experiences, though this relational orientation is independent of their level of object representation.

SEPARATION DURING ADOLESCENCE IN FEMALES

The task of object relinquishment and consequent object finding is more difficult for females due to their primary maternal relationship. "The girl struggles with object relations more intensely during her adolescence: in fact, the prolonged and painful severance from the mother constitutes a major task of this period" (Blos, 1962; p. 66). Deutsch (1944) similarly noted females' "more persistent" and "more intense" relationship with their maternal world, as they retain their preoedipal maternal identification to a greater degree than males. As such, Deutsch believed that females are more prone to certain transitional symptomatic "solutions" in an attempt at separation-individuation. For example, the college woman may find a female best friend with whom she has an intense and intimate relationship, or a boyfriend who ostensibly represents a transition into heterosexual relationships, but who in reality enables her to continue feeling intimate and close. Such behaviors may function as transitional phenomena which create links to preoedipal maternal representations. Volkan (1981) refers to such linking, or transitional phenomena as a "reactivation of a [earlier] form of psychological relatedness" (p. 374).

For females, separation in adolescence from mother and/or other intimate relationships may represent a more dramatic and intensely anxiety producing psychological experience than for males, at least at the conscious level. Thus, relational concerns are such a predominant theme for females who seek treatment in college counseling centers. Adolescence, as Deutsch notes, is a period when women must make the transition from their earlier, more dependent maternal ties to more autonomous functioning, while also establishing new heterosexual object ties. However, it is apparent that the forced separation initiated by the moving off to college brings these psychodynamics to the forefront for both women and men.

CLINICAL ILLUSTRATIONS

Mary, an 18 year old woman, sought treatment with me toward the end of her freshman year in college. Her primary complaint was of unsatisfactory relationships with men. Separation issues were quite apparent from the beginning of psychotherapy. On average, Mary called home four to five times a week. She felt compelled to check with her parents (particularly her mother) before making even minor decisions or plans, such as going off somewhere with her friends for the weekend. Mary stated that her parents' intrusiveness was a significant problem and terribly upsetting. However, she did not recognize her own part in encouraging this relationship.

Mary had been an excellent student in high school and graduated a year early. Clearly, her accelerated academic progress served as an attempt to liberate her, albeit superficially, from her overinvolved relationship with her mother. After entering college, Mary became quite focused on dating and finding a boyfriend, though she had dated very little before college.

During the initial interview, Mary stated that she had dated many men during the past year, but that all these men seemed to be interested in was sex. She longed for a relationship which was intimate in nonsexual ways, but claimed that she had been unsuccessful in finding men who could meet these needs. Her solution was one of pseudopromiscuity, quickly entering into sexual relationships with each new boyfriend, not for the genital pleasure of sexual activity, but because she "liked to be held afterwards." The regressive pull of this behavior was obvious, serving as a compensation or substitution in lieu of a more successful separation/liberation from her preoedipal mother. In this case, Mary's pseudopromiscuity can be viewed as a transitional phenomenon which linked her to her preoedipal object world.

Another vignette illustrates the separation related phenomena of a depressed college man who did not seek treatment. Henry, a college senior, was quite confused over what to do following graduation. He spent much time ruminating over whether to accept a job immediately or to continue his business education in graduate school. Although intelligent and capable, his academic performance had been mediocre, taking a back seat to fraternity and other social activities. Henry was quite popular and well known on campus, and could almost always be found with a number of friends, both male and female. Moreover, he had developed somewhat of a reputation as a "ladies' man" based on his stories of sexual conquest and others' observations of his behavior with women. To others, Henry was confident, self-assured, silver tongued, and ready to conquer the world after graduating from college.

However, as graduation neared, Henry became more anxious over the prospect of moving out on his own. He did not fear his prospective professional responsibilities as much as his emotional independence. He spent even less time with his studies and more time drinking, socializing, and pursuing women sexually. To his friends, he was carefree, independent, and enjoying himself immensely. However, intrapsychically, Henry struggled tremendously over separation and was terribly afraid of being alone. At the same time, he was quite threatened by intimacy. Henry's mother was a dominant woman who smothered him emotionally. On the one hand, he struggled to escape from what he experienced as her tight grasp on him. On the other hand, however, his relationship with her provided a sense of safety, security, and nurturance.

Henry's dynamic compromise was to continue to act out his conflicts over separation through promiscuous behavior. By winning over a continual stream of women he maintained a sense of being worthwhile and adequate. As a defense against his underlying self-doubts, descriptions of his conquests always contained the suggestion of how these women desired him. A long time athlete, Henry would describe his sexual achievements using sports analogies, for example telling his buddies how he had "scored." Feelings of loneliness, dependency, and depression were fended off in this way, despite the higher level genital facade. This behavior also served the function of satisfying preoedipal wishes to be nurtured and reassured that he was his mother's "darling baby," as his mother would call him. At the same time, the fear of merger and loss of self was defended against through the avoidance of intimacy inherent in his refusal to remain in any one relationship. In this way, Henry's ostensible exaggerated independence was a defensive effort in response to the anxiety associated with the threat of regression to the experience of a more undifferentiated state.

When confronted with the prospective separation from the emotional supports that college provided, Henry was faced with a crisis. Emotionally, Henry was quite dependent on his mother, despite his facade which indicated otherwise. His sense of self-worth was dependent on constant affirmation from others. He attempted to obtain this through his promiscuous behavior. His "scores," as he termed them, were experienced as validations of his self-worth and of others needing him (a projection of his own dependency needs). Moreover, they enabled him brief and, therefore, less threatening contacts with others. Unfortunately, he was not willing to seek psychotherapy and confront the painful issues necessary to arrive at more healthy and adaptive solutions. Although his decision to continue his education in graduate school may very well have been the correct one academically, it appeared to have been primarily determined by his inability to resolve these separation issues. By continuing school, Henry could remain in an environment where he would rarely be alone and "bored" (a term he used to describe what appeared to be the experience of depression when he was alone) and could easily continue to act out his conflicts over separation and intimacy through his promiscuous encounters.

THE CONCEPT OF ANACLITIC
AND INTROJECTIVE DEVELOPMENTAL LINES

The preceding vignettes illustrate how both men and women struggle with the separation process, but can manifest this differently. However, to conclude that "the task of becoming a separate individual [is] . . . more difficult for girls than for boys" (Mahler, Pine, and Bergman, 1975; p. 106), or that women struggle more with separation because their separation related difficulties are often manifested in more obvious form or are more accessible to conscious experience, albeit in derivative form, appears oversimplified.

It may be that men and women manifest their depressive experiences within different developmental lines. Blatt and Shichman (1983) proposed that there exist two fundamental, but separate, developmental lines: (1) an anaclitic line, and (2) an introjective line. The anaclitic developmental line was proposed to lead to the establishment of mature and satisfying interpersonal relationships. According to this formulation, "[anaclitic] disturbances can range from the more global and fundamental issues of relatedness that occur in the mother-infant dyad to issues of relatedness based on the oedipal triadic configuration . . . the anaclitic configuration is based on the common denominator of attempts to establish [and maintain] satisfactory intimate interpersonal relations" (pp. 201-202).

The introjective developmental line was postulated to lead to a stable, realistic and positive self-identity. Disturbances within this line were proposed to reflect misguided attempts at establishing and/or maintaining a positive, realistic, and stable concept of the self.

This reformulation enables one to examine men's and women's predominant depressive concerns without comparing them in hierarchical terms. Moreover, it is apparent that men's and women's separation related depressive symptoms are often manifested within these different developmental lines, as was portrayed in the preceding clinical vignettes. For example, while Mary's separation related symptoms were more obvious, Henry's took form in a pseudoindependent facade that masked his anxiety over emotional separation. Consequently, his symptomatic presentation appeared more introjective than anaclitic in nature. Nonetheless, Henry's behavior, like Mary's, was symptomatic of underlying separation difficulties and served as a transitional phenomenon which provided a soothing and comforting function in response to his fear of being alone.

In both so called normal and clinical populations, men and women experience struggles over separation-individuation. The psychological importance of, and concomitant denial of, these concerns on the part of men is revealed in such behavior as fraternity bonding through physical horseplay, or greeting one another with a brief (but macho) embrace, followed by a punch in the arm to ensure that this apparent affection is not misconstrued. To this end, it is interesting to note the common phenomenon of intoxicated fraternity brothers (but also many college men in general) hugging one another, professing their friendship and loyalty. Can it be that these needs are more apparent in men only when in regressed states? Moreover, what connection might this have to men's higher incidence of drug and alcohol abuse during college?

It is important that we as psychotherapists recognize that the predominance of women who seek help through psychotherapy is probably due to their proclivity toward affiliation and more relational modes of acquiring help. This, however, should not lead us to conclude that men do not struggle with separation. Theorists such as Chodorow, Gilligan, and Fox-Keller have accused men of abandoning their preoedipal ties and ignoring the importance of their early object relationships. Psychotherapists must not collude with men's misleading facade. It is therefore imperative that we recognize and address men's separation related symptomatology, albeit in its many disguised forms.

REFERENCES

Bebbington, P. E., Hurry, J., Tennant, C., Sturt, E., & Wing, J. K. (1981). The epidemiology of mental disorders in Camberwell. *Psychological Medicine, 11,* 561-580.

Beckham, E. E., & Leber, W. R. (1985). The comparative efficacy of psychotherapy and pharmacotherapy for depression. In E. E. Beckham & W. R. Leber (Eds.), *Handbook of depression: Treatment, assessment, and research* (pp. 316-340). Homewood, Illinois: Dorsey Press.

Blatt, S. J. (1974). Levels of object representation in anaclitic and introjective depression. *Psychoanalytic Study of the Child: Vol. 29.* (pp. 107-157). New Haven: Yale University Press.

Blatt, S. J., D'Afflitti, J. P., & Quinlan, D. M. (1976). Experience of depression in normal young adults. *Journal of Abnormal Psychology, 85,* 383-389.

Blatt, S. J., Quinlan, D. M., Chevron, E. S., McDonald, C., & Zuroff, D. (1982). Dependency and self-criticism: Psychological dimensions of depression. *Journal of Consulting and Clinical Psychology, 48,* 226-239.

Blatt, S. J. & Shichman, S. (1983). Two primary configurations of psychopathology. *Psychoanalysis and Contemporary Thought,* 187-254.

Blatt, S. J., Wein, J. S., Chevron, E., & Quinlan, D. (1979). Parental representations and depression in normal young adults. *Journal of Abnormal Psychology, 88,* 388-397.

Blos, P. (1962). *On Adolescence: A Psychoanalytic Interpretation.* New York: The Free Press.

Boyd, J. H., & Weissman, M. M. (1981). Epidemiology of affective disorders: A reexamination and future directions. *Archives of General Psychiatry, 38,* 1039-1046.

Chevron, E. S., Quinlan, D. M., & Blatt, S. J. (1978). Sex roles and gender differences in the experience of depression. *Journal of Abnormal Psychology, 87,* 680-683.

Chodorow, N. (1974). Family structure and feminine personality. In M. Z. Rosaldo & L. Lamphere (Eds.), *Woman, culture, and society* (pp. 43-66). Stanford: Stanford University Press.

Chodorow, N. (1978). *The reproduction of mothering.* Berkeley: University of California Press.

Clayton, P. J. (1983). Gender and Depression. In J. Angst (Ed.), *The origins of depression: Current concepts and approaches,* (pp.77-89). Berlin: Springer-Verlag New York Inc.

D'Andrea, V. J., & Martinez, A. M. (1989). Psychiatric hospitalization and academic achievement. Paper presented at the Annual Meeting of the American College Health Association, May 26, 1989, Washington, D.C.

Deutch, H. (1944). *Psychology of Women,* Vol. I, New York: Grune & Stratton.

Egeland, J. A., & Hostetter, A. M. (1983). Amish Study I: Affective disorders among the Amish. *American Journal of Psychiatry, 140,* 56-61.

Egeland, J. A., Hostetter, A. M., & Eshleman, S. K. (1983). Amish Study III: The impact of cultural factors on bipolar diagnosis: *American Journal of Psychiatry, 140,* 67-71.

Fox-Keller, E. (1985). *Reflections on gender and science.* New Haven: Yale University Press.

Gilligan, C. (1982). *In a different voice.* Cambridge: Harvard University Press.

Gold, M. S., and Pottash, A. L. C. (1983). Thyroid dysfunction or depression? In F. J. Ayd, I. J. Taylor, & B. T. Taylor (Eds.), *Affective disorders reassessed: 1983* (pp. 179-191). Baltimore: Ayd Medical Communications.

Halbreich, U., Endicott, J., & Nee, J. (1983). Premenstrual depressive changes. *Archives of General Psychiatry, 40,* 535-542.

Johnson, L. D., O'Malley, P. M., & Bachman, G. (1988). Illicit drug use, smoking and drinking by America's high school students and young adults: 1975-1987. *National Institute on Drug Abuse,* U.S. Dept. of Human Services, DHHS Publication #89-1602. Rockville, MD, 1988.

Kovacs, M., Feinberg, T. L., Crouse-Novak, M. A., Paulauskas, S. L., & Finkelstein, R. (1984). Depressive disorders in childhood I: A longitudinal study of characteristics and recovery. *Archives of General Psychiatry, 41,* 229-237.

Mahler, M. S. (1968). *On human symbiosis and the vicissitudes of individuation.* New York: International Universities Press.

Mahler, M. S., Pine, F., & Bergman, A. (1975). *The psychological birth of the human infant.* New York: Basic Books, Inc.

Mann, T. (1988). Gender orientation and its influence on the psychodynamics underlying the depressive experiences of females and males. *Dissertation Abstracts International,* University Microfilms No. 8819314.

Parry, B. L. & Rush, A. J. (1979). Oral contraceptives and depressive symptomatology: Biologic Mechanisms. *Comprehensive Psychiatry, 20,* 347-358.

Pitt, B. (1982). Depression in childbirth. In E. S. Paykel (Ed.), *Handbook of affective disorders* (pp. 361-378). New York: The Guilford Press.

Schwartz, A. J. (1990). The epidemiology of suicide among students at colleges and universities in the United States. *Journal of College Student Psychotherapy, 4* (3-4), 25-44.

Silverman, L. H. (1983). The subliminal activation method: Overview and comprehensive listing of studies. In J. Masling (Ed.), *Empirical Studies of Psychoanalytic Theories.* New Jersey: Analytic Press.

Volkan, V. D. (1981). *Linking Objects and Linking Phenomena.* New York: International Universities Press.

Weissman, M. M. & Klerman, L. (1977). Sex differences and the epidemiology of depression. *Archives of General Psychiatry, 34,* 98-111.

Whitaker, L. C. (1990). Countering cultural myths to help prevent college student suicide. *College Student Suicide* (pp. 79-98). New York: The Haworth Press, Inc.

Whitaker, L. C. (1987). Macho and morbidity: The emotional need vs. fear dilemma in men. *Journal of College Student Psychotherapy, 1,* 33-47.